Weak versus Strong Sustainability

To my students, the past, current and future ones

Weak versus Strong Sustainability

Exploring the Limits of Two Opposing Paradigms

Third Edition

Eric Neumayer

Professor of Environment and Development,
Department of Geography and Environment and
Associate, Grantham Research Institute on Climate Change
and the Environment,
London School of Economics and Political Science, London, UK

Edward Elgar
Cheltenham, UK • Northampton, MA, USA

Published by
Edward Elgar Publishing Limited
The Lypiatts
15 Lansdown Road
Cheltenham
Glos GL50 2JA
UK

Edward Elgar Publishing, Inc.
William Pratt House
9 Dewey Court
Northampton
Massachusetts 01060
USA

A catalogue record for this book
is available from the British Library

Library of Congress Control Number: 2009937892

ISBN 978 1 84844 872 8 (cased)
ISBN 978 1 84844 873 5 (paperback)

Printed and bound by MPG Books Group, UK

Contents

Figures

Tables

Variables

A	Pollution abatement
AC	Average resource extraction costs
C	Consumption
	Cost function
D	Resource discoveries
E	Harvest of renewable resources
F	Production function
G	'Human induced' growth of renewable resources
GS	'Genuine saving'
H	Hotelling rent
	Hamiltonian
K	Stock of man-made capital
L	Labour
M	Stock of human capital
M_E	Share of energy in total production costs
N	Investment in human capital
P	Stock of pollution
	Price
R	Resource depletion
RC	Resource receipts
S	Stock of non-renewable resources
SI	Sustainable income
T	Time variable
U	Utility function
X	Stock of accumulated resource discoveries
Z	Stock of renewable resources
a	Natural growth function (renewable resources)
b	Natural restoration function (pollution)
c	Exponent in production function
d	Exponent in production function
e	Exponent in production function
f	Expenditure function for non-renewable resource extraction
g	Expenditure function for resource exploration
h	Expenditure function for renewable resource harvesting

i	Expenditure function for pollution abatement
j	Expenditure function for investment into human capital
k	Rate of 'resource augmenting' technical progress
m	Rate of Hicks-neutral technical progress
n	Reserves to production ratio
p	Exponent in production function
q	Exponent in production function
r	Rate of interest
	Discount rate
s	Exponent in production function
t	Time index
u	Average rate of consumption growth
v	Parameter
w	Parameter
z	Static reserve index
π	Profit
σ	Elasticity of substitution
α	Elasticity of output with respect to man-made capital
	Parameter
β	Elasticity of output with respect to non-renewable resources
	Parameter
γ	Conversion factor converting production into pollution units
λ	Shadow value of man-made capital
	General Lagrangian multiplier
μ	Shadow value of the stock of non-renewable resources
ω	Shadow cost of the stock of resource discoveries
ϕ	Shadow value of the stock of renewable resources
ψ	Shadow cost of the stock of pollution
ξ	Shadow value of the stock of human capital
ρ	Pure rate of time preference
η	Elasticity of the marginal utility of consumption
Γ	Lagrangian

Abbreviations and Acronyms

Abbreviations that are rather unfamiliar are explicated in the main text on their first appearance. Familiar abbreviations are used without further explanation throughout.

AIDS	Acquired Immune Deficiency Syndrome
AES	Allen partial Elasticity of Substitution
bn	billion (thousand million)
CBA	Cost-benefit analysis
CES	Constant Elasticity of Substitution
CFC	Chlorofluorocarbons
CO_2	Carbon Dioxide
CSERGE	Centre for Social and Economic Research on the Global Environment
CV	Contingent Valuation
DICE	Dynamic Integrated Model of Climate and the Economy
DNA	Deoxyribonucleic Acid
DDT	Dichlorodiphenyltrichloroethane
EF	Ecological Footprint(s)
EKC	Environmental Kuznets Curve
ENetS	Extended Net Saving
FAO	Food and Agricultural Organisation
GEF	Global Environmental Facility
GPI	Genuine Progress Indicator
gNNP	green Net National Product
GDP	Gross Domestic Product
GNP	Gross National Product
GREENSTAMP	Greened National Statistical and Modelling Procedures
GS	Genuine Savings
HDI	Human Development Index
IPCC	Intergovernmental Panel on Climate Change
ISEW	Index of Sustainable Economic Welfare
LDC	Less Developed Country

MF	Material Flows
MRS	Marginal Rate of Substitution
NPP	Net Primary Productivity
NO_x	Nitrogen Oxides
OECD	Organisation for Economic Co-operation and Development
OPEC	Organisation of Petroleum Exporting Countries
R&D	Research and Development
RICE	Regional dynamic Integrated Model of Climate and the Economy
SD	Sustainable Development
SERI	Sustainable Europe Research Institute
SHDI	Sustainabile Human Development Index
SI	Sustainable Income
SMS	Safe Minimum Standard
SNI	Sustainable National Income
SO_x	Sulphur Oxides
SS	Strong Sustainability
UK	United Kingdom
UNDP	United Nations Development Programme
UNEP	United Nations Environment Programme
US	United States of America
WS	Weak Sustainability
WBCSD	World Business Council on Sustainable Development
WTA	Willingness-to-accept
WTP	Willingness-to-pay

Preface to the Third Edition

This third edition of *Weak versus Strong Sustainability* is a substantially revised version of the second edition (Neumayer 2003c), which followed the first edition, originally published in 1999 (Neumayer 1999a). The revisions affect all chapters. In particular, I have updated all graphs and tables and I discuss the literature published since the last edition was published. This has affected all sections to some extent, but section 2.4 most dramatically. With the publication of the Stern (2007) Review, the debate on climate change has considerably moved on and this new edition reflects this.

In writing this book I have tried to ensure that it is open to a broad audience. Chapter 3 should be accessible for interested readers from all backgrounds who for the first time come across the issues of resource availability for sustained economic growth and the environmental consequences thereof. Equally, Chapter 4 examines the preservation of natural capital in a world of risk, uncertainty and ignorance without abstract mathematical modelling. Chapter 5, on measuring weak sustainability, is more advanced, presents a more formal analysis and presupposes a more substantial economic background. Chapter 6 is again perfectly understandable by all those interested in the measurement of strong sustainability. I hope that I have written a book that is of use to everybody with an interest in the two opposing paradigms of weak and strong sustainability, be they economists or not.

This book builds upon articles in refereed journals and it has therefore benefited greatly from many comments of anonymous referees. In addition, parts of the book have been presented at research seminars at various academic institutions and international academic conferences. It has benefited much from discussions with the participants of these events as well as from comments from James Putzel (special thanks), Brian Barry, James K. Boyce, Lord Meghnad Desai, Simon Dietz, Paul Ekins, Salah El Serafy, Henk Folmer, Mathias Hafner, Kirk Hamilton, Friedrich Hinterberger, Michael Jacobs, David Pearce, Tom Tietenberg, Jeroen C.J.M. van den Bergh and Mathis Wackernagel. All errors are mine as are all views expressed here.

Eric Neumayer
London School of Economics and Political Science

1. Introduction and Overview

Starting from the early 1990s support for 'sustainable development' (henceforth: SD) has become very widespread. At the Rio summit in 1992 the vast majority of nation-states have formally committed themselves to SD in signing Agenda 21 (UNCED 1992) — a commitment renewed at the 2002 World Summit on Sustainable Development in Johannesburg. Especially since then, there has been hardly any politician, academic or businessperson who does not call for making development sustainable. In some sense this is not surprising: SD is like freedom or peace — that is, something to which no reasonable person would overtly object. Development always sounds good and that it has to be sustainable seems self-evident.

In this book two economic paradigms of SD — 'weak sustainability' and 'strong sustainability' — will be analysed with the objective of exploring their limits. 'Weak sustainability' (henceforth: WS) is based upon the pioneering work of two neoclassical economists: Robert Solow (1974a, 1974c, 1986, 1993a, 1993b), a Nobel Laureate, and John Hartwick (1977, 1978a, 1978b, 1990, 1993), a famous resource economist. WS can be interpreted as an extension to neoclassical welfare economics. It is based on the belief that what matters for future generations is only the total aggregate stock of 'man-made'[1], human and 'natural' capital[2] (and possibly other forms of capital as well), but not natural capital as such. Loosely speaking, according to WS, it does not matter whether the current generation uses up non-renewable resources or dumps CO_2 in the atmosphere as long as enough machineries, roads and ports as well as schools and universities are built in compensation. Because natural capital is regarded as being essentially substitutable in the production of consumption goods and as a direct provider of utility, I call WS the 'substitutability paradigm'.

In opposition to WS stands 'strong sustainability' (henceforth: SS). While WS is a relatively clear paradigm in that it builds upon a well-established core of neoclassical welfare economics, SS is not. It is more difficult to define SS and pin down its implications, as many different scholars have contributed their own views on what SS should be. However, the essence of SS is that natural capital is regarded as non-substitutable, in the production of consumption goods ('source' side of the economy), in its capacity to absorb pollution ('sink' side of the economy) and as a direct provider of utility in the form of environmental amenities. Hence, I call SS the 'non-substitutability paradigm'.

The objective of this book is to explore the limits of the two opposing paradigms of sustainability. In particular, it will assess whether either paradigm can provide a clear course of action and a measure[3] for whether sustainability is achieved or not. The book is thus an exercise in exploring the limits of what we can know about the requirements of sustainability.

The book is structured as follows. Chapter 2 discusses conceptual, ethical and paradigmatic issues of SD. The definitions, assumptions and the methodology of the analysis in the book are laid down. Then some arguments are presented which make SD plausible as an ethical choice. A kind of time-inconsistency problem of SD is discussed which results from the fact that the current generation can only commit itself, but not coming generations, to SD. Finally, two misunderstandings about what sustainability requires are corrected. It is shown that SD neither locks society into eternal poverty if it is poorly endowed at the start nor demands the choice of greatly inferior utility paths. These ethical issues of SD are dealt with before a distinction is made between WS and SS, because they apply to both paradigms equally.

Next in Chapter 2 the two opposing weak and strong paradigms of sustainability are characterised. It is shown that WS can be interpreted as an extension to neoclassical welfare economics with the additional requirement of non-declining utility over time. The implications of the substitutability assumptions are explained. As regards SS, two differing possible interpretations are given. One calls for preserving natural capital in value terms,[4] the other one calls for preserving the physical stocks of certain forms of so-called critical natural capital. The implications of the non-substitutability assumption are explained.

Finally, Chapter 2 stresses the importance of the substitutability assumption using climate change as a case study. It is shown that cost-benefit analysis, as exemplified by the approach taken by Nordhaus (1991a, 1994, 2008), comes to the conclusion that only minor emission cut-backs are efficient and therefore optimal, unless the discount rate used is very low as in the Stern (2007) Review. The predominant critique of Nordhaus has concentrated on the rate of discount to be used. I argue that the more important issue is Nordhaus's implicit assumption of substitutability of natural capital. If one accepts the substitutability assumption, then it is very questionable whether one can make a very persuasive case for using a relatively low discount rate. I therefore argue that substitutability should be the main issue in dispute, not discounting.

Chapter 3 analyses the validity of the basic assumptions of both paradigms. As mentioned, WS regards natural capital as being essentially substitutable both in the production of consumption goods and as a more direct provider of utility. SS, in contrast, regards natural capital as being essentially non-substitutable. Chapter 3 first examines theoretical and empirical evidence on the availability of natural resources for the production of consumption goods. Four propositions of resource optimism are stated and critically assessed. These propositions imply that a natural resource can either be substituted with another resource or man-made capital, or that the feedback mechanisms triggered by rising resource prices and technical progress will work to overcome any apparent constraint. Second, it discusses whether future generations can be compensated for long-term environmental degradation. It argues that an answer to this question must be speculative to some extent as we cannot know the preferences of future generations. It also argues that there are good reasons against both extreme positions; that is, neither unlimited substitutability nor perfect non-substitutability of natural capital as a provider of utility seems reasonable. As will be explained in Section 2.3.1, p. 21, WS tends to be rather optimistic about the environmental consequences of economic growth, however. Therefore it has to rely less on the assumption that natural capital is substitutable as a direct provider of utility. In other words, it has to rely less on the assumption that increased consumption opportunities can compensate future generations for the loss of natural capital in the form of long-term environmental degradation. Chapter 3 therefore analyses thirdly the link between economic growth and environmental degradation. The theoretical case both in favour of environmental optimism, which suggests economic growth is good for the environment at least over the long run, and environmental pessimism, which contends the opposite, are put forward. However, since the likely environmental consequences of future economic growth cannot be solved theoretically, the existing empirical evidence on this question is examined as well.

In short, Chapter 3 comes to the conclusion that neither paradigm of sustainability is falsifiable. As is so often the case for extra-paradigmatic disagreements, support for one paradigm or the other depends much on basic beliefs (here about possibilities of substitution and technical progress) which are non-falsifiable and can therefore not be conclusively decided. The book offers an alternative explanation to that of Norton (1995) who argues that the debate between proponents of weak and strong sustainability cannot be resolved because there is no agreement on the scope of the true subject matter nor a consensually accepted methodology. Chapter 3 argues that it would still be impossible to resolve the debate even if there was agreement on the subject matter and a consensually accepted methodology.

That, strictly speaking, both paradigms of sustainability are non-falsifiable does not imply of course that scientific research cannot help in informing policy-making for sustainability. Chapter 4 takes up the discussion where it ended in Chapter 3 and argues that a combination of the distinctive features of natural capital with the prevalence of risk, uncertainty and ignorance make a *persuasive* case for the preservation of certain forms of natural capital that provide basic life-support functions. It argues that, in principle, there are good reasons for the protection of global life-support resources such as biodiversity, the ozone layer and the global climate as well as the restriction of the accumulation of pollutants, unsustainable harvesting and soil erosion. Conversely, no explicit protection policy for non-renewable resources used in the production of consumption goods seems warranted. In essence, therefore, Chapter 4 argues that there is more support for WS with regard to the 'source' side of the economy, while there is more support for SS with regard to the 'sink' side of the economy and with regard to natural capital as a direct provider of utility in the form of environmental amenities

Chapter 4 discusses various ways of coping with risk, uncertainty and ignorance, from the traditional neoclassical economic approach to alternatives in the form of the precautionary principle and safe minimum standards (SMS). The traditional economic approach deals with risk, uncertainty and ignorance via including option and quasi-option values into environmental valuation. Such an approach is helpful, but critics argue insufficient. The alternatives have their problems as well and these are discussed at some length for SMS in particular. A further question is how much cost society should be willing to incur in order to preserve certain forms of natural capital. One option is to deliberately ignore opportunity costs. Given uncertainty and ignorance about the consequences of depleting natural capital one might choose to refrain from any marginal decisions and call for the preservation of the remaining totality of certain forms of natural capital. From this perspective, it is better to incur the definite and potentially large costs of preservation in order to prevent the uncertain, but potentially tremendous, costs of depletion. It is argued in Chapter 4, however, that it is better to face the fact that every policy decision for preserving natural capital implies an opportunity cost that has to be balanced against the benefits of preservation.[5] Deliberately ignoring opportunity costs is tantamount to avoiding the often awkward decisions on how to spend scarce resources for which there are several competing claims. Chapter 4 therefore argues in favour of applying SMS for the forms of natural capital identified as being in need of preservation subject to the condition that preservation costs must not be 'unacceptably high', with preservation costs defined in net terms as opportunity costs minus the expected benefits of preservation.

It is argued in the concluding section of Chapter 4 that such a position is in effect broadly compatible with a moderate deontological or rights-based approach, which obliges the current generation to prevent imposing deliberate harm on the future unless the costs of following this prescription become excessive. Scientific research can help society in providing information on the likely benefits and costs of preservation. But it cannot tell society what it should regard as 'unacceptably high' costs. That is, it cannot tell society how risk averse it should be with regard to the depletion of natural capital. The precautionary principle and safe minimum standards imply that opportunity costs may exceed the expected preservation benefits by a certain factor. Economic valuation techniques provide best available information on both benefits and costs. But what are 'unacceptably high' costs is an ethical and political question, not a scientific one.

Chapter 5 assesses whether weak sustainability, as defined in this book, can be measured in practice. A dynamic optimisation or optimal growth model is presented in order to show how 'genuine savings' (GS), the theoretically correct measure of WS, can be derived. The model is set up for the case of a closed economy and the necessary amendments for the open economy case are discussed. Then a series of problems for practical measurements of GS are put forward. The World Bank's (2009a) estimates of GS, the most serious and comprehensive attempt to measure WS so far, are critically assessed. I show that the World Bank's conclusions about the dismal performance of many developing countries with respect to sustainability are largely reversed if the El Serafy method is used for estimating the value of natural resource depreciation instead of the Bank's method. The analysis then turns to the Index of Sustainable Economic Welfare (ISEW) or Genuine Progress Indicator (GPI), an alternative indicator of WS. Again, I show that its conclusions concerning the dismal performance of all examined countries with respect to 'sustainable economic welfare' depend on a few, rather problematic assumptions and, sometimes, methodological errors.

Next, Chapter 6 turns to measuring SS. The analysis in Chapter 4 implies that the second interpretation of SS should be favoured over the first one: it is more sensible to preserve the physical stocks of certain forms of natural capital (at least up to a certain extent). In contrast, preserving natural capital in value terms does not preclude the possibility that certain forms of natural capital providing basic life-support functions are endangered or become irreversibly lost. It is therefore not surprising that all indicators of SS we look at here are either physical indicators or hybrid indicators, which combine the setting of environmental standards in physical terms with monetary valuation.

In the first section on physical indicators, I present the justification and basic idea of the concept of ecological footprints (EF) and the concept of material flows (MF) as the two most important and popular physical indicators of SS. With respect to EF, I show that strong unsustainability fails to be detected if the necessary land area for absorbing carbon dioxide emissions is counted in terms of the required land area for replacing non-renewable with renewable energy resources rather than in terms of land area required for carbon capture via forestry. Since the current rate of carbon dioxide emissions is clearly in violation of SS, however, this puts doubt on whether EF can really provide an indicator of SS. With respect to MF, I argue that the call for general reductions in MF is economically inefficient and is not guaranteed to be ecologically effective. Because of the latter, it is also highly doubtful whether the concept of MF really provides an indicator of SS, as suggested by its proponents. If one distinguishes MF according to their potential to threaten critical functions of natural capital, then the concept of MF holds much greater promise, however.

The second section of Chapter 6 looks at hybrid indicators. All of these indicators are inspired by Hueting's (1980) early path-breaking work, which is briefly discussed, and they all set environmental standards for certain forms of natural capital. The concept of sustainability gaps measures the gap between current practice and the defined standards. It also proposes to estimate the costs of achieving the standards, that is of closing the gaps, in monetary terms. This is done under the ceteris paribus assumption in a partial equilibrium framework, where relative prices are assumed to remain unchanged. Two other hybrid indicators — the Greened National Statistical and Modelling Procedures (GREENSTAMP) and the 'Sustainable National Income according to Hueting' — abandon the problematic *ceteris paribus* assumption and model the costs of achieving the set of environmental standards in a general equilibrium framework. This is their great advantage and disadvantage at the same time as the modelling character makes the indicator difficult to understand as well as highly dependent on model assumptions.

Chapter 7 provides conclusions from the main analysis. More formal derivations of basic principles and results can be found in the accompanying appendices.

NOTES

1   A more neutral term from a gender perspective would be 'human-made' capital. To distinguish this form of capital more clearly from 'human' capital I shall refer to it as 'man-made' capital, however.
2   Capital is defined here broadly as a stock that provides current and future utility. For more detail see Section 2.1, p. 7.
3   Note that throughout the book I use the terms 'measure' and 'indicator' interchangeably.
4   Value of capital should be interpreted throughout the book in real terms in the sense that the value has to be adjusted for inflation.
5   The usage of the terms 'benefits' and 'costs' might at points be confusing to the reader. Whether something counts as a benefit or a cost depends on the reference point and on the perspective one takes. The benefits of preserving natural capital are the costs of depleting natural capital. Similarly, the benefits of depleting natural capital are the costs of preserving natural capital.

2. Sustainable Development: Conceptual, Ethical and Paradigmatic Issues

This chapter will lay the foundation for the main analysis in the subsequent chapters. Section 2.1 defines the major terms used, describes the main simplifying assumptions and the methodology that will be employed. Section 2.2 discusses a few ethical issues of SD. It provides some justification for choosing SD, discusses a time-inconsistency problem of SD and resolves two misunderstandings about SD. Those readers who are most interested in WS versus SS itself might want to skip this section and go straight to Section 2.3, which introduces in more detail the two opposing paradigms. There it is explained what their major differences are with respect to the possibilities of substituting for natural capital. Section 2.4 provides a case study on climate change, which illustrates vividly the importance of the substitutability assumption. It is argued that the conflict between those who demand drastic emission reductions and those who demand only minor reductions should really be about the substitutability of natural capital rather than about the right rate of discount.

2.1 DEFINITIONS, ASSUMPTIONS, METHODOLOGY

In this book the analysis is confined to two starkly differing *economic* paradigms of SD, namely weak and strong sustainability.[1] They are the most influential paradigms within debates and policy discussions about SD. Let us start with some definitions and assumptions. In some sense, SD is a vague concept — so much so that Pezzey (1992b) can present a whole gallery of differing definitions. Nevertheless, a definition most proponents of an *economic* concept of SD would be likely to accept is the following: development is defined here to be *sustainable if it does not decrease the capacity to provide non-declining per capita utility for infinity*.

For the analysis that follows, those items that form the capacity to provide utility are called capital. Capital is defined here broadly as a stock that provides current and future utility. Natural capital is then the totality of nature –

non-renewable and renewable resources, plants, species, ecosystems and so on – that is capable of providing human beings with material and non-material utility. It follows that those items of nature that provide disutility to human beings do not count as natural *capital*. The most conspicuous examples are viruses and bacteria that cause diseases. Man-made capital is what has traditionally been subsumed under 'capital', that is factories, machineries, roads, infrastructure and so on. Human capital is knowledge and human skills. Note that I use the terms 'conserving capital' and 'preserving capital' interchangeably. The same applies to the terms 'utility' and 'welfare'.

Obviously the definition of SD used here is anthropocentric. Nature has value if, and only if humans value nature. Humans might value nature for whatever reasons, however, and not merely because it contributes to the production of consumption goods or directly produces utility through environmental amenities. Humans might very well value nature as such and for its own sake in attributing to it 'intrinsic' value. But it is still humans who determine the value. There is no value independent of human valuation in the definition of sustainability used here.

Note that SD is defined here as development that maintains the *capacity* to provide non-declining per capita utility for infinity. In other words, it is defined in terms of maintaining the capital that is necessary to provide non-declining future utility. It is not defined in terms of non-declining utility for infinity itself. In the real world, the current generation has no control over how future generations use the capacity they inherit. One must not demand more from the current generation than it can possibly achieve. This might sound as a merely semantic distinction, but prominent environmental philosophers have similarly distinguished non-declining utility from non-declining opportunities (for example Page 1983, p. 53; Barry 1991, p. 262).

Note that my definition of SD is not utilitarian. That is, I do *not* embrace a definition of SD as '*maximised present-value* utility non-declining for infinity' which can be represented in compact form as

$$SD = \arg\max \int_0^\infty U(t) \cdot e^{-\rho t} dt \text{ s.t. } dU/dt \geq 0 \ \forall t \tag{2.1}$$

where U is again (per capita) utility, ρ is pure rate of time preference and t is time. I reject utilitarianism for my definition of SD for mainly two reasons: first because SD is defined here in terms of maintaining the capacity to provide non-declining future utility, not in utility terms itself (see above). Second, I reject utilitarianism because I regard it to be too restrictive an assumption. Utilitarianism leaves no space for free choice: utility *must* be shifted inter-temporally so as to maximise the discounted stream of utility over infinite time (subject to the non-decline constraint). *Voluntary* sacrifices of the current generation for the sake of future generations are not allowed according to this social decision rule: the sacrifice would either increase or decrease the discounted stream of utility; in the first case, the current generation *must* make the sacrifice, in the second case it is *forbidden* to do so.

On the other hand, utilitarianism has some advantages as well: the first is again tractability, which is one of the reasons why it is so commonly used in economics. The second is that present-value maximisation as the most common form of utilitarianism has some desirable ethical properties as well when it comes to discounting the future. Note, first of all, that the pure rate of time preference in (2.1) could be set to zero, as indeed many authors demand for reasons of inter-generational fairness: being later in time should be no reason for counting less (for example, Ramsey 1928; Pigou 1932; Rawls 1972; Broome 1992; Cline 1992; Azar and Sterner 1996; Stern 2007). If ρ is set greater than zero, then this is often called utility discounting. And yet, even with ρ set to zero there are good reasons for discounting the future within a utilitarian framework if one expects the future generations to be better off than the present one. This is often called consumption or growth discounting and it is compatible with utilitarianism since more weight is given to the more present (and by presumption less well-off) generations. Note that this argument for discounting does not involve any bias against future generations *per se*. The argument for the potential ethical desirability of discounting within a utilitarian framework is formalised in Appendix 2, p. 198, where the so-called Ramsey rule is derived from a dynamic optimisation model.

Clearly, my definition of SD does not give a complete social decision rule, since there are likely to be an almost infinite number of development paths that maintain the capacity to provide non-declining utility for infinity. It follows that there has to be some decision criteria, a social welfare function in the language of economists, to choose from different paths. The utilitarian criterion is to take that path of non-declining utility which maximises the present (that is, the discounted) value. But an infinite number of other decision criteria exist, the most prominent of which are listed in any textbook on welfare economics — see, for example, Ng (1983). My definition of SD just calls for 'maintaining the capacity to provide per capita utility non-declining for infinity' whatever the complementary social decision criterion is. Note, however, that I use a utilitarian framework at various places throughout the book in analysing WS, because utilitarianism is usually embraced by proponents of WS (subject to the sustainability constraint). The same holds true for Section 2.4, p. 27, where the importance of the substitutability assumption for the case of climate change is stressed. This is because the analysis there focuses on the neoclassical approach towards climate change, as represented by Nordhaus (1991a, 1994, 2008), which is clearly utilitarian.

Proponents of WS and SS have radically differing beliefs about which forms of capital are necessary for providing non-declining utility. In order to highlight this difference and to make the analysis in the book possible, I will assume for simplicity that the utility of a representative individual can sufficiently be described by a utility function of the following form

$$U = U(C,Z,P), \tag{2.2}$$

$$\partial U/\partial C, \ \partial U/\partial Z \ > 0, \ \partial U/\partial P < 0$$

where C is consumption, Z is the stock of renewable resources providing environmental amenities and P is the stock of pollution. The first two components contribute positively to utility; hence their partial first derivatives are positive. The last component, pollution, on the other hand, reduces utility; hence its first derivative is negative. Note that I have split up natural capital into the stock of renewable resources and the stock of pollution which, of course, is a capital 'bad' rather than a capital good. I have done so to keep the presentation consistent with later chapters. Nothing of substance would change if I had put Z and P together into one variable for natural capital (or rather Z and some variable for the pollution-assimilative capacity of the environment).

Why are the *stocks* of renewable resources and pollution included in the utility function rather than the resource and pollution *flows*? The reason is that if people have preferences for environmental quality, it makes sense to assume that they care about the whole stock of directly utility-relevant renewable resources and pollution and not just incremental changes to the stock, that is, flows. It has become increasingly common in the environmental economics literature to put the *stock* of natural capital into the utility function rather than the *flows* derived from the stock — see, for example, Bovenberg and Smulders (1995); Beltratti (1995); Tahvonen and Kuuluvainen (1993); and Barrett (1992).

Why are *non-renewable* resources not included in the utility function? Because non-renewable resources are important for the production of consumption goods, but do (mostly) not produce any direct utility. Nobody derives direct utility from mineral and energy resources, but from renewable resources such as forests, wildlife and so on.[2] Of course, non-renewable resources provide indirect utility via consumption. For the same reason, man-made capital is not included in the utility function: it does not provide any direct utility, but is a major input into the production of consumption goods.

Population growth is exogenous to the analysis. Whatever the size of the population, SD calls for maintaining the capacity to provide non-declining *per capita* utility. This requirement seems to be reasonable since the present generation is responsible for population growth. It can either reduce population growth or increase the capacity to provide utility to comply with the *per capita* requirement. I concede that keeping population growth exogenous to the analysis is not satisfactory. But as Solow (1986, p. 149) has put it: "The welfare economics of an endogenously changing population is altogether murky."[3] Population growth makes achievement of SD typically more difficult than if population were stationary (Hamilton and Atkinson 2006, ch. 3; World Bank 2006, ch. 5). But note that technical progress is a force in the other direction.

That the capacity to provide non-declining per capita utility should be maintained *for infinity* is more for convenience. Doing so ensures better mathematical tractability. What is actually meant with 'for infinity' is that development cannot be sustainable if it maintains the capacity to provide non-declining utility only temporarily and leads to a decline in this capacity after some finite time.

Speaking of the 'present' and 'future' generations is of course a fictitious simplification. Every day some people are born while others die so there is a permanent flow of people into and out of the present generation, while 'future' generations are not a given but are contingent on the 'present' generation's actions. One has to interpret the notions of 'present' and 'future' generations as ideal types in Max Weber's (1922) usage of the term. Therefore, they are not really existent but they help enormously in conceptualising and analysing problems.

The analysis of this book mainly looks at *inter*-generational as opposed to *intra*-generational distributional questions. Inter-generational fairness questions are at the centre of concern of most proponents of SD, but that is not a good reason to exclude intra-generational conflicts per se.[4] Heyes and Liston-Heyes (1995, p. 3) are presumably correct in arguing that "it may be that those embroiled in the environmental sustainability debate have become so obsessed with intergenerational equity that intragenerational equity considerations have been swept under the rug".

My justification is that I want to focus on inter-generational distributional questions here.[5] Ignoring to a large extent intra-generational distributional issues makes the analysis much easier. And again, this admittedly restrictive assumption ensures tractability, because then I can let different generations be represented by a representative agent of each generation. At certain points I shall loosen this assumption somewhat, however, and ask what consequences the unequal intra-generational income distribution has on the likelihood of achieving sustainability. This will be the case, for example, in Section 2.4, p.

27, on climate change and in Section 4.5, p. 118, on the opportunity costs of preserving natural capital.

The methodology I am using is that of the boundedly rational individual who attempts to maximise his or her utility. This methodology is usually called the economic paradigm although it is debatable whether there can be anything like *the* economic paradigm when economists themselves disagree about the specifics of 'their' paradigm (on this see, for example, Sen 1987 and Hausman 1992). I want to put emphasis on the word *boundedly*. I am interested in real-world problems and I do not want to dispose of those problems by simply assuming them away. Hence I do not assume the presence of either perfect information, or perfect foresight, or boundless computational capacity. For a good case for this view on 'rationality', see Simon (1982).

The motivation for choosing the economic paradigm as methodology is not that I am convinced that it reflects actual human behaviour at all times and to all extent correctly. There is more to human life than being a rational utility maximiser. But there is no better alternative to the economic paradigm and especially so if one is looking for something tractable. The main reason for sticking to the economic methodology is a different one, however: I want to grant the paradigms of sustainability I am looking at the most favourable conditions, especially because of my primary interest in exploring their limits. Since I am looking at economic paradigms of sustainability, it seems only fair to analyse them according to their own standards. It is all too easy to dismiss a paradigm as pure nonsense from a perspective outside the discipline. I am taking WS and SS seriously as economic paradigms; but I can only do so by basing my analysis on the economic methodology.

In Section 2.2, p. 13, I present some arguments of why it is justifiable to pursue SD. After that, it will simply be assumed that the ethical decision to strive for SD as defined here has already been taken. I assume that policy makers act in accordance with the SD goal without pursuing any other interest that would contradict this aim; that is, they are credibly committed to SD. In terms of political economy this assumption is utterly naive, of course. It fits nicely into the analysis here, however, which is essentially about exploring the limits of the two paradigms of sustainability as if they were the central goal for policy makers.

What about consumer sovereignty? It is a central value for many economists, but it can only refer to the sovereignty of the present generation's consumers since future generations are not present today and cannot reveal their preferences in today's markets. Of course, with overlapping generations and parents who are somewhat altruistic towards their offspring, there exists some protection for the welfare of future generations (Howarth and Norgaard 1993; Barro and Sala-i-Martin 1995, pp. 128–37). Indeed, depending on how exactly parents value the welfare of their offspring, SD might not clash with consumer sovereignty. But, in general, there is no guarantee that private altruism will lead to sustainable or socially optimal outcomes, both because this parental altruism might very well be of insufficient reach and because the welfare of future generations has to a certain extent the characteristics of a public good since what is beneficial for my own children often will be beneficial to others as well (Sen 1967).[6] Hence, consumer sovereignty could well conflict with SD. I assume here, however, that either consumers also act in accordance with the SD goal or — in case of conflict — that consumer sovereignty is overridden by policy makers. This, of course. leaves open the question why consumers should vote for policy makers who override their preferences. However, I am assuming away any problems of political economy in order to focus on my central research questions which presuppose that society is committed to SD. In this sense, the danger of "some tyranny of decision-making in the name of sustainability" (Pearce 1998, p. 48) is excluded in my analysis *by assumption*.

In some instances I shall present models to prove a point or for reasons of analytical rigour. These will mainly be simple models and I shall always explain the intuition behind the models presented. It is of great importance to me that I write clearly and concisely in a manner that is understandable not only by trained economists but also by everybody interested in SD with some basic knowledge of economics.

2.2 THE ETHICS OF SUSTAINABLE DEVELOPMENT

Why is it that — past concern about the welfare of coming generations notwithstanding — scrutinising the consequences of economic activity on the capacity for generating future utility has only relatively recently become an explicit academic enterprise? The answer is that it is only now that humankind itself *and* its economic activity has reached a scale that is potentially big enough to threaten the welfare prospects of future generations. The exponential rise in human numbers and in human resource appropriation and environmental destruction especially over the last few centuries is unprecedented in history. Also, human activity has now reached a scale that is capable of generating new environmental hazards. Climate change is an example which shows that the uncertainties mankind has to cope with have vastly increased (IPCC 2007a).

But this fact alone is not enough to make a case for SD. Ethical principles — and the aim to maintain the capacity to provide non-declining per capita utility forever is such a principle — never follow from facts alone. Hence this section briefly discusses the ethics of SD before the following main chapters take the commitment to SD for granted. Section 2.2.1 presents arguments for committing to SD. Section 2.2.2 discusses a kind of time-inconsistency problem of SD, that is, the incentive problems that arise from the hazard that coming generations might deviate from SD. Section 2.2.3 resolves two misunderstandings about what SD actually requires and clears the way for the main analysis in later chapters.

2.2.1   Reasons for Committing to Sustainable Development

Before actually providing some arguments to derive SD as an ethical principle let us first make explicit what everybody understands intuitively: why is it that the welfare of future generations cannot simply be left to their own care? The answer is of course that their very existence and the conditions of their existence are dependent on the present generation's actions. Future generations are 'downstream in time' so to speak and are therefore vulnerable to the choices made 'upstream in time'. This vulnerability is exacerbated by the fact that future generations almost by definition are not present in today's market and political decisions, that they have no present voice or vote or market power. However, the fundamental asymmetry between the present and the future really goes both ways: everything the present does can affect the future, nothing that the future does can affect the present any more. Harm that is undertaken now cannot as such be undone in the future, but, equally, present sacrifices for the benefit of the future cannot be compensated for by the future because by that time the present generation will no longer be around. This fundamental asymmetry puts the present generation into a strong position of dominance: it is an inter-temporal dictator, not even by its own choice but simply due to the fact that the flow of time is unidirectional and cannot be reversed. A natural seductive question is then: why not exploit this unequal position and maximise our own utility without any concern for the future? 'Après nous le déluge?' Indeed, why not?

One answer could be that since people have children this shows their concern for the future. The problem with this argument is that not all people have children, that some who do have them, treat them rather badly and that while people might care about their own children and grandchildren and great-grandchildren maybe, as soon as we consider the distant future things have become already so remote that nobody could claim direct kinship relations any more. Immediate offspring concern does not reach as far as the consequences of our economic activity do — climate change being a case in point.

More generally, the fact that people have children does not answer the question *why* we should care for the future. As I said, normative principles do not follow from facts. So let us come up with a normative argument. Maybe we should care for the future because it is right or just to do so. But not a lot has been gained therewith, the question then being why is concern for the future right or just?

One possible answer was given by Immanuel Kant's deontological moral theory which found its most widely known expression in his categorical imperative: "Act only according to that maxim by which you can at the same time will that it should become a universal law" (Kant 1785, p. 51, my translation). Following this imperative, we should not only care for the future as such, but even espouse the principle of maintaining the capacity to provide non-declining future utility. This is because we could not wish that any other principle should become a universal law since this would imply that we possibly would have been worse off due to decisions of others in the past, which is not in our own interest.

However, the next question is then 'why should we follow the categorical imperative?' As with all moral principles, there can be no conclusive, definitive answer that could not be questioned for some reason or other. Nevertheless, a good argument for following the categorical imperative can be made by applying the 'veil of ignorance' of John Rawls's (1972) *A Theory of Justice*.[7] According to Rawls, moral principles are considered just or fair if they could be chosen by a representative rational individual in an 'original position' behind a virtual veil of ignorance concerning his or her future position both in time and space and his or her social position in society.[8] They are considered fair precisely because, due to this ignorance, the representative individual cannot construct principles that are directly designed to further his or her own advantage. What is important for our analysis here is that the representative individual would not know which generation he or she would belong to. Hence accepting the categorical imperative as a moral norm, and the principle of sustainability following therefrom, could be said to lie in the best self-interest of the individual: if I do not know which generation I shall belong to, then the categorical imperative and the principle that no generation is allowed to gain at the expense of future generations could be said to protect my interests best.[9]

Note, however, that the imperative does not follow compellingly from the original position. If the representative individual behind the veil of ignorance exhibited strong risk preference he or she might be willing to accept a 'first come first serve' rule in which the first generations are allowed to improve their own lot at the expense of the welfare and, indeed, the existence of later generations, on the hope that he or she would end up in an earlier generation. On the other hand, the acceptance of the categorical imperative does not depend on extreme risk averseness, as the 'maximin' or 'difference' principle does, which Rawls himself derived from his theory of the original position.[10]

For more on the distinction between the principle of sustainability and the maximin principle see Section 2.2.3.1, p. 17.

To summarise, arguments derived from Kant's deontological moral philosophy and from a Rawlsian 'original position' point of view can make SD plausible as an ethical choice. Of course, many ethical issues have not been discussed here (such as Parfit's (1983) 'non-identity-problem'). But this book is in general not about moral philosophy. The limited purpose of this small section was to give a start-up motivation for committing to SD and to show that the principle of sustainability is not an implausible moral norm for inter-generational decision making.

2.2.2   The Time-inconsistency Problem of Sustainable Development

In this section a problem is highlighted that is rarely recognised in the literature on SD. The problem is as follows: assume that the present generation commits itself to SD, that is commits itself to maintain the capacity to provide non-declining per capita utility *into the indefinite future*. Obviously, it can only control the present, but not the indefinite future. It can make present sacrifices that it expects not to contradict SD, but it cannot force the next generation, and the next after the next and so on to commit themselves to SD. There is a time-inconsistency problem here: the present generation would like, but is unable to bind all coming generations to its own ethical choice for SD. Some future generation might well find it appropriate to deviate from SD or to abandon it completely. But this possibility has severe repercussions on the incentives for the current generation to opt for SD in the first instance: what is the point in making present sacrifices if the benefits of those sacrifices that were thought to benefit all future generations can be reaped by some single future generation that opts out from SD?

There is no easy solution to the fundamental time-inconsistency problem of SD. At the end of the day, the only thing the current generation can do is to influence coming generations such that they regard their enduring commitment to SD as a decent and 'right' decision. Surely, the current generation cannot influence very distant generations directly, but it can influence the next generation through the education of the current children and adolescents. If each generation instructs its offspring to regard SD as a desirable goal then the problem of time-inconsistency could be overcome. Admittedly, there is no guarantee that future generations will stick to SD, but the current generation might well be sufficiently convinced that they feel undeterred from incurring costs for the benefit of the future due to the still existing possibilities that their efforts will be frustrated by coming generations.

2.2.3   Two Misunderstandings about Sustainable Development Resolved

There are two main misunderstandings about SD that should be corrected at the beginning of this analysis because if they represented valid claims then the justification for the book would be severely put into doubt.

2.2.3.1 'SD might lock society into eternal poverty'
The first one is that sticking to SD will lock society into eternal poverty if it is poorly endowed at the start. Solow (1974a) developed this concern when he examined how applying Rawls's (1972) maximin rule to the inter-generational problem of the optimal depletion of a given stock of a non-renewable resource and the accumulation of man-made capital would affect current and future utility. Richter (1994, p. 46) and Dasgupta (1994, p. 35) have raised similar concerns. I shall not reproduce Solow's model since his proposition is easy to understand intuitively. The argument is as follows:

1. The maximin-rule means that the utility of the worst-off generation has to be maximised.

2. It follows that utility has to be constant throughout time, that is, utility has to be equal for all generations. Why? Imagine otherwise: some generation has higher utility than other generations. But then the maximin criterion would call for shifting utility away from this generation to others who are worse off. The same applies vice versa if some generation has lower utility than other generations. Only, this time, utility has to be shifted towards this generation. Equilibrium is where all generations have equal utility. Hence utility has to be constant throughout time. (In Solow's model utility can be shifted to and from generations simply by allocating more or less of the available stock of the non-renewable resource to them.)

3. It follows that the initial generation cannot be asked for even the smallest sacrifice in the consumption of their share of the resource that would allow investment into man-made capital and an accumulation of this form of capital over time because that would make it worse off than future genera-tions. Hence if the initial situation is such that society is poor, humankind will be locked into poverty throughout time.[11] That is, the welfare proper-ties of the maximin criterion depend very much on "the mercy of the initial conditions" (Solow 1974a, p. 33).

If the argument was valid, then it would establish a huge rebuff for the SD case because society would be required to stick to constant utility when it might have had rising utility throughout time due to the accumulation of man-made capital if only some initial small sacrifice was made. It would be rather difficult then to do justice both to the present and to future generations. Fortunately, the argument is based on a misunderstanding of SD.

There are two possible ways to show this. The rather pragmatic counter-argument says that we are presently in a situation that is no longer character-ised by an initial lack of wealth. That earlier generations have made sacrifices for us, we cannot change any more. It is futile to imagine how poor we would still be, had earlier generations already applied the maximin criterion. Now that we are no longer poor, applying the maximin criterion does not lock future generations into eternal poverty. Dasgupta and Heal (1979, p. 311) seem to endorse this argument for rich countries. But one of the problems with this line of thought is just that: it does not apply to poor countries and arguably most of the developing countries are still poor by any measure. An-other problem is that it still locks society into a constant utility time path, although maybe from a higher initial level of utility.

Fortunately, the second counter-argument does not depend on the present generation being rich and refutes the supposition that sustainability locks society into a constant path of utility over time. It simply says that SD neither is equivalent to, nor implies the maximin criterion: SD is *not* calling for con-stant or equal utility, but for maintaining the capacity to provide non-declining utility. This might appear as a minor difference in the choice of words, but it produces a huge difference in its ethical prescriptions. For SD, properly interpreted, allows earlier generations to make *voluntary* sacrifices in order that coming generations can enjoy higher utility whereas the maximin criterion does not. In some sense this counter-argument turns the debate over SD from its head back to its feet. The 'locked into eternal poverty' argument sprang from concern over the present generation's utility, whereas SD was genuinely developed out of concern for the utility of future generations. No proponent of SD ever denied the present generation the right to make *volun-tary* sacrifices for the future (nor, to be fair, did Solow do so; he was only exploring the consequences of applying the maximin criterion). SD rules out 'mortgaging the future', so to speak, but it does not rule out bequeathing a better world. On the other hand, nor does SD *require* to bequeath a *better* world. Barry's (1991, p. 267) claim that:

> if one believes that successive generations made sacrifices in the (no doubt vague) expectation that each generation would pass on more than it inherited, this would constitute a prima facie case for saying that the present generation has a certain obligation to continue with this process

is not backed by the principle of sustainability. SD as defined here only calls for *maintaining* the capacity to provide non-declining future utility.

A different, and still unresolved question is whether the obligation to some future generation changes if an earlier generation deviated from the principle of sustainability – see the discussion of the time-inconsistency problem in section 2.2.2, p. 16. Does this generation have to compensate for the devia- tion of the past or does it simply have to maintain the now lower capacity to provide non-declining utility? Strictly speaking, sustainability would only require the latter, but compensation might be expected if the costs of doing so are low. There really is no general answer to this question, however.

2.2.3.2 'SD demands the choice of greatly inferior utility paths'
A similar argument as that under Section 2.2.3.1 holds that SD requires soci- ety to prefer very low constant utility paths to a persistently rising path that has a temporary very small decline in utility somewhere along the path. Re- member from section 2.1, p. 7, that SD was not defined in direct utility terms, but in terms of maintaining the capacity to provide non-declining future wel- fare. Nonetheless, for the sake of refuting the argument, assume that a society

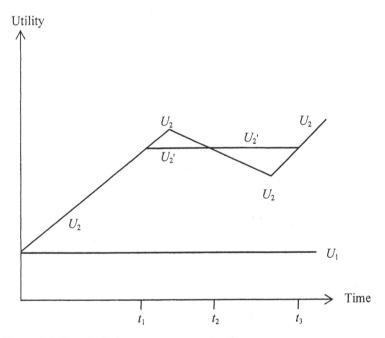

Figure 2.1 Non-declining versus constant utility

committed to SD could directly choose a utility path over time and assume for simplicity that there are only two utility paths which society could choose from: U_1 provides constant utility forever, U_2 provides higher utility than U_1 everywhere, but with a temporary dip along the path. Look at Figure 2.1 on p. 19 which is taken from Pezzey (1995, p. 4) with amendments. The argument asserts that SD requires that U_1 is preferred over U_2. Beckerman (1994, p. 196) therefore concludes that sticking to SD would force society to choose greatly inferior utility paths. Again, if the argument was valid it would present a huge rebuff against the case for SD. Fortunately, it is not valid.

The counter-argument runs as follows: if the economy is 'productive' in the sense that saving a share of current income for investment leads to a net increase in future utility (Pezzey 1995, p. 12), then the utility path with the temporary decline in utility can be modified into a path that is non-declining along the whole path by saving a certain amount before the decline is supposed to occur and then using those savings later on to prevent the decline. Referring to Figure 2.1, ensuring sustainability would mean starting 'extra-saving' from time t_1 to t_2 and to use these 'extra-savings' to prevent a decline in utility from time t_2 to t_3. That is, from t_1 to t_3 society deviates from U_2 to follow the utility path U'_2, after t_3 society returns to the original path U_2.

The assumption that the economy is 'productive' is not very restrictive, so applying SD does not force society to choose greatly inferior utility paths. What it does, however, is to require earlier generations to save more so that later generations do not have to experience a decline in utility. Hence, the earlier generations' utility does not rise as much if the sustainability constraint is binding as it would without the constraint. But, then again, this is what SD is all about.

2.3   WEAK VERSUS STRONG SUSTAINABILITY

In Section 2.1, p. 7, SD was defined as development that does not decrease the capacity to provide non-declining per capita utility for infinity. But what does that mean and how is it to be ensured? This, of course, is the point of divergence and it opens fundamental disagreements that are not to be confused with semantic disputes about the meaning of the term. SD is a contestable concept and there is real struggle over its interpretation in practice.

In this section the two opposing paradigms of sustainability relevant for the analysis are presented. Their main difference derives from starkly contrasting assumptions about the substitutability of natural capital. I call WS the substitutability paradigm, whereas SS can be perceived as the non-substitutability paradigm. Section 2.3.1 presents WS and Section 2.3.2 presents SS. The distinction between WS and SS should presumably be credited to Pearce et al. (1989).

2.3.1 The Paradigm of Weak Sustainability

WS is often called 'Solow–Hartwick sustainability' (for example, by Gutes 1996, p. 150) because it is based on the work of Nobel Prize winner Robert Solow (1974a, 1974c, 1986, 1993a, 1993b) and John Hartwick (1977, 1978a, 1978b, 1990, 1993). WS requires keeping *total net investment*, suitably defined to encompass all relevant forms of capital, above zero. This can be interpreted as a generalisation and extension to the so-called *Hartwick rule* (Hartwick 1977). WS is built on the assumption of substitutability of natural capital (as well as any other form of capital). Because of this assumption I call WS the 'substitutability paradigm'. Hence its investment rule, whilst covering all relevant forms of capital, need not distinguish between specific forms of capital. If investment in man-made and human capital is big enough to compensate for the depreciation of natural capital, an explicit policy of sustainable development is not even necessary for then sustainability is guaranteed quasi-automatically.[12] If not, apply suitable measures (for example, a resource tax, saving subsidy or environmental regulation) to keep total net investment above zero (Mikesell 1994, p. 85) — see Section 5.1, p. 126, for more detail.

Note that usually the relevant literature speaks of savings rather than investment and uses the term 'genuine savings' (GS), a term introduced by Hamilton (1994), for total net investment. To add to the confusion, the World Bank now uses the term 'net adjusted savings' to refer to genuine savings in its flagship statistical publication *World Development Indicators*. In my view, which is shared by Dasgupta (2001b) and Arrow et al. (2004, 2007), genuine investment would be a better term to use than genuine savings. The reason is that in macroeconomics, savings are often defined as private savings. For example, in a closed economy, private savings is equal to investment plus government expenditures minus taxes. Savings in the usage of genuine savings instead refers to the sum of private plus public savings (taxes minus government expenditures), which generates the equality between total savings and investment. For the rest of this book, I shall speak mainly of savings instead of investment to maintain harmony with the usage of terms in most of the relevant literature.

WS is built upon the assumption that natural capital is either abundant or substitutable both as an input into the production of consumption goods and as provider of direct utility. This means that natural capital can be safely run down as long as enough man-made and human capital is built up in exchange. In the words of Solow: "Earlier generations are entitled to draw down the pool (optimally, of course!) so long as they add (optimally, of course!) to the stock of reproducible capital" (Solow 1974a, p. 41).

With respect to natural capital as an input into the production of consumption goods, proponents of WS hold that:

- natural resources are super-abundant;
- or the elasticity for substituting man-made capital for resources in the production function is equal to or greater than unity, even in the limit of extremely high output–resource ratios;
- or technical progress can overcome any resource constraint.

Quite clearly, given the assumptions about the availability of natural resources and possibilities for substitution for natural capital in the production of consumption goods, WS is a paradigm of resource optimism — see Section 3.2, p. 48. As regards natural capital as a provider of direct utility, the reader might be uncomfortable with the proposition that the components in the utility function are substitutes for each other. It means that a rise in consumption (C) can compensate future generations for a decline in the stock of renewable resources (Z) or a rise in the pollution stock (P). It is important to note therefore, that WS holds that there are good reasons to presume that with rising incomes and hence rising C, Z will *eventually* rise as well and P will *eventually* fall. That is, WS holds that economic growth or a rise in consumption C will eventually be good for the environment as well. Because the proponents of WS believe that, eventually, with rising incomes the state of the environment will improve as well, I call them environmental optimists – see Section 3.3, p. 74.

Note that although WS is deeply rooted within neoclassical economic thinking given its assumption of substitutability of natural capital, it is still conceptually different. What makes it different are two things: first is the willingness of its proponents to take natural capital both as an input into production and as a direct source of welfare seriously and include it into their models (compare Colby 1991). Second, WS differs from 'present-value maximisation', the reigning utilitarian paradigm of neoclassical welfare economics, in postulating the constraint that the capacity to provide non-declining utility must be maintained at any point in time. Whilst Beckerman (1994) provides an excellent defence of neoclassical welfare economics, he is therefore wrong in saying that WS "offers nothing beyond traditional welfare maximisation" (p. 191). More formally, WS in effect denies the validity of *potential* Pareto improvements in an inter-generational context and demands *actual* compensation if future generations would suffer from an action that benefits the current generation. That is for inter-generational allocation decisions, WS rules out the validity of the so-called Hicks–Kaldor test (Hicks 1939; Kaldor 1939) that is the common decision criterion in traditional welfare economics. Present-value maximisation and sustainability can strikingly conflict with each other. Appendix 1, p. 196, provides a stylised example showing that applying present-value maximisation as the decision criterion could even lead to the optimal (efficient) choice of a path that finally ends up in catastrophe, that is to zero utility and therefore to the extinction of humankind![13] I do not claim that this stylised example is particularly realistic, but it shows that, in principle, applying present-value maximisation can lead to utmost unsustainability. As Chichilnisky (1996) has shown, the clash between present-value maximisation and sustainability holds true even for less restrictive definitions of sustainability. Her definition only rules out dictatorship of the present and the future, that is, giving no weight to the distant future or no weight to the present, but does not rule out declining utility along the path. Not surprisingly, since present-value maximisation with any positive constant discount rate gives only infinitesimal small weight to the distant future it clashes with this definition of sustainability as well.

2.3.2 The Paradigm of Strong Sustainability

Proponents of SS are not against achieving WS. Rather, they would regard achieving WS as an important first, but insufficient, step into the right direction. In a sense, SS encompasses WS, but adding further requirements. In this perspective, WS is better than traditional neoclassical economics, but it is still a far cry away from what is needed for SD.

Herman Daly's (1992a) book *Steady-state economics*, first published in 1977, might mark the foundation of SS. Daly, one of the founders of the International Society for Ecological Economics (ISEE), and Robert Costanza, co-founder and until 1997 the president of the ISEE, have also been two of the most prominent proponents of SS (Daly 1991, 1992a, 1992b, 1994, 1995a, 1996, 2005; Daly and Costanza 1992). Many others have also made early contributions to the creation of the paradigm. To list just a few: Robert Goodland (for example, Goodland and Daly 1992), Roefie Hueting (for example, Hueting 1980), Richard Norgaard (for example, Norgaard 1994), John Proops (for example, Faber, Manstetten and Proops 1992), Charles Perrings (for example, Perrings 1989), Brian Barry (for example, Barry 1991), Michael Jacobs (for example, Jacobs 1991) and Clive Spash (for example, Spash 1993). David Pearce and his colleagues have also provided arguments for stronger versions of sustainability (for example, Pearce, Barbier and Markandya 1990; Turner and Pearce 1992) without necessarily subscribing to the paradigm of SS. The many contributions to SS render its definition somewhat more difficult than the one of WS.

In spite of SS being more difficult to define than WS, the essence of SS is that it regards natural capital as fundamentally non-substitutable through other forms of capital. I therefore call SS the 'non-substitutability paradigm'. There are two differing interpretations of SS in the literature. In one interpretation SS is the paradigm that calls for preserving natural capital itself in value terms. Note that SS in this interpretation does not demand the preservation of nature as it is. For example, SS does not require never using non-renewable resources such as coal, as Klepper and Stähler (1998, p. 489) erroneously suggest. It requires, however, reinvesting the receipts from coal mining into the development of renewable energy sources in order to keep the aggregate value of the total natural resource stock constant (Hohmeyer 1992). More generally, Barbier, Pearce and Markandya (1990) have suggested compensating depreciation in the natural capital stock with adequate shadow projects.

One of the problems of this definition of SS is that it does not constrain at all substitutability within natural capital. This is clearly at odds with the spirit of SS. To put it drastically, it would be strange to assume that more man-made capital cannot substitute for a bigger hole in the ozone layer, but an increased number of whales can. Clearly, substitutability within natural capital needs to be constrained as well, which is what the second interpretation of SS achieves.

In this second interpretation, SS is not defined in value terms, but calls for the preservation of the *physical* stock of those forms of natural capital that are regarded as non-substitutable (so-called critical natural capital) (see, for example, Ekins, Folke and De Groot 2003; Ekins 2003). Also note that this interpretation does not allow for any substitutability among different forms of 'critical' natural capital. Nor does it imply keeping nature as it is, however. Indeed, such a task would be impossible. But it calls for maintaining its functions intact. If the flows from these forms of natural capital are used, then their regenerative capacity must not be exceeded, so that their environmental function remains intact (Goodland 1995; Hueting and Reijnders 1998). Hueting and Reijnders (1998, p. 145) give the example that "the rate of erosion of topsoil may not exceed the rate of formation of such soil due to weathering". More generally, management rules for preserving critical natural capital would include the following (Daly 1992a, p. 256):

- Use renewable resources such that their stock does not deteriorate. That is: Harvest *at maximum* the maximum sustainable yield.

- Use the environment as a sink for pollution only to the extent that its natural absorptive capacity does not deteriorate over time.

At least some of the proponents of SS are quite pessimistic about the availability of non-renewable natural resource availability and believe that past levels of resource depletion ("the onetime bonanza of fossil fuel consumption", Daly 1992b, p. 244) cannot be sustained into the future. As an additional requirement they would therefore demand that the current generation needs to compensate the future for its use of non-renewable resources with investment into replacement renewable resources that are functionally equivalent.

In Chapter 4, I shall argue that the second interpretation of SS is more plausible. There I shall also discuss some reasons for justifying the assumption of non-substitutability. In short, the main suggested reasons for non-substitutability is a combination of the following factors (see Turner and Pearce 1992, p. 7):

- We are largely uncertain and ignorant about the detrimental consequences of depleting natural capital.
- Natural capital loss often is irreversible.
- Some forms of natural capital provide basic life-support functions.
- Individuals are highly adverse to losses in natural capital. A stronger suggestion would be that individuals cannot be compensated for any environmental degradation via increased consumption opportunities (Spash 1993, 2002).

To distinguish SS clearly from the substitutability assumption of WS, it will be implied for the analysis in this book that SS holds that rising consumption cannot compensate future generations for rising environmental degradation, that is, it cannot substitute for a declining stock of directly utility-relevant renewable resources and a rising stock of pollution. Such a position is often derived from a normative rights-based theory of intergenerational justice. Sen (1982, p. 346), for example, argues that "lasting pollution is a kind of calculable oppression of the future generation", which he regards as being similar in character to torture. Consequently, Sen (1982, p. 347) rejects the idea that future generations could be compensated for 'lasting pollution' via increased material welfare:

> Even if the future generation may be richer and may enjoy a higher welfare level, and even if its marginal utility from the consumption gain is accepted to be less than the marginal welfare loss of the present generation, this may still

not be accepted to be decisive for rejecting the investment when the alternative implies long-term effects of environmental pollution.

Similarly, Barry (1991, p. 264) regards environmental pollution as not amenable to compensation by doing future generations some other good, as he makes clear in drawing the following analogy:

> We will all agree that doing harm is in general not cancelled out by doing good, and conversely that doing some good does not license one to do harm provided it does not exceed the amount of good. For example, if you paid for the re-alignments of a dangerous highway intersection and saved an average of two lives a year, that would not mean that you could shoot one motorist per year and simply reckon on coming out ahead.

Maybe the most elaborate and explicit argument for non-compensability was put forward by Spash (1993, 1994, 2002). He makes it very clear that in his view "compensation does not licence society to pollute, provided the damages created are less than the amount of compensation" (Spash 1993, p. 127) and postulates an "inviolable right of future generations to be free of intergenerational environmental damages" (ibid.).

Proponents of SS also tend to be pessimistic with respect to the environmental consequences of economic growth. Goodland and Daly (1992, p. 129) and Daly and Goodland (1994, p. 76), for example, define throughput growth as an increase in the capture of resources and the pollution of more sinks, while development is seen as an improvement in productivity and efficiency. Daly (1992a) calls an economy that develops but does not grow anymore a 'steady-state economy'.[14] Reaching a steady-state is seen as the ultimate goal: "Sustainable development ... necessarily means a radical shift from a growth economy and all it entails to a steady-state economy, certainly in the North, and eventually in the South as well" (Daly 1996, p. 31).

Whilst WS could be interpreted as an extension to neoclassical economics, SS calls for a paradigmatic shift away from neoclassical environmental and resource economics towards an 'ecological economics'. Daly (1996, p. 45) demands a drastic change in "the basic framework of our thinking" towards a vision of the macroeconomy as a subsystem of the finite ecosystem. If the macroeconomy was not envisioned as 'the whole' anymore, but as part of the larger ecosystem, the question of an optimal scale of the macroeconomy would naturally arise (Daly 1991). The scale is optimal where the benefits of a marginal increase in the macroeconomy just equal the costs. An ecological economics would pay priority attention to both the limitedness of resource input ('source') and the limitedness of the waste and pollution absorbing capacity of the environment ('sink'). It would thus embed the economy into the bigger ecosystem and stress the constraints that are put on its growth:

> The necessary change in vision is to picture the macroeconomy as an open subsystem of the finite natural ecosystem (environment), and not as an isolated circular flow of abstract exchange value, unconstrained by mass, balance, entropy and finitude. (Daly 1996, p. 48)

> Historically, in the 'empty world' economy, manmade capital was limiting and natural capital superabundant. We have now, due to demographic and economic growth, entered the era of the 'full world' economy, in which the roles are reversed. More and more it is remaining natural capital that now plays the role of limiting factor. (Daly 1995a, p. 50)

An ecological economics would encompass neoclassical economic theory with its emphasis on an efficient *allocation* of resources, but superimpose on this the criterion of a just inter-generational *distribution* and an optimal *scale* of the macroeconomy. Thus, SS would represent a higher level paradigm in the sense of Kuhn (1962, p. 95) rather than a mutually exclusive alternative to neoclassical economic theory. We have already seen, in discussing the difference between WS and neoclassical welfare economics, that the question of a 'just' inter-generational distribution is different from an efficient allocation of resources. But so, Daly argues, is the question of an optimal scale different in kind from the optimal (efficient) allocation of resources (see also Daly et al. 2007). Daly's favourite example is that of a boat that sinks in spite of the load being optimally allocated on board — simply because the overall weight is too much (Daly 1991, p. 257).

The optimal scale is rather thought of as a theoretical leitmotif than a practical device, however, because "discontinuities, thresholds, and complex webs of interdependence make a mockery of the idea that we can nicely balance smoothly increasing ecosystem costs with the diminishing marginal utility of productions at the macro level" (Daly 1996, p. 54). This has implications for how risk, uncertainty and ignorance are dealt with — see Chapter 4, p. 97.

2.4   THE IMPORTANCE OF THE SUBSTITUTABILITY ASSUMPTION: THE CASE OF CLIMATE CHANGE

In this section it will be stressed how important the assumption of substitutability is, using climate change as a case example. The economics of climate change as well as perceptions of what is the verdict of the mainstream economic profession on action on climate change have dramatically changed since the publication of the so-called Stern Review (Stern 2007), which was commissioned by the UK government, and the ensuing controversy that followed its publication. As Heal (2009, p. 18) has put it in answering his rhetorical question of what we have learned from the Stern Review and the ensuing debate: "I think this should change the presumption that economists hold about the need for strong action on climate change from largely negative (prior to Stern) to positive."

Before the Stern Review, the best-known cost-benefit analysis of the expected consequences of climate change was the one of William Nordhaus from Yale University — see Nordhaus (1991a, 1994), Nordhaus and Popp (1997), Nordhaus and Boyer (2000) and Nordhaus (2008). Nordhaus found that large-scale greenhouse gas abatement is unwarranted and that only modest policy measures should be undertaken that would not prevent a substantial increase in accumulated greenhouse gases in the atmosphere. As I will show in this section, Nordhaus's analysis implicitly presupposes the validity of the substitutability assumption of the paradigm of WS.

Most of Nordhaus's critics have concentrated on the issue of discounting and demanded that a lower discount rate should be applied for reasons of inter-generational fairness: being later in time should be no reason for counting less (for example, Broome 1992; Cline 1992; Azar and Sterner 1996; Stern 2007). Other critics have questioned whether consumption growth can compensate for environmental degradation caused by climate change. In their view, discounting is not the main issue, but substitutability is: any call for aggressive emission abatement must directly attack the substitutability assumption (see, for example, Spash 2002; Neumayer 1999b, 2007; Helm 2008).

I select climate change as a case example because its features — current economic activity has large-scale long-term future consequences on both environmental amenities, food, water, human health and the capacity to provide material goods — suggest it as an ideal object of study for questions of sustainability. The major impacts of climate change will not be felt for another 50 years or so (IPCC 2007a). That is, climate change will mainly impact upon future generations but less so upon the current one. Hence the benefits of abating greenhouse gas emissions will be mainly enjoyed by future generations, while the costs of abating greenhouse emissions would have to be borne already by the current generation. Much of what will be said here could similarly be applied to other global long-term environmental problems, however, such as biodiversity loss, and the problem of radioactivity caused by nuclear waste.

Discussing climate change is no easy task: the science and economics of climate change is very complex (see IPCC 2007a, 2007b, 2007c), there are numerous highly technical models for cost-benefit analysis and there is a vast and continually growing literature discussing the pros and cons of controlling CO_2 and other greenhouse gas emissions.[15] Quite clearly, I cannot and do not want to discuss all the details of this debate. I shall restrict my discussion to the cost-benefit analysis of the 'DICE-model' and 'RICE-model' of William Nordhaus (1991a, 1994, 2008) and to the Stern Review (Stern 2007) as well as the controversies around both sets of studies.

2.4.1 The Nordhaus Approach Towards Climate Change

Nordhaus's (2008) DICE–2007 model — the Dynamic Integrated Model of Climate and the Economy — is a dynamic optimisation economic growth model based on Ramsey (1928) in which a social planner maximises the integrated sum of the utility of per capita consumption. The RICE-model — the Regional dynamic Integrated Model of Climate and the Economy — is the regionalised counterpart. Output is produced by a constant returns to scale Cobb–Douglas production function. Output production generates CO_2 emissions which lead to climate change which leads, in turn, to losses in output. Nordhaus (2008) comes to the conclusion that the optimum cost-efficient policy is to reduce emissions by 25 per cent in 2050 and by 45 per cent in 2100, relative to the projected emissions increase that would happen without any climate control policies in place (baseline case). Note that because uncontrolled emissions are expected to grow tremendously over time, Nordhaus's optimal policy recommendation does not call for any emission cuts relative to, say, the level in 1990, but for further and substantial increases in greenhouse gas emissions over time. In the optimum CO_2 emissions would be allowed to increase from 7.4 billion tons of carbon per year in 2005 to about 12.4 billion tons per year in 2100, with more emission cuts relative to the baseline case in later rather than earlier periods – a policy recommendation that Nordhaus calls the 'policy ramp'. Nordhaus expects this to lead to an increase in global mean temperature by 2.6 and 3.4 degrees Centigrade in 2100 and 2200, respectively (ibid., p. 14), which he expects to generate a present value residual damage cost from climate change in the order of $17 trillion, down from $22.6 trillion in the baseline case without any climate policy in place.

Nordhaus implicitly assumes the validity of the substitutability assumption which is at the heart of the paradigm of WS. He does so in two closely related ways: first, all benefits and costs are meshed together and computed as shares of total output — regardless of whether they are connected to environmental amenities or not. The only costs due to climate change are costs in the form of output losses. Note that Nordhaus (2008) does not simply ignore environmental amenities. Indeed he states explicitly that "consumption should be viewed broadly to include not only food and shelter but also nonmarket environmental amenities and services" (Nordhaus 2008, p. 34). However, substitutability amongst these items is not restricted (Sterner and Persson 2008). This is valid only if future generations do not care about whether, say, the costs of climate change are connected to environmental amenities that provide them with direct utility or restrain their capacity to consume material goods.

Second, Nordhaus presumes substitutability in the way he discounts the future. His formula for discounting is the so-called Ramsey formula which is formally derived and discussed in Appendix 2, p. 198. The formula is as follows:

$$r = \rho + \eta(C) \cdot \frac{\dot{C}}{C} \qquad (2.3)$$

The social discount rate r should be equal to the sum of the pure rate of time preference ρ and the product of the elasticity of the marginal utility of consumption $\eta(C)$ and the per capita growth rate of consumption $\dot{C}/C$. If $\rho > 0$, this is called (pure) utility discounting. Nordhaus (1994, p. 123) calls discounting because $\eta(C)\dot{C}/C > 0$, 'growth discounting'.

The specific discount rate has undergone several modifications throughout the years from the early versions of DICE to DICE-2007. However, these changes relate more to the individual components of the Ramsey formula, rather than the resulting overall figure for a discount rate. Nordhaus does not base the discount rate on ethical principles (so-called prescriptive approach), but calibrates the individual components of the Ramsey formula to be such that they fit his estimate of actual, observed real rates of return on capital and savings rates (so-called descriptive approach toward discounting). This distinction is very important and makes Nordhaus's analysis radically different from the one provided in the Stern Review (Stern 2007), as we will see below.

Estimates of the real rate of return on capital, which is also called the opportunity cost of investment, vary, but they usually lie in the range of 4 per cent to 10 per cent per annum in developed countries (Nordhaus 1991a, p. 926). Manne and Richels (1995, p. 5) believe that 5 per cent represents a lower bound, Pearce (1993a, p. 60) thinks that 7 per cent comes close to the long-run average real rate of return, Cline (1992, p. 262) estimates it to be about 8 per cent. The World Bank usually does not accept any project with a rate of return of less than 10 per cent (Markandya and Pearce 1991, p. 140).

How does Nordhaus arrive at a particular discount rate then? Nordhaus (1994, p. 11) sets the pure rate of time preference ρ equal to a constant rate of 3 per cent. In the updated version of Nordhaus and Boyer (2000, p. 16) the pure rate of time preference is assumed to decrease slightly to 2.3 per cent in 2100 and 1.8 per cent in 2200 "because of the assumption of declining impatience", which is not further motivated, however. Nordhaus (1994, pp. 11f) assumes a logarithmic utility function for which $\eta(C)$ is equal to 1 and projects global $\dot{C}/C$ to be about 3 per cent in the first few years, declining slowly in later decades (ibid., p. 125). Hence his overall discount rate is approximately 6 per cent to start with. In his most recent analysis, Nordhaus (2008) lowers the pure rate of social time preference from 3 per cent to 1.5 per cent. As this would, ceteris paribus, generate a lower discount rate than what he regards as the real rate of return on capital, he recalibrates the utility function to match this real rate of return, which prompts him to use a value of $\eta(C)$ equal to 2. His estimate of future global consumption growth is also somewhat lower at an average of around 1.9 per cent in the first half century of projections. Together this gives a discount rate of around 5.5 per cent for the first half century of projections, which he regards as a good, conservative estimate of the real rate of return on capital.

Whatever the specific values that enter the Ramsey formula, the underlying assumption is substitutability of natural capital. To see why, recall the ethical rationale for the inclusion of $\eta(C)\dot{C}/C$ in the Ramsey formula: given that $\eta(C)\dot{C}/C > 0$, the future should count less because it is then presumed to be *better off* due to the increase in consumption (weighted by the elasticity of the marginal utility of consumption). That is, future losses arising from climate change, for example, in the form of environmental amenities, are implicitly assumed to be compensable by an increase in other consumption goods. Natural and other forms of capital are substitutes.

One might think that if the current generation was committed to WS this would demand higher emission abatement than found by Nordhaus since he does not explicitly take WS as a side constraint to his cost-benefit analysis. This is not the case, however. Solely judged from the requirements of WS it is most likely that no explicit abatement policy whatsoever is warranted! The reason is that if natural capital is substitutable then the very large projected increase in per capita income implies that future generations are likely to be materially much better off than the current generation and there is no need to combat climate change for reasons of sustainability — given the validity of the substitutability paradigm. Why does Nordhaus then come to the conclusion that some emission reductions are optimal? The answer is that Nordhaus endorses a utilitarian framework in which it so happens that even though the future is better off than the present, the current generation is still called upon to provide some additional sacrifices which make it still worse off in comparison to the future. This will be the case if the future benefits after discounting are higher than the present costs of sacrifice that bring the future benefits into effect. In this sense, Nordhaus's computations are more friendly to future generations than a mere commitment to WS would be. Note, however, that WS should be regarded as traditional neoclassical welfare economics plus the *additional* requirement to maintain the capacity to provide non-declining welfare over time. Thus interpreted, WS would come to the same conclusion as Nordhaus does.

2.4.2   Critique of the Nordhaus Approach (I): Discounting the Future

Many aspects of the Nordhaus approach have been criticised (Ayres and Walter 1991; Chapman, Suri and Hall 1995; Cline 1996; Ekins 1996; Howarth 1996; Tol 1994; Price 1995; Sterner and Persson 2008; Weitzman 2009a, 2009b). See, in particular, Weitzman (2009a, 2009b) who argues that Nordhaus's and other standard cost-benefit analyses of climate change neglect structural uncertainty regarding low-probability extreme-impact outcomes. I shall concentrate here on the two most important criticisms: the rate of discount used to value future costs and benefits and, in the next sub-section, the issue of substitutability of natural capital. I shall argue that the likely non-substitutability of natural capital loss inflicted by climate change provides the more persuasive criticism of Nordhaus's approach.

Most critics of Nordhaus have focused on the discount rate chosen. Lowering the applied discount rate would drastically increase the warranted emission abatement as confirmed by studies of Cline (1992), Fankhauser (1994), Chapman, Suri and Hall (1995) and, more recently and certainly most prominently, Stern (2007). The Stern Review advocates drastic and immediate action in order to stabilize emissions somewhere in the range of 450 to 550 parts per million CO_2 equivalent. The reason why a lower discount rate dramatically changes the optimal policy recommendation of a cost-benefit analysis of climate change lies in the distribution function of the net costs of climate change, which is heavily skewed towards the distant future. The lower the discount rate the more count the long-term damages of climate change in present value terms relative to the more near-term abatement costs.

As mentioned already, Nordhaus follows a descriptive approach towards discounting: the discount rate applied to climate change economics should mirror the real rate of return on capital. The descriptive approach can be justified on efficiency grounds. Efficiency requires that investments should be evaluated at their opportunity cost. If investments generate a 5-6 per cent real rate of return, then investments into climate change policies must generate the same rate of return to be considered optimal. Using a different, say lower, rate would channel scarce resources away from investments that provide the future with a higher real rate of return.

Let us now turn to the critique to Nordhaus's approach towards discounting. Dietz and Stern (2008) argue that to look for market rates of return as guidance on the choice of social discount rate used for decision making on climate change is misguided. The reason is that market rates are not socially optimal rates and that it is not clear what rates to use for the case of climate change, given that there is very little market information for investments concerning the very long run. In other words, Dietz and Stern (2008) argue that even if one wanted to follow the descriptive approach, it is not clear that this would necessarily lead to the high discount rates used by Nordhaus. Rates of return on long-term government bonds in the UK and US are much lower at around 1.5 per cent than private rates of return on capital (Stern 2008, p. 13).

Morever, many economists and philosophers have long since demanded that when it comes to long-term decision making, the discount rate should be set on ethical grounds, following the prescriptive instead of the descriptive approach. They have also typically demanded to set the pure rate of time preference equal to zero for reasons of inter-generational fairness: being later in time should as such be no reason for counting less (for example, Ramsey 1928; Pigou 1932; Rawls 1972; Broome 1992; Cline 1992; Azar and Sterner 1996; Stern 2007). The main argument is that future generations are excluded from today's market and political decisions (for example, Broome 1992, pp. 89f). If future generations could reveal their preferences they would surely opt for higher investments for the benefit of the future, thus driving down the real rate of return on investment. Since we cannot know counter-factually what the real rate of return on investment would be if future generations were not excluded from today's market and political decisions, it can be said to be fair to set the pure rate of time preference equal to zero: being later in time should be no reason for counting less.

Going beyond the issue of the pure rate of time preference, Azar and Sterner (1996, pp. 177ff) have further abandoned the assumption of a world-wide representative consumer and have examined the consequences of *intra*-generational unequal distribution. They argue as follows: if it is right to apply the Ramsey formula to future generations and ask what their marginal utility of rising consumption is, then it must also be right to to take into account the marginal utility of the much poorer people in the present-day and future developing world. It was taken as a justification for discounting that future generations are expected to be better off in Ramsey's formula. For the same reason Azar and Sterner (ibid., p. 178) argue "that a given ... cost which affects a poor person (in a poor country) *should be valued as a higher welfare cost than an equivalent cost affecting an average OECD citizen*". Because the costs of climate change are relatively higher in developing countries than in developed countries due to their greater vulnerability and their more restricted capacity for adaptation (IPCC 2007b), adjusting the discount rate along the lines of Azar and Sterner (1996) substantially increases the level of abatement that is warranted by a cost-benefit analysis of climate change.

Weitzman (1998) has provided an argument for declining discount rates. His argument is that there is fundamental uncertainty about the long-term future, which means we do not know what interest rate will then apply. It also means that only a state of the long-term future with low discount rates has any relevance for today as all other states of the world have become irrelevant due to the power of compound discounting at a high rate. Hence, whilst we can apply a high discount rate for the immediate future, the rate should decline for values in the long-term future. Weitzman's (1998) idea has sparked new interest in the issue of so-called hyperbolic or discounting at a declining rate (see, for example, Portney and Weyant 1999). Hyperbolic discounting will also result in more emission reductions than would be deemed optimal with conventional discounting. Heal (2009, p. 8), however, points out the weakness of a declining discount rate, namely its time inconsistency: "Any intertemporal plan constructed using such a discount rate will be dynamically inconsistent, in the sense that if we follow it for a period of time and then stop and ask what is the best continuation from where we are, it will not be the plan that we originally adopted."

The Stern Review (Stern 2007) is not the only, but certainly the most prominent study to have shown that applying a low discount rate favours much more drastic and immediate action compared to Nordhaus's analysis. There are of course many aspects that distinguish the Stern Review from previous studies. Some of them are based on laudable innovations, such as the more comprehensive treatment of future uncertainty and its acknowledgement that the expected growth rates of consumption, and therefore one part of the discount rate, are endogenous to future paths of emissions and damage from climate change. It is impossible to do justice to the detail, breadth and depth of a report of almost 700 pages here. Instead, I will concentrate on the issue of the discount rate, which has an overwhelming impact on the economics of climate change. Stern (2007) endorses the prescriptive approach and sets the pure rate of time preference, ρ, essentially to zero. He also assumes a value of one for $\eta(C)$, which implies logarithmic utility in the social welfare function and, thus, some mild aversion against income inequality. Concretely, it is assumed that equal proportional (that is, percentage) increases in consumption are of equal social value independently of the consumption level of the individual or generation. In plain terms, if the current generation has consumption level 10 and some future generation has consumption level 20, then one extra unit of consumption to the poorer current generation (equivalent to 10 per cent extra consumption for the present) is counted equal to two extra units of consumption to the future generation that is twice as rich (also equivalent to 10 per cent extra consumption for the future). A pure rate of time preference of essentially zero added to the forecasts of future consumption growth made by Stern (2007) multiplied by an elasticity of marginal utility of consumption of one, together generate an overall discount rate of something like 1.4 per cent in the review, but variable depending on emission and climate change paths.

Critics of the review have been quick to pick up the crucial role of the discount rate (Mendelsohn 2006; Dasgupta 2007; Nordhaus 2007, 2008; Tol and Yohe 2006). Some argue that low discount rates like those employed in the review are simply inconsistent with the allocation of income toward consumption and savings by the current generation. Specifically, if the current generation were serious about employing such a low discount rate, it would have to consume far less now and invest the enhanced savings for the benefit of the future. That it does not do so is taken as evidence by critics that the current generation does not embrace such low discount rates and that therefore higher discount rates should be employed.

Although I have some sympathy for the arguments in favour of a low discount rate, ultimately I think they are not persuasive as long as one does not simultaneously abandon the substitutability assumption. While it is true that future generations are not present in today's markets, the actual rate of discount used by the present generation does not violate the WS constraint *if* consumption is rising over time. If future generations were around and could reveal their preferences in today's markets, investment into man-made and human capital would be higher, the real rate of return on capital and hence the discount rate would be lower and consumption would rise *still faster* over time. But if the substitutability assumption is valid, then there is no compelling justification to lower the rate of discount for reasons of sustainability if non-declining utility can already be ensured by the higher rate of discount that mirrors existing real rates of return on capital. Furthermore, low discount rates are contestable on ethical grounds as well. This becomes clear by looking at worst-case scenarios. Assume that the world fails to follow the review's recommendations and that it will achieve only very modest emission reductions over the next decades. In this case, the review predicts a substantial loss of output (consumption) for far-off future generations, possibly up to 20 per cent or even up to 35.2 per cent. However, because of baseline consumption growth the future will still be very much better off than the present, despite climate change damage. For example, based on the assumptions in the review, even in the worst-case scenario the future generation of 2200 will still be eight times better off than the present one (rather than 12.3 times better off without climate change). Within the cost-benefit analysis (CBA) framework of the review allowing such damage to occur is clearly sub-optimal and inefficient. But the worst that can happen if the world fails to heed the review's advice and employs a higher discount rate is that the distant future is only much, much better off than the present instead of being much, much, much better off. That is too bad, but it is not really a tragedy.

If future generations are far better off than the present anyway, then there is no compelling ground for employing a low discount rate on grounds of inter-generational fairness. As Lind (1995, p. 384) has put it:

> Can we justify current generations sacrificing 2–3 per cent of GWP [gross world product, E.N.] to increase the wealth of future generations who even after deduction for the high damage scenario are 2–15 times richer than the present generation? The answer is clearly no on the basis of intergenerational equity, which must weigh in favour of the current generation.

Again, clearly such reasoning depends on the validity of the substitutability paradigm.

What about the argument of Azar and Sterner (1996)? Here things are somewhat different. If we discount future values because they accrue to richer people in the future then it is consistent to count values that accrue to the future *intra*-generational poor differently from those that accrue to the rich. With climate change, there will be winners and losers and it could be argued that the future beneficiaries of emission abatement are located mainly in some of the future developing countries whereas those who are likely to undertake the abatement investments are located mostly in the present developed countries. Furthermore it could be argued that due to this difference in location the future beneficiaries will not be better off (very much) than the current people asked to undertake sacrifices: even if the now poor will be much better off in 100 years they need not be much better off, if at all, than the currently rich. Hence it would follow that, given a zero pure rate of time preference, the discount rate should be equal to 0 per cent or only slightly above. It might even be negative!

Azar and Sterner's (ibid.) reasoning is consistent with the spirit of the Ramsey formula. But their reasoning is inconsistent with the actual provision of aid from the current rich to the current poor which is of a rather limited magnitude.[16] As Schelling (1995, p. 397) has put it:

It would be strange to forgo a per cent or two of GNP for 50 years for the bene-fit of Indians, Chinese, Indonesians and others who will be living 50 to 100 years from now — and probably much better off than today's Indians, Chinese, and Indonesians — and not a tenth of that amount to increase the consumption of contemporary Indians, Chinese, and Indonesians.

But such a policy would also be hugely inefficient, even if the current rich were ready to make large sacrifices for the sake of people living in developing countries either now or in the future. Given the validity of the substitutability assumption, there are many much more attractive investment options from the viewpoint of the beneficiaries than investing in emission abatement. As Nord-haus (1991b, p. 57) notes, real rates of return to investment into education are extraordinarily high in poor countries: about 26 per cent for primary educa-tion, 16 per cent for secondary and 13 per cent for higher education. No doubt, poor people would be much better off if scarce resources were invested in these opportunities rather than in combating climate change. Given substi-tutability, Schelling (1995, p. 401) is right in expecting that "if offered a choice of immediate development assistance or equivalent investments in carbon abatement, potential aid recipients would elect for the immediate" — as would their future descendants if they had a voice.

2.4.3 Critique of the Nordhaus Approach (II): Substitutability of Natural Capital

The discussion about the 'correct' discount rate to use is an important one, but it fails to deal with what I regard as the weakest point of Nordhaus's ap-proach, namely the assumption of substitutability of natural capital. Given this assumption, large-scale emission abatement is *either* ethically dubious be-cause future generations are better off than the present generation anyway and inconsistent with the observed magnitude of current savings, *or* it is inconsis-tent with the behaviour of the currently rich towards the currently poor and imposes upon the poor inefficient investments whose financial resources they would rather use for different purposes if given a choice.

One way or another, other critics of Nordhaus have therefore made argu-ments that point in the direction of limited substitutability or even non-substitutability of natural capital (Gardiner 2004; Helm 2008; Neumayer 1999a, 2007; Page 2006; Philibert 1999; Rabl 1996; Spash 2002; Sterner and Persson 2008; Weitzman 2009b). While the Stern (2007) review does not explicitly make such an argument or formally models limited substitutability in its quantitatiave analysis, many of the arguments put forward in the review in its wider qualitative analysis can in fact be seen as making such a case. On this, see also Dietz, Hope and Patmore (2007).

The suggestion to treat environmental costs and benefits differently from other values is not a new one. In a seminal contribution from the 1970s, Krutilla and Fisher (1975) put forward an argument that became known as the Krutilla–Fisher approach. They presume that environmental benefits are likely to increase *relative* to other benefits in the economy — for example because future richer people will appreciate relatively more environmental amenities if the income elasticity of demand for environmental amenities is bigger than one (that is, if it is a luxury good). *De facto*, this increase in relative value means that environmental benefits are discounted at less than other values or maybe even not at all. If the relative importance of environmental benefits grew sufficiently strong, they could even count more than their nominal value so that, *de facto*, they would be 'discounted' at a negative rate. Krutilla and Fisher also presume that some of the benefits from environmental destruction are likely to depreciate over time. The developmental benefits from dam construction, for example, are likely to depreciate over time as superior technologies become available. *De facto*, this depreciation in relative value means that these benefits are discounted more heavily than other, especially environmental, values. Note the words *de facto*: formally, the same uniform discount rate is applied to all values, it is rather the values that appreciate or depreciate, respectively, before they are uniformly discounted to present values. Philibert (1999), on the other hand, also stresses that the value of non-reproducible environmental assets should be assumed to increase in the future, but calls for discount rates that slowly decrease over time.

Rabl (1996) has applied the Krutilla–Fisher rationale to climate change under the presumption that the environmental benefits of combating climate change are likely to rise over time. Similarly, but without recourse to the Krutilla–Fisher approach, Tol (1994) examines the effect of letting intangible goods, whose values increase over time with per capita income, enter the utility function. Not surprisingly, Rabl and Tol find that higher emission abatement is warranted than Nordhaus did. Sterner and Persson (2008) use Nordhaus's DICE model with modifications, showing that under the assumption that the supply of environmental services is negatively affected by climate change and that environmental services enter a utility function with a constant relative risk aversion, then much more aggressive emission reductions will follow from DICE, despite using the same discount rate as Nordhaus does.

The Krutilla–Fisher approach and related arguments go some way in departing from the substitutability paradigm. What it says is that natural capital becomes more difficult to substitute over time as its relative value increases. At the same time, the approach still assumes some form of substitutability. Not surprisingly, proponents of SS with their belief in the non-substitutability of natural capital go all the way and represent the opposite extreme to Nordhaus's computations. Their argument is that climate change threatens to impose non-substitutable damage to and loss of natural capital. While not every effect of climate change will be detrimental to natural capital, a consensus is emerging (see IPCC 2007a) that it will lead to or at least can lead to:

- a drastic loss of biodiversity;
- a change in the species composition of forests with the possible loss of species and the disappearance of entire forestry types;
- an increase in the frequency and the range of pests, pathogens and fires;
- an increase in desertification;
- a disruption in mountain resources of food and fuel for indigenous people;
- an increase in the salinity of estuaries and freshwater aquifers;
- a disruption of saltwater marshes, mangrove ecosystems, coastal wetlands, coral reefs, coral atolls and river deltas due to, among others, increased coastal flooding;
- an increase of heat waves with damaging effects on ecosystems and human health;
- an increase in the potential transmission of infectious diseases like malaria and yellow fever.

In putting ecosystems under severe stress, climate change can therefore damage the capacity of natural capital:

- to provide food, fibre, medicines and energy;
- to process and store carbon and other nutrients;
- to assimilate waste, purify water and regulate water runoff;
- to control floods, soil degradation and beach erosion;
- to provide opportunities for recreation and tourism.

Given this list of potentially severe damages to natural capital due to climate change, it should come as no surprise that SS calls for aggressive policies to combat climate change since natural capital as such should be kept intact. While some warming might be unavoidable, SS would try to ensure that the future is harmed as little as possible, even if it is materially better off than the present. According to this view, climate change will degrade natural capital and since natural capital cannot be substituted for, climate change has to be contained as much as possible quite regardless of the costs of doing so (Spash 2002). This position is shared by many environmentalists (see, for example, Leggett 1990) and it stands in marked contrast to Schelling's (1991,

p. 221) belief that "any disaster to developing countries from climate change will be essentially a disaster to their economic development".

The proponents of SS and the environmentalists regard the disturbance of the global atmospheric cycle as a harm to future generations that cannot be compensated for by higher consumption even if future generations are materially much better off. Their argument is that climate change, at least when above a certain threshold, damages the utility of future generations to an extent that they are worse off than the present generation, whatever the baseline consumption growth. This may sound implausible to many neoclassical economists, but only because they often overestimate the extent to which consumption growth leads to actual utility gains (see Easterlin 2003). Once it is acknowledged that further consumption growth may only lead to a small rise in utility, then the proposition that climate change may actually decrease utility despite consumption growth is not too far fetched. Of course, such an argument must ultimately rest on a normative judgement. This is for two reasons. First, there is no way of knowing future generations' preferences. Second, there is similarly no way of adequately valuing the utility loss from, say, the loss of glaciers, wetlands, forests and coral reefs, the damages to coastal, marine, arctic, mountain and other ecosystems and the likely massive rise in the rate of species extinction, which are all likely to be associated with already moderate temperature increases.

In consequence, SS calls for limiting climate change, which should be set as an explicit policy objective. That lowering the discount rate would coincidentally achieve the same result on this aspect should not distract from the main message, namely that climate change threatens to inflict irreversible and non-substitute damage to and loss of natural capital. In some sense, Nordhaus himself is much clearer about this than some of his opponents. His recommendation to those who want to limit climate change because of perceived limits to the substitutability of natural capital is that they should not mess around with the discount rate to achieve the desired outcome, but should argue for the desired outcome explicitly and directly. This becomes clear from the following quotation (Nordhaus 1999, p. 145):

> The best approach will generally be to identify the long-term objective and to directly override market decisions or conventional benefit–cost tests to achieve the ultimate goals. Focusing on ultimate objectives shows trade-offs explicitly, makes the cost of violating benefit–cost rules transparent, and allows public decisionmakers to weigh options explicitly rather than allowing technicians to hide the choices in abstruse arguments.

2.4.4   The Real Controversy

Whether and how to act against climate change cannot be decided on the basis of 'hard numbers' because there are no 'hard numbers' when it comes to climate change. To outsiders, the CBA studies of economists may suggest otherwise. But those who understand what the studies do, also know two things. First, many effects of climate change simply cannot be adequately monetarily valued. Second, what can be valued needs to be transformed from values in the far distant future to present values and any CBA recommendation is therefore crucially dependent on the discount rate used, which is in turn inextricably linked to normative value judgements.

Of course, the issue of the right discount rate is somewhat more complex than I have portrayed it in Section 2.4.2, p. 32 – I refer readers to, for example, Yang (2003); Tol (2004); Weikard and Zhu (2005); Dasgupta (2007); Quiggin (2008) and Stern (2008). I merely wish to emphasize that there is no 'right' discount rate, particularly not for such long time spans as those relevant to climate change (that is, several centuries). The choice of the pure rate of time preference as well as the elasticity of marginal utility of consumption[7] necessarily derive from ethical value judgements that, because they are normative judgements, can and will always be contested.[18] One way or the other, decision making toward climate change is heavily influenced by ethical choices. But it is important to face the real issues when making ethical choices and orient the discussion toward what matters to people.

I contend that those who believe that the current generation should take immediate and decisive action against climate change need to go beyond arguing for a low discount rate. Otherwise, the case for action crucially depends on asking the current generation to make substantial sacrifices for cushioning consumption losses to future generations that are much better off than the present generation anyway. This will not be very popular once voters understand what they are being asked to do. It will be even less popular when critics point out that the very favourable cost-benefit ratios of action presented by the Stern Review diminish and even turn negative with different, and *a priori* no less valid, assumptions about the components of the discount rate.

I also contend that the non-substitutability issue is much closer to the real concerns of people. By contrast, CBA studies of climate change and the debate on the discount rate are strangely out of touch with reality. Voters and politicians who favour decisive and urgent action surely do not do so because they want to save much better off future generations from some consumption loss that, even if it happened, would still leave them much better off than the present generation (see Sterner and Persson 2008 for a similar view). Instead, they are concerned that climate change is like no other and that its sheer scale and extent of damage threatens to create a new bio-physical world that either leaves the future worse off or violates their inalienable rights to enjoy natural capital, despite consumption growth. Article 2 of the United Nations Framework Convention on Climate Change calls for "stabilization of greenhouse gas concentrations in the atmosphere at a level that would prevent dangerous anthropogenic interference with the climate system", not for maximizing the present discounted value of an inter-temporal social welfare function built on questionable assumptions about substitutability of natural capital.

2.5   CONCLUSION

This chapter has laid the foundations for the analysis of the coming chapters. In Section 2.1 SD was defined as development that does not decrease the capacity to provide non-declining per capita utility for infinity. Notably, SD was not defined in direct utility terms, but in terms of the capacity to provide utility. The relevant terms were explained and the economic paradigm was chosen as methodology because both WS and SS are essentially economic. In Section 2.1 it was merely assumed that the current generation is committed to SD, but in Section 2.2.1 some reasons based on Kant's deontological moral theory and Rawls's 'Theory of Justice' were provided for why such a commitment might be a reasonable choice. The commitment might suffer from a time-inconsistency problem, however, as argued in Section 2.2.2. No definite solution to this problem could be provided, but the argument was put forward that if each generation tries to p the next generation through the education of its children that a commitment to sustainability is a 'just' thing to do, then there might be a chain of commitment such that the time-inconsistency problem can be mitigated, if not overcome.

In Section 2.2.3 two popular misunderstandings about SD were resolved. It was shown that SD does not lock society into eternal poverty if it is poor at the start of its commitment to sustainability because SD does not require constant utility throughout time. Hence sacrifices for the sake of future generations are anything but ruled out. It was also shown that SD does not demand the choice of greatly inferior utility paths if a temporary decline in utility along the path can be avoided via increased saving before the expected decline. Section 2.2.3 is important for the later analysis because if these claims about SD were true, a commitment to sustainability could hardly be seen as a defensible choice for society to make. Section 2.3 presented the two paradigms of sustainability. The essence of WS is its assumption that natural capital is substitutable. In contrast, the essence of SS is that it regards natural capital as non-substitutable. In order to highlight the importance of these differing assumptions Section 2.4 looked at the case of climate change. It was shown that whether natural capital is regarded as substitutable as in the WS paradigm or non-substitutable as in the SS paradigm has major consequences for decision-making on climate change. If natural capital is substitutable, then there is little compelling justification to strongly reduce carbon dioxide and other greenhouse gas emissions. If, on the other hand, natural capital is non-substitutable, then the massive damage to and irreversible loss of natural capital inflicted by climate change justifies drastic and immediate action. The proper conflict between those who demand an aggressive abatement policy and those who call for only minor abatement efforts should therefore mainly be about the substitutability of natural capital, not about the 'correct' rate of discount. The next chapter takes a closer look at the validity of these opposing assumptions with respect to the substitutability of natural capital

NOTES

1   For a short overview of sustainable development views from other disciplines, see Heinen (1994) and Redclift (1994).
2   Except for jewellery perhaps and even there it could be said that gold, silver, diamonds and so on are used to produce the consumption good jewellery and are therefore not directly contributing to utility.
3   For a discussion of some ideas concerning an 'optimal' size of population see, for example, Hammond (1988); Daily, Ehrlich and Ehrlich (1994); Broome (1996) and Dasgupta (1998).
4   Note, however, that the so-called Brundtland Report (World Commission on the Environment and Development 1987), which was quite influential in promoting the debate on sustainability, put emphasis on both inter- and intra-generational justice. From this report stems also the best-known non-academic definition of SD as development that 'satisfies the needs of the present without compromising the needs of the future' (Chapter 2, paragraph 1). Also, in 'Southern' debates about SD, the notion of intra-generational fairness features prominently (for example, Guha 1989; Agarwal and Narain 1991).
5   In other writings I have put priority on questions of intra-generational fairness. See, for example, Neumayer (2000a).
6   A (pure) public good is characterised by two characteristics: first, non-rivalness in consumption and, second, non-excludability. The former means that the consumption of a public good by any individual does not diminish the consumption possibilities for any other individual. The second characteristic is more problematic. It means that nobody can be excluded from consuming the good. While this might sound rather innocuous, it has the negative consequence that in general there is no sufficient incentive for any private individual to produce the good. This is because since nobody can be excluded from consumption, nobody can be made to pay for the costs of providing the good either. But if the costs cannot be recovered, the good will not be privately produced in the first instance. This is the reason why public goods are usually referred to as prime examples for the necessity of government intervention.
7   Rawls (1972, p. 140) himself claims that the notion of the veil of ignorance is already implicit in Kant's moral philosophy.
8   Rawls actually spoke of many individuals, but given his information assumptions the number of individuals can be reduced to one representative individual without loss of generality.

9   Anand and Sen (2000) provide a complimentary justification for sustainability under the notion of 'usufruct rights', where each generation has the right to enjoy the fruits of accumulated capital without depleting it.

10 Note, however, that Rawls (1972, pp. 284ff) did not apply his principle to intergenerational matters.

11 This holds true as long as there is no *exogenous* technical progress, that is, technical progress that is independent of the accumulation of man-made capital which is the underlying assumption in Solow (1974a).

12 This is an important point to note. Statements such as 'sustainability is a very tough objective for industrial societies to meet' (Jacobs 1997a, p. 371) are contingent on a different definition of sustainability than WS.

13 Of course, much depends on the exact model specifications. But there are present-value maximisation models (for example, Dasgupta and Heal 1974 and Solow 1974a) with either sub-exponential or zero technical progress that lead to eventual catastrophe for *any* positive constant discount rate (Pezzey 1995, p. 11).

14 Note that Daly's use of the term differs from the standard economic definition of a steady-state as a 'situation in which the various quantities' of an economy 'grow at constant rates' (Barro and Sala-I-Martin 1995, p. 19).

15 Throughout the book I concentrate mostly on CO_2 emissions since CO_2 has contributed in the past and is expected to contribute in the future 'about 60 per cent of the radiative forcing from the increase in the greenhouse effect' (Cline 1991, p. 906). The reader should always keep in mind, however, that an efficient strategy to combat climate change would have to take into account all greenhouse-relevant emissions.

16 I would guess that Azar and Sterner (1996) would demand to raise this level of aid so as to maximise world social welfare, if only to remain consistent with their own approach.

17 This elasticity need not be constant, but could be a function of future expected consumption growth. I, for one, do not think that giving up 1 per cent of consumption today for the purpose of giving 1 per cent extra consumption to much better off future generations is ethically desirable.

18 Note that this is not equivalent to uncertainty about the discount rate and therefore not subject to Weitzman's (1998) argument for declining discount rates in the long run. His argument applies to uncertainty about the growth rate of future consumption, but not to the choice of the pure rate of time preference or the elasticity of marginal utility of consumption. Economists and other social scientists are not uncertain about these, but simply differ in their choice because of differing value judgements.

3. Resources, the Environment and Economic Growth: Is Natural Capital Substitutable?

This chapter discusses a natural question that comes to the reader's mind after having been confronted with the two paradigms of sustainability: if they have so starkly differing assumptions about the substitutability of natural capital, how can we know which paradigm is 'correct'? I will argue that both paradigms ultimately rest on non-falsifiable beliefs about the future. There can therefore be no clear answer on whether natural capital is substitutable or not.

Section 3.1 puts the discussion into context in giving a brief history of resource and environmental concern. Section 3.2 looks at natural capital as an input into the production of consumption goods. It suggests that the resource optimism of WS can be expressed in four propositions and critically assesses each one of them. It looks at:

- Substitution of a resource with other resources.
- The role of prices in overcoming resource constraints.
- Substitution of natural resources with man-made capital.
- The role of technical progress in overcoming resource constraints.

Then, Section 3.3 turns to environmental degradation. Section 3.3.1 looks at the substitutability of natural capital as a direct provider of utility and examines whether future generations can be compensated for long-term environmental degradation with increased consumption opportunities. Section 3.3.2 analyses the environmental consequences of economic growth. It presents the theoretical case for environmental optimism, which holds that economic growth is good for the environment, at least in the long run, and the theoretical case for environmental pessimism, which holds that economic growth is bad for the environment. Since theory is shown to be unable to resolve the dispute, the empirical evidence is assessed. Section 3.4 concludes that both paradigms are non-falsifiable.

3.1   A SHORT HISTORY OF RESOURCE AND ENVIRONMENTAL CONCERN

Modern concern that limited availability of natural resources will constrain the possibilities for consumption growth or, for that matter, even non-declining consumption dates back at least to Malthus (1798). He was convinced that the limitedness of land put an absolute scarcity constraint on food consumption growth. While population rose at a geometric (exponential) rate, the production of food could only be expanded at an arithmetic (linear) rate, Malthus thought. Hence, he believed that population could grow only until the minimum subsistence level of per capita food consumption was transgressed and had to decline sharply afterwards — only to grow and hit the absolute scarcity constraint afterwards again in an apparently endless vicious circle. Later on, Jevons (1865) warned against a running out of coal as an energy resource and expressed concern about detrimental consequences of rising coal extraction costs on economic growth and the competitiveness of British industry.

We know by now, of course, that both had been wrong: population grew tremendously in the 19th century and in 2008 worldwide proven reserves of coal would last for another 122 years at current consumption rates (BP 2009). Moreover, coal is not seen as an essential resource any more. Malthus and Jevons committed mistakes other resource pessimists repeated later on. Malthus did not consider the power of technical progress and he was not aware of the fact that, as Ricardo (1817) first realised, land availability is more a question of relative as opposed to absolute scarcity; that is, land is a heterogeneous resource and it is possible to get the same amount of nutrition out of an ever lower quality acre by investing increasing inputs. Jevons, for his part, underestimated the scope for exploration and finding new reserves of coal and neglected the powerful possibilities of substituting other energy resources for coal. One has to keep in mind, however, that concern about the availability of natural resources was deeply rooted in mainstream economic thinking of that time and many classical economists, most notably Mill (1862) and Ricardo (1817), shared the belief that the economy had to stop growing sooner or later due to a resource constraint.[1] In those days economics had a reputation as a 'dismal' science (Barnett and Morse 1963, p. 2).

It was not before the so-called marginal revolution and the rise of neoclassical economics at the turn of the century, mainly due to Alfred Marshall, Léon Walras and Irving Fisher, that concern about resource availability vanished. In its leading macroeconomic metaphor, the income–expenditure cycle, the depletion of natural resources is non-existent in a seemingly endless circular exchange of value in which households provide labour for producing goods for which they receive income which is in turn exchanged for the produced goods. Reality seemed to buttress this new thinking: the economy kept on growing, especially in the 'golden years' after the Second World War and even if it did not, as in the Great Depression, the reasons were no longer sought in limited natural resources. This is not to say that there were no pessimistic outlooks. The US President's Materials Policy Commission (1952a, p. 1), for example, saw 'many causes for concern' in its examination 'of the adequacy of materials ... to meet the needs of the free world in the years ahead' for the struggle against the 'threats of force and of a new Dark Age which rise from the Communist nations'. On the whole, however, resource optimistic perspectives prevailed.

Concern about natural resource availability emerged again with the publication of the Club of Rome's 'Limits to Growth' report (Meadows et al. 1972). This concern became popular and widespread after the quadrupling of world oil prices, as OPEC first boycotted the US and the Netherlands for their support of Israel in the Yom Kippur War in 1973 and soon learned to exercise leverage over the OECD countries.[2] Meadows et al. prophesied that the exhaustion of essential mineral and energy resources would make economic growth infeasible some time in the 21st century. Therefore, a halt to economic growth and even an eventual economic contraction might be enforced through resource scarcity. Essentially the same message was echoed by the Global 2000 Report to the President of the US in 1980 (Barney 1980) and twenty years after their first report, Meadows et al. published an updated, but hardly revised restatement of their argument (Meadows et al. 1992).

Economists, contrary to the wider public, this time did not share the concern about resource availability. Only some 'outsiders', often regarded as eccentrics by the mainstream economist community, had sympathy with the report's motivation and goal, without overlooking the criticisms that could be raised against it (Daly 1992a, first published in 1977; Georgescu-Roegen 1971, 1975; Mishan 1974). In economic terms Meadows et al. were naive in extrapolating past trends without considering how technical progress and a change in relative prices can work to overcome apparent scarcity limits. This criticism was put forward vigorously in a fierce attack by neoclassical economists and other scientists who rejected the report(s) as pure nonsense (Beckerman 1972, 1974; Cole et al. 1973; Solow 1974b; Nordhaus 1973, 1992). For them the depletion of non-renewable resources had to be tackled with traditional economic instruments and had to be taken on board by neoclassical economics (Solow 1974a, c; Dasgupta and Heal 1974; Stiglitz 1974) — but limits to growth due to resource constraints were not a problem.

For a long time, environmental problems were regarded as temporary rather than enduring and were thus by most people not perceived as a fundamental problem of industrialisation and economic growth per se. The public

awakened to the detrimental side-effects of industrialisation and rapid economic growth in the early 1960s, when Carson (1962) expressed her fear
about a 'silent spring' due to the death of birds being exposed to DDT. The
book became very popular and so, albeit slowly, became the environmental
movement popular (for an overview, see McCormick 1989). It was not before
the ozone layer depletion, climate change, and biodiversity loss became major
issues in the 1980s, however, that environmental degradation was perceived
as a potential constraint to economic growth as such. Interest by that time
shifted away from natural resource availability towards the environment as a
medium for assimilating wastes (from 'source' to 'sink') (Pearce 1993b).

Indicative of this trend is that the second and third 'Club of Rome' reports
by Meadows et al. (1992, 2004) were much more concerned with environmental degradation than the first report (Meadows et al. 1972). Nevertheless,
environmental pessimists believe that economic growth in the long run is
constrained both by resource availability and by its detrimental effects on the
environment. Again, mainstream economists, although expressing some concern about environmental pollution, do not believe in environmental limits to
growth (Ravaioli 1995).

The following section starts with the 'source' side of the economy in analysing the availability of resources for the production of consumption goods.
So far, the pessimists have been wrong in their predictions. But one thing is
also clear: to conclude that there is no reason whatsoever to worry on the
basis that the pessimists have been wrong in the past is tantamount to commi-
ting the same mistake the pessimists are often guilty of — that is the mistake
of extrapolating past trends. The future is something inherently uncertain and
it is humans' curse (or blessing, if you like) not to know with certainty what
the future will bring. The past can be a bad guide to the future when circumstances are changing. That the alarmists have regularly and mistakenly cried
'wolf!' does not imply that the woods are safe.

3.2   RESOURCE AVAILABILITY

First, let us have a look at natural capital as an input in the production of
consumption goods. Just how scarce are natural resources and can they easily
be substituted for by man-made capital or technical progress?[3] The resource
optimism of WS can be summarised in four propositions (see the box over-
leaf).

If resource optimism is correct, then there is no need to worry about the
depletion of natural resources: either the world will not run out of a resource

or it will not matter if it does since another resource or man-made capital will function as a substitute.

A summary of resource optimism in four propositions

Resource optimism holds that if some resource A is becoming scarce in an economic sense[4] its price will rise, which triggers the following four mutually non-exclusive effects:

a) Demand shifts away from resource A and another resource B becomes economical and replaces resource A.
b) It becomes economical to explore and extract as well as recycle more of resource A. As a consequence, the price of resource A will decline again, thus signalling an ease in economic scarcity.
c) Man-made capital will substitute for resource A.
d) More effort is put into technical and scientific progress in order to reduce the necessary resource input per unit of output, thus easing any resource constraint. Also technical and scientific progress make resource extraction cheaper and thus the extraction of a resource's lower-quality ores economical. As a consequence prices will decline again, signalling an ease in economic scarcity.

3.2.1 Substitution with Other Resources

Let us first look at proposition (a) of resource optimism which essentially says that a resource B will substitute for resource A if the latter is running out. If the proposition is correct, then there is no need to worry about the depletion of resource A and, since A could be any resource, there is no need to worry about the depletion of any resource at all. The point is that the depletion of a resource does not matter economically if it is or becomes unnecessary for production. It was this Beckerman (1972, p. 337) had in mind when he commented rather cynically on the first 'Limits to Growth' report from the Club of Rome:

> Why should it matter all that much whether we do run out of some raw materials? After all ... economic growth has managed to keep going up to now without any supplies at all of Beckermonium, a product named after my grandfather who failed to discover it in the nineteenth century.

Conversely, the existence of a resource does not matter economically as long as it is without an economic use. As Ray (1984, p. 75) observes:

All materials used by industry were 'new' at some point in history; they have become 'resources' as a result of scientific and technological advance discovering them and developing their use. Bauxite did not even have a name before it was discovered that it could be processed into a new metal: aluminium.

It is clear, that proposition (a) taken to its logical limit only applies to resources B that are quasi-undepletable, be they renewable or non-renewable. An example of the former is renewable energy from solar influx that will vanish some time in the very long run, but will provide its daily service for all plausible human time understanding. An example of the latter is nuclear fusion, which is based on a non-renewable resource and which might provide services some time in the future at reasonable costs without an immediate or even intermediate risk of running out. These two examples make clear that ultimately resource B must be something close to what economists call a 'backstop technology'. A backstop technology is a resource that can provide services at constant marginal costs in infinite amounts (Dasgupta and Heal 1974). If such a resource exists, then the economy can be saved from doomsday for an indefinite time (Prell 1996).

Is a backstop technology possible? Strictly speaking, neither of our two examples is really a backstop technology, because the amount of services potentially provided, although very huge indeed, is still finite. Presumably, there cannot be any backstop technology in the strict sense, because the first law of thermodynamics (conservation of mass) states that energy cannot be created anew and because the second law of thermodynamics states that entropy in a closed system is monotonically increasing over time, that is useful energy is used up and cannot be used over and over again (Söllner 1997, pp. 181, 183). For all human relevance the universe is a closed system. But note: it is the universe that is a closed system, not the earth itself which is an open system in the sense that it is getting a steady, constant, finite influx of energy from the sun. It is a closed system only in so far as it does not exchange matter with the outside. Georgescu-Roegen's (1975, p. 370) suggestion that every car built today implies 'fewer plowshares for some future generations, and implicitly, fewer future human beings, too' due to the laws of thermodynamics is *not* correct in a system that receives a steady, constant, finite influx of energy where it is not compelling that entropy permanently increases.[5]

Now, controlled civil use of nuclear fusion may remain a natural scientist's dream for ever, but solar energy comes close to a backstop technology for energy resources, at least in principle: the solar energy influx exceeds total world energy demand at about three orders of magnitude (Norgaard 1986, p. 326; Hohmeyer 1992, p. 10). Hence, solar energy and hydrogen produced from solar energy (Blanchette 2008), complemented by other renewable energy sources such as wind, tidal power, biomass etc., hold the greatest promise (Ayres 2008). Whether these renewable energy sources can be used at reasonable economic costs is less clear, however. Lenssen and Flavin (1996, p. 772) optimistically suggest that, due to rapidly declining provision costs, solar and wind energy as well as geothermal technologies will become fully competitive with fossil energy resources in the near future. They believe that the current energy infrastructure which is based mainly on oil, gas and coal will gradually be replaced by an energy infrastructure based mainly on solar energy and other renewables and using hydrogen as the medium to transfer primary energy to final energy users. Martinot (2006, p. 40) similarly contends that 'with concerted effort, renewables could realistically comprise more than half of global primary energy by 2040'. For further optimistic out-looks, see, for example, Smil (2003), Kammen (2006) and Lackner and Sachs (2005, p. 216) who argue the case 'that the known energy resource base is more than sufficient to provide a growing world population with energy on the scale to which the industrial countries have grown accustomed and to which the developing countries now aspire'.

A different picture is painted by Trainer (1995) who represents the oppo-site, and rather pessimistic view. He believes that the prospects of renewable resources providing sufficient energy at reasonable economic costs are vastly over-estimated in neglecting the difficulties of 'conversions, storage and sup-ply' of renewable resources 'for high latitudes' (ibid., p. 1009). He suggests that if the world must depend on renewable energy resources only, then it 'must be based on materially simple lifestyles, a high level of local economic self-sufficiency, and a steady-state or zero-growth economy' (ibid., p. 1025). Huesemann (2003, p. 21) similarly contends that 'it will be extremely difficult to switch to an industrial and economic system based solely on renewable resources'.

Which of the two projections will be closer to *future* reality we do not know. Projections are highly dependent on prophesying the *future* develop-ment of scientific and technical progress; the *future* growth of economies, populations and world energy demand; and on predicting *future* changes in energy and environmental policies. Beyond the very immediate time span, these projections *necessarily* become closer and closer to sophisticated guesses and speculations lacking a sound and reliable scientific basis. Mis-takes in past projections represent a case in point: many reports in the early 1970s overestimated the amount of nuclear power the world would be using in the mid-1990s by a factor of six, while leading studies in the early 1980s overestimated the cost of a barrel of oil by almost a factor of five (Lenssen and Flavin 1996, p. 770). These flawed estimates should remind us that our ability to project world energy supply and its composition and world energy demand and prices is very limited indeed in the intermediate and distant future. In the end, at what time and under what conditions solar energy will become widely available is contingent on our efforts in developing this renewable resource and in bringing its costs down. As early as 1952, the US President's Materials Policy Comission (1952b) called on the USA to provide an outstanding contribution to world welfare by investing aggressively in the field of solar energy. More than half a century later, this call is still valid.

So far we have only dealt with energy resources. Whether solar energy and other renewable energy resources can substitute for non-renewable non-energy resources is even less clear. Direct substitution possibilities might be low, but a backstop energy technology has another advantage as well: if it provides services at not too high a cost, it can boost the availability of other resources that can be extracted economically — at least if we assume that ever-lower-quality ores can be extracted with ever-rising energy and other inputs and that the costs of extraction do not rise steeply and quickly. It was this that Adelman (1990, p. 1) referred to in stating that 'the total mineral in the earth is an irrelevant non-binding constraint', for the question really is whether it will be possible or not to extract ever-more resources from ever-lower quality ores at reasonable economic costs. Energy is the one and only real limiting factor in the long run, because given enough energy there will always be enough natural non-energy resources extractable from the crust of the earth.

However, there does not seem to exist any serious study that has tried to compute the prospects of backstop technologies to substitute on a large scale for the depletion of non-energy resources in the long run or to facilitate the mining of resource ores of low concentration. What we have are more or less optimistic statements, but no comprehensive, detailed analysis — see, for example, Gordon et al. (1987), Scott and Pearse (1992), Beckerman (1995) or Goeller and Zucker (1984, p. 456) who assure the reader that they:

> believe that, with a few exceptions, the world contains plentiful retrievable resources that can supply mankind with the necessary materials for the very long term, and that these resources can probably be extracted and converted to useful forms indefinitely with acceptable environmental consequences and within the boundaries of foreseeable economic constraints.

A more pessimistic view is taken by Ayres (2007, p. 126):

> ... while there is plenty of room for substitution and some possibility of major breakthroughs (...) the pessimists – those who espouse the notion of "strong sustainability" appear to be closer to the truth than the optimists who believe in more or less unlimited substitution possibilities.

3.2.2 The Role of Prices in Overcoming Resource Constraints

Now let us look at proposition (b). It highlights more than any of the other four propositions the role resource prices play in overcoming resource constraints. Prices serve different functions in an economy, the most important being that they signal economic scarcity and that they act as a coordination mechanism pushing the economy towards efficiency and triggering technical progress. Resource pessimists have persistently either ignored or downplayed the role that prices play in easing resource constraints. It is naive, as Meadows et al. (1972) and many others have done, to compare current amounts of resource use with current proven reserves and simply extrapolate from the past that hence the resource will be depleted in x years. For the gradual depletion of a resource affects its price which affects supply and demand to which the economy adapts permanently. This dynamic process makes a mockery out of simple-minded static computations of a resource's remaining life-time.

To highlight the role that prices play for resources let us introduce the famous Hotelling rule (Hotelling 1931). The rule states that, under some restrictive assumptions (on which more will be said later on), the resource rent (that is, the price of the resource for the marginal unit minus the marginal cost for extracting this unit) in a perfectly competitive economy must rise at a rate equal to the interest rate for a given stock of a non-renewable resource.[6] The resource rent can be interpreted as the net marginal profit for the resource extractor and is often called 'Hotelling rent'. The rule holds true, with some amendments, for renewable resources as well — see Appendix 2, p. 198. Because of their much higher importance as an input into production, the analysis here refers solely to non-renewable resources.[7]

The intuitive reason why the rule must hold in a context of rational utility-maximising agents is as follows: imagine otherwise, for example, that the resource rent rose at a rate lower than the interest rate. Then it would pay the resource owner to liquidate more of the resource, deposit his or her receipts in a bank and earn interest on his or her account — which gives him or her a higher net rate of return than leaving the resource in the ground since by assumption resource rents rise at a lower rate than the interest rate. It would pay to liquidate more of the resource up until marginal extraction costs rise so much that the resource owner is just indifferent between extracting a marginal resource unit and leaving this unit in the ground. It might be profitable to even liquidate the whole resource stock! Now imagine instead that the resource rent rose at a higher rate than the interest rate. Then it would pay the resource owner to leave more of the resource in the ground in order to extract it later on, thus getting a higher net rate of return than if he or she had extracted the resource right now and had put the receipts in a bank account. In other words, the Hotelling rule requires that the present value of resource rents are the same in all periods, that is, it is a profit-maximising condition of intertemporal arbitrage (Livernois 2008). The deeper reason why the Hotelling rule must hold is that for the resource owner a stock of non-renewable resource is just another asset in his or her portfolio, so it has to earn an equal net rate of return as the other portfolio assets do. Hence equilibrium is where resource rent rises at a rate equal to the interest rate, where the interest rate stands for a representative rate of return on other assets.

The following simple model derives the Hotelling rule:[8] a representative resource extracting firm maximises its profit π from a given resource stock S over an infinite time horizon. Since we assume perfect competition, the firm takes the price P as given. The problem of the firm is to

$$\underset{R}{Max}\ \pi = \int_0^\infty \left\{ P(t)R(t) - C[R(t)] \right\} \cdot e^{-rt} dt \tag{3.1}$$

$$\text{s.t.}\ \dot{S}(t) = -R(t) \tag{3.2}$$

$$\text{and } \int_0^\infty R(t)dt = S(0) \tag{3.3}$$

where t is a time index, P the price of the resource, R the quantity of resource extracted at each instant of time and C the total cost of extraction. r is the interest rate that is exogenously given to the model and used by the firm to discount future profits to its present value. That is, in equation (3.1) the firm chooses a suitable R that maximises the present (discounted) profit of the resource. Equation (3.2) is an equation of motion, where $S(t)$ is the total remaining stock of the resource at each instant of time and the dot above S indicates the derivative of S with respect to t. Equation (3.2) simply says that the resource stock decreases by the amount of extraction. Equation (3.3) is an integral constraint which says that the integrated sum of all resource depletion should be equal to the initial resource stock $S(0)$. In other words, as time reaches infinity the total stock should be exhausted which is demanded by efficiency: the firm would forgo profits if it did not use up its stock.

The problem is solved by forming the Lagrangian Γ and maximising with respect to R:

$$\underset{R}{Max}\ \Gamma = \int_0^\infty \left\{ P(t)R(t) - C[R(t)] \right\} \cdot e^{-rt} dt - \lambda R(t) \tag{3.4}$$

where λ is the (constant) Lagrange-multiplier. Assume the cost function to be 'well behaved', that is, strictly convex, continuous and twice differentiable, so that $d^2C/dR^2 > 0$ and the necessary first-order condition is also sufficient for a maximum:

$$(P - \frac{dC}{dR}) = \lambda e^{rt} \quad (3.5)$$

Define H to be the resource rent:

$$H \equiv (P - \frac{dC}{dR}) \quad (3.6)$$

λ is constant for this so-called isoperimetric problem (Chiang 1992, pp. 139–43, 280–82). Differentiating (3.5) with respect to time and dividing the result by (3.5) leads to

$$\frac{\dot{H}}{H} = r \quad (3.7)$$

that is, in the optimum the resource rent rises at the rate of interest (Hotelling rule). The basic result does not change if the firm maximises profits over a *finite* time period. Neither does the basic result depend on the firm being a price taker. If the firm is a price-setting monopolist for example, it is marginal revenue minus marginal cost that rises at the interest rate and resource depletion is in general slower than under perfect competition (Pearce and Turner 1990, pp. 284–86). The form of market structure is of no further interest to the analysis here, however.

That the resource rent rises at the interest rate holds true more generally, however, only in a setting of certainty about, for example, the size of the resource stock, the date of exhaustion, the existence and marginal costs of a backstop technology and so on.[9] Deshmukh and Pliska (1985) show that the resource rent need not rise at the rate of interest if uncertainty is introduced. One important aspect is the exploration of new reserves. Pindyck (1978) is the seminal paper showing how prices (and resource rent) can fall over time as the exploration of new reserves increases the available resource stock.

To see this, look at the following very simple setting: assume that the marginal costs of resource extraction are constant and equal to zero. Before the discovery of new reserves the resource stock was of size S. The resource rent had to increase at the rate of interest (equation 3.7) and economic efficiency demands that the stock is fully exhausted at time $t = \infty$ (equation 3.3), so the price P_0 that was initially set at time $t = 0$ is specified as well (see Figure 3.1).

As new reserves become known at time $t = t_1$, the available stock rises. The resource rent still has to rise at the interest rate and economic efficiency still requires that the resource stock is fully exhausted at time $t = \infty$. But the available resource stock has increased, so it follows that the price set at time $t = t_1$ after the discovery of new reserves must lie below the price at time $t = t_1$ just before the discovery. That is, the price at time $t = t_1$ decreases because of new discoveries. If new discoveries are frequent and large enough, the overall trend in the resource rent can be downwards over time, as Figure 3.1 shows. Hence actual resource rents might not only fail to rise at the interest rate, but even fall over some time period if unexpected discoveries are made. Note that this does not contradict the Hotelling rule which demands resource rent to rise at the interest rate only for a *given* stock of resources, that is excluding new formerly unknown resources. And ultimately, of course, the Hotelling rent and therefore the resource price have to rise again because the total resource stock in the earth is finite.

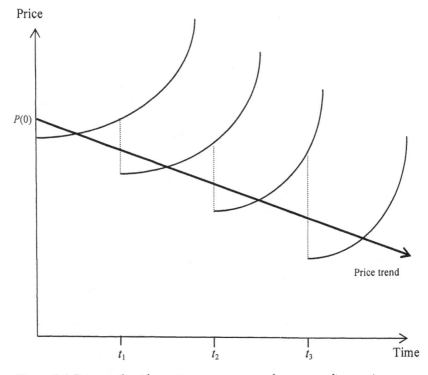

Figure 3.1 Price path with continuous unexpected resource discoveries

I have derived this qualification to the Hotelling rule in a particularly simple context and looked at unexpected discoveries in an otherwise static environment. But the main result holds true for more complicated contexts as well (see Hartwick and Olewiler 1986; Perman, Ma and McGilvray 1996, pp. 154–59): the resource rent is responsive to changes in the underlying economic scarcity of a resource which suggests resource rent to be a good indicator of economic scarcity. The resource rent reflects the opportunity cost of current resource extraction, that is, the trade-off between resource extraction now and resource extraction in the future. It is a measure of anticipated scarcity of the resource. Rising resource rents would indicate rising scarcity, whereas falling resource rents would indicate falling scarcity and no rise or fall would suggest no change in scarcity.

Unfortunately, resource rent is not directly observable and hence inherently difficult to measure. This is the reason why attempts to validate Hotelling's rule empirically have resulted in contradictory conclusions — see for example Miller and Upton (1985) versus Farrow (1985) and Halvorsen and Smith (1991) who reject the Hotelling hypothesis (for an overview, see Berck (1995) and Livernois (2008)). Swierzbinski and Mendelsohn (1989) explain the apparent contradictory results as follows: Miller and Upton (1985) demonstrate that stockholders use the Hotelling rule at each moment of time to forecast the value of their stocks. That time-trend tests of the Hotelling rule (for example, Farrow 1985 and Halvorsen and Smith 1991) have generally failed to support the rule is due to the fact that because of dynamic uncertainty and consistent updating in information the true mean rate of change in the resource price persistently deviates from the deterministic Hotelling rule. Because of that, it is hard to validate or reject the Hotelling rule. Mackellar and Vining (1989, pp. 522f) even suggest that due to:

> changing unit extraction costs, producers' price expectations, imperfect competition, exploration, inefficient capital markets, durability and recycling of the resource in question, and so on, virtually any path of real resource prices over the last century could be judged consistent with the theory [of Hotelling, E.N.].

Note, however, what Farrow (1985) and Halvorsen and Smith (1991) really reject is not the Hotelling rule as such, which *must* hold in a context of rational utility maximisers, but the simplistic proposition that actual resource rent is rising at the interest rate. One has to keep in mind that the Hotelling rule as introduced above only holds for some rather restrictive assumptions. Hartwick and Hageman (1993, p. 222) have made this point clear:

> We can summarize Hotelling's rule this way: *if,* under quite restrictive assumptions regarding (a) mineral quality, (b) market uncertainty including stock size

uncertainty, (c) agents' foresight, and (d) the functioning of futures markets, mineral stock owners are extracting at each date so as to maximize the discounted future profits from their mineral holding, *then* the rental earned on the marginal ton extracted will increase over time at the rate of interest. ... Failure to demonstrate that 'rent rises at the rate of interest' might reflect the invalidity of any one of the assumptions on which this prediction is based. What such failure does not imply, however, is that mineral stock owners are not maximizing discounted future profits (that is, the current market value of the mineral deposit).

Because of the difficulties in measuring resource rent, studies of resource scarcity have come up with two alternative indicators: unit extraction costs, that is, the value of factor inputs per unit of output of the resource-extracting industry; and relative resource prices, that is, the ratio of a resource price index to an overall price index.

The relative resource price indicator is closest to resource rent. It includes the current extraction cost plus the resource rent, that is, the opportunity cost of current extraction. Its rationale is that with approximately constant marginal extraction costs the change in the overall resource price is a good proxy to the change in the unobservable resource rent, so that with rising resource scarcity the overall resource price would rise relative to a suitably defined overall price index. Its chief advantage is that it is easily observable: 'In today's closely integrated global marketplace, most natural resource commodities trade at a single, US dollar-denominated price' (Mackellar and Vining 1989, p. 525). The rationale for using unit extraction costs instead is that if resource extraction is a Ricardian process that is, it starts from the high-quality ores and moves continually to the lower-quality ores, then one would expect unit extraction costs to rise with rising resource scarcity. In a competitive context it is reasonable to presume that resource extraction follows a Ricardian process, for then 'the market serves as a sensing-selective mechanism, scanning all deposits to take the cheapest increment or tranche into production' (Adelman 1990, p. 3). Unit extraction costs are less easy to observe, at least in highly integrated resource industries, because it becomes difficult to isolate resource extraction costs proper from other costs such as transportation and processing costs (Mackellar and Vining 1989, p. 519).

The classical study of resource scarcity is Barnett and Morse (1963). It examined unit extraction costs for the period 1870–1957 for agricultural, mineral and forest resources in the United States, finding a general downward trend with the exception of forestry. Barnett (1979) and Johnson, Bell and Bennett (1980) updated the original study to the 1970s coming to the same principal conclusions of falling unit extraction costs, which they interpreted as a decline in resource scarcity.

At the beginning of the 1980s the studies undertaken by Slade (1982) and Hall and Hall (1984) shed some doubt on these findings. Slade (1982) examined relative resource prices for several mineral and energy resources, finding evidence for 'U-shaped' price trends; that is after prices had fallen over a substantial period of time they then started to rise. Slade (ibid., p. 136) concluded that 'if scarcity is measured by relative prices, the evidence indicates that non-renewable natural-resource commodities are becoming scarce'. Similarly Hall and Hall (1984, p. 363) found evidence for 'measurable increasing scarcity of important natural resources' in studying both unit extraction costs and relative resource prices for energy and forestry products in the United States. Both studies claimed that part of the rise in oil prices in the 1970s was due to rising scarcity and not simply an artefact of the exercise of market power by OPEC (Slade 1982, p. 136; Hall and Hall 1984, p. 373). More recent studies have mostly failed to support these findings of rising scarcity.[10] Slade (1988, p. 200) herself admitted later on that there was no statistically significant upward trend in resource prices and in 1992 she concluded that there was no evidence of an increase in unit extraction costs and that 'when we consider a century of data, the most striking feature is the decline in the relative price of the majority of mineral commodities' (Slade 1992, p. 7). A study by Uri and Boyd (1995) equally failed to find any increase in unit extraction costs or relative resource prices for several mineral resources. At the beginning and middle of this decade, many resource prices, including that of oil, increased rather drastically – only to be followed by an equally drastic fall in prices when the world economy entered into a slump in 2008. There is thus great volatility in resource prices, but looked at over the long run there is not much evidence for rising resource prices. Figure 3.2 on the next page shows both nominal and inflation-adjusted oil prices from 1948 to 2009, in which great volatility without a clear upward trend are visible.

Can one conclude, therefore, that resources have not become more scarce in an economic sense over the past and will not become scarce in the future? There are two objections to doing so:

1. As pointed out, empirical studies do not measure resource rent, the theoretically correct indicator, but a surrogate indicator. Unfortunately, the forward-looking properties of the surrogate indicators are poor. They can be very misleading, that is suggesting the opposite of the true underlying scarcity trend. What is more, they can be contradictory: Brown and Field (1978) detected a rising trend in the relative resource price of lumber while at the same time the unit cost was falling. Why is it that the indicators can be misleading and contradictory?

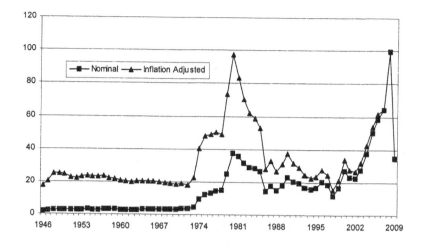

Source: Illinois Oil and Gas Association (www.ioga.com).

Figure 3.2 Crude oil prices (1946 to 2009)

Take unit extraction costs first. If the resource is becoming scarce, unit
extraction costs will rise if resource extraction follows a Ricardian process.
However, improvements in the extraction technology counter this effect,
and if technical change is sufficiently strong, unit extraction costs can *fall*
in spite of *rising* future economic scarcity (Farzin 1995, p. 118). Unit extraction costs only measure the costs of extracting already discovered
deposits but do not reflect the costs of future extraction (Fisher 1979, p.
257). It is a backward-, not a forward-looking indicator: 'The unit cost
measure does not warn us of impending physical exhaustion' (Brown and
Field 1979, p. 219). This is no mere theoretical possibility; for example:

> In the 19th century, technical progress steadily reduced unit extraction cost
> in the US lumber industry despite the fact that forest resources were disap-
> pearing at a rapid rate. The number of some whale species in the oceans has
> dwindled while superior hunting methods have steadily reduced unit extrac-
> tion costs. (Mackellar and Vining 1989, p. 520)

Relative resource prices are in principle better suited to predict future
resource scarcity, since expectations about the future should enter current
prices. In the absence of a complete set of futures markets, however, relative resource prices also fail to reflect future scarcity accurately; that is
relative resource prices are only an imperfect forward-looking indicator.

To give an example: Farrow (1995) suggests that the market did not anticipate the end of hunting of passenger pigeons which became extinct 'with hardly a ripple in its commercial price' (Brown and Field 1978, p. 241). More generally, often market prices do not or, rather, cannot take into account ecological thresholds and irreversibilities in depleting natural capital. Resource prices would be much higher if the environmental externalities were internalised. Equally, they cannot work for resources that are characterised by open access.

Since resource prices are supposed to function as a proxy for the unobservable resource rent, problems arise if the link between the price and the rent is rather weak. This will be the case if, for example, substitution among other factor inputs in the processing of the resource is high, because then the price will rise less than the rent. Similarly, if the raw resource (for example, bauxite) has a small share in the production costs of the final good (for example, aluminium), then the price for the final good will be much more influenced by changes in other factor prices than by the resource rent. Another major problem is the selection of an appropriate deflator or numeraire to transform nominal into real resource prices. As Hartwick and Olewiler (1986, pp. 148ff) report from other studies, trends in resource prices can be quite divergent depending on which deflator — for example, index of factor inputs, index of intermediate goods, index of final goods and services — is used.

The most fundamental objection against using relative resource prices as an indicator for resource scarcity was provided by Norgaard (1990, 1991). His argument is as follows: in an ideal system of complete markets, including futures and options markets, relative resource prices should reflect present and future scarcity accurately. The problem is that this full set of markets is not existent and that therefore traders in natural resource markets have to form their own expectations about scarcity and the future price paths. Since these traders are boundedly rational utility maximisers with imperfect information and imperfect foresight, they might well be badly informed about real resource scarcity. The same holds true if their only concern is over the next 5–10 years, as Aage (1984, p. 108) suspects, or the next 10–20 years, as Ray (1984, p. 76) suggests. But if that is the case, then:

> the cost and price paths their decisions generate are as likely to reflect their ignorance as reality. To control for whether or not allocators are informed, however, we would have to know whether resources are scarce. Since this is the original question, the exercise is logically impossible. (Norgaard 1990, p. 19f)

Inferring the real underlying scarcity trend from the time series of the indicator is therefore flawed from the beginning. Norgaard (1991, p. 195) suggests that the only thing one can really test is whether or not allocators *believe* that a resource is scarce and not real scarcity.

2. Past trends cannot simply be extrapolated into the future (and most definitely not into the far future). That the resource constraint is not binding yet does not imply that it will not be so in due course. Even with a rather modest growth rate for the global economy of two per cent per annum, world economic output doubles approximately every 35 years. It is not all that clear whether there are sufficient resources for such a tremendous growth of output. The point is that resource pessimists are concerned whether there will be enough resources to satisfy a demand that tremendously exceeds past levels of demand.

What about the prospects of recycling, that proposition (b) also refers to? These prospects are limited as well. Strictly speaking, given a backstop energy technology, the second law of thermodynamics imposes no physical constraint on the possibilities of recycling material. In principle, given an unlimited supply of energy, all material could be recycled — a fact that follows directly from the first law of thermodynamics (conservation of mass) and that was at first denied by Georgescu-Roegen, but later on accepted (Georgescu-Roegen 1986, p. 11). However, there is an economic constraint since, for many materials, the costs of recycling material are likely to become prohibitively high as the recycling rate tends towards 100 per cent. Recycling can ease a resource constraint for some time, but it cannot overcome it in the end. For a detailed discussion of the physical principles governing the possibilities of recycling material, see Georgescu-Roegen (1986), Biancardi et al. (1993, 1996), Khalil (1994), Kummel (1994), Mansson (1994) and Converse (1996).

3.2.3   Substitution with Man-made Capital

Now let us turn to proposition (c). Evidently, proposition (a) cannot be a satisfactory solution, if there is no backstop technology that can substitute for all economically relevant resources and substituting for them with renewable resources is either infeasible or would hugely overstretch their regenerative capacity. Equally, proposition (b) cannot be a satisfactory solution if we take on a very long-run perspective, because in the end a non-renewable resource is just that: non-renewable and it will be depleted in some finite time. The resource might still be substituted for with man-made capital then.

But can man-made capital substitute for an ever-diminishing resource stock? Daly (1994, p. 25) tries to refute the possibility of substituting man-made capital for natural capital (here: natural resources) with a general argument:

> One way to make an argument is to assume the opposite and show that it is absurd. If man-made capital were a near perfect substitute for natural capital, then natural capital would be a near perfect substitute for man-made capital. But if so, there would have been no reason to accumulate man-made capital in the first place, since we were endowed by nature with a near perfect substitute.

Daly's argument is incorrect, however. It says that if A is a near-perfect substitute for B, then B must be a near-perfect substitute for A. However, the conclusion does not follow from the premise. A might have some additional desirable properties that B does not have: for some production purposes A and B are almost near-perfect substitutes with almost linear isoquants. But for other purposes, A has some desirable properties that B does not have. Hence, A can substitute for the totality of B, but not vice versa. Hence, there is reason to accumulate A and substitute for B.

Solow (1974a) and Dasgupta and Heal (1979) have proved that, in theory at least, man-made capital can substitute for an ever diminishing natural resource.[11] Dasgupta and Heal (1979) examine under which conditions a non-renewable resource is essential and when it is inessential, where an essential resource is defined as a resource for which 'feasible consumption must necessarily decline to zero in the long run' (p. 199). To make analysis possible they have to assume some sort of production function and they take the constant elasticity of substitution (CES) production function, which is the most prominent production function in economics, for reasons of simplicity. Since they assume that labour is constant, one can as well normalise it to one and suppress it and put only man-made capital K and resource input R as arguments into the function. Hence the constant elasticity of substitution refers to the elasticity of substitution between reproducible man-made capital and the non-renewable resource. Let us call this elasticity σ. The CES function can be represented as follows:

$$F(t) = \left\{ \alpha K(t)^{(\sigma-1)/\sigma} + \beta R(t)^{(\sigma-1)/\sigma} + (1-\alpha-\beta) \right\}^{\sigma/(\sigma-1)} \tag{3.8}$$

where F is produced output and α, $\beta > 0$, $\alpha+\beta < 1$, and

$$\sigma = \frac{d\ln\left(K/R\right)}{d\ln\left|MRS_{K,R}\right|} \Rightarrow \sigma \geq 0 .^{12} \tag{3.9}$$

where MRS is the marginal rate of substitution between K and R:

$$MRS_{K,R} = \frac{dK}{dR} = -\frac{\partial F/\partial R}{\partial F/\partial K} = \frac{P_R}{P_K} \tag{3.10}$$

and P_K, P_R is the price of the man-made capital factor and resource factor price, respectively. The higher is σ, the better can resources be substituted with man-made capital. There are three cases to distinguish: first, $\sigma > 1$; second, $\sigma = 1$, and, third, $\sigma < 1$.

The first case is trivial and therefore uninteresting. To see this, note that with $\sigma > 1$ all exponents become greater than zero and since resources enter the production function only in an additive way, they are inessential. However, for the same reason it is possible to have $F(K,0) > 0$, that is production without any input of resources, which contradicts the first law of thermodynamics. That something can be produced without any resource input is a physical impossibility. $\sigma > 1$ can therefore be dismissed.

The third case is uninteresting as well. Note that for this case the average product of the resource, F/R, is

$$F(t)/R(t) = \left\{\alpha K(t)^{(\sigma-1)/\sigma} + \beta R(t)^{(\sigma-1)/\sigma} + (1-\alpha-\beta)\right\}^{\sigma/(\sigma-1)} \cdot R(t)^{-1} \tag{3.11}$$

or equivalently

$$F(t)/R(t) = \left\{\alpha\left(\frac{R(t)}{K(t)}\right)^{(1-\sigma)/\sigma} + \beta + (1-\alpha-\beta)R(t)^{(1-\sigma)/\sigma}\right\}^{\sigma/(\sigma-1)} \tag{3.12}$$

and it is bounded above as the resource becomes depleted, because as $R \to 0$, F/R becomes

$$\lim_{R\to 0} F(t)/R(t) = \beta^{\sigma/(\sigma-1)} \tag{3.13}$$

With a finite resource stock and no technical progress, the boundedness of the average product F/R implies that total output is finite so that output must decline to zero as time goes to infinity. In the limit with $\sigma = 0$ the CES-function degenerates into a so-called Leontief production function of the form $F(K,R) = \min(vK, wR)$ with $v > 0$, $w > 0$, which means that all substitution possibilities are ruled out and we reached perfect complementarity (Varian 1992, p. 20).

In the second case, with $\sigma = 1$ the CES function is formally undefined but can be shown to collapse into a function that is known by economists as the Cobb–Douglas production function (Chiang 1984, pp. 428ff). It takes the following form:

$$F(t) = K(t)^{\alpha} \cdot R(t)^{\beta} \tag{3.14}$$

It is apparent, that the resource is not trivially inessential since without resources ($R = 0$) no production is possible, that is $F = 0$. However, dividing F by R and taking the partial derivative of F with respect to R shows that

$$\frac{F}{R} = \frac{K^{\alpha}}{R^{(1-\beta)}} \quad \text{and} \quad \partial F / \partial R = \beta \left(\frac{F}{R} \right) \tag{3.15}$$

so for $\sigma = 1$ both the average (F/R) and marginal product $\partial F / \partial R$ of the resource are unbounded and both F/R and $\partial F / \partial R \to \infty$ as $R \to 0$. This combination ensures that the case $\sigma = 1$ is non-trivial: it is not a priori clear whether the resource is essential or not. Dasgupta and Heal (1979, pp. 200–205) prove that the resource is not essential if $\alpha > \beta$, that is if the elasticity of output with respect to man-made capital is higher than the elasticity of output with respect to the non-renewable resource. There is no direct intuition for this result beyond the mathematical necessity. However, since in a competitive economy these elasticities are equal to the share of total income going to the factors man-made capital and resources, respectively (Euler's theorem), Dasgupta and Heal (1979, p. 200) circumscribe the condition $\alpha > \beta$ with the condition that man-made capital is 'sufficiently important in production'. Solow (1974a, p. 39), Hartwick (1977, p. 974) and Dasgupta and Heal (1979, p. 205) suggest that man-made capital's share is as much as four times higher than the share of resources, so that resources are not essential for the Cobb–Douglas case.[13]

There are several objections that can be raised against being optimistic as a consequence of this analysis, however:

1. The first objection is that we do not know whether σ is greater than, equal to or smaller than 1. In one of the rare attempts to estimate elasticities of

substitution for non-energy resources, Brown and Field (1979, p. 241) found high elasticities of substitution for steel, copper, pulp and paper through man-made capital and labour. Deadman and Turner (1988, p. 91) present qualitative evidence for low elasticities of substitution for beryllium, titanium and germanium. There are more econometric studies on the relationship between man-made capital and energy. Table 3.1 summarises the findings of several studies. It is important to note that the reported values are not the σ's as defined above, but so-called 'Allen partial elasticity of substitution' values, $\sigma(AES)$, with

$$\sigma(AES) = \frac{\partial \ln K}{\partial \ln P_E} \bigg/ M_E \qquad (3.16)$$

where P_E is the price of energy and M_E is the share of energy in total production costs. $\sigma(AES)$ is not bounded below by zero and its values are not directly transferable into values of σ. However, negative values of $\sigma(AES)$

Table 3.1 Estimates of the capital–energy Allen partial elasticity of substitution

$\sigma(AES)$	Sample	Type of data	Source
−1.39	US	1947–71 time-series	Hudson and Jorgenson (1974)
−3.22	US	1947–71 time-series	Berndt and Wood (1975)
1.07 / 1.03	US/9 OECD countries	1955–69 cross-section	Griffin and Gregory (1976)
1.22	7 OECD countries	1963–74 time-series	Özatalay et al. (1979)
−2.32	Netherlands	1950–76 time-series	Magnus (1979)
0.36–1.77	10 OECD countries	1963–73 time-series	Pindyck (1979)
−3.8	US	1971 cross-section	Field and Grebenstein (1980)
2.26	Australia	1946–75 time-series	Turnovsky et al. (1982)
−1.35	US	1971–76 cross-section	Prywes (1986)
2.17	Taiwan	1956–71 time-series	Chang (1994)

signal complementarity between man-made capital and energy and the more negative is $\sigma(AES)$ the higher is the complementarity. Vice versa for positive values of $\sigma(AES)$ which signal substitutability (Allen 1938, p. 509).

Table 3.1 shows extreme variance in results ranging from complementarity to substitutability. There is much dispute about possible explanations for these 'notably contradictory' (Solow 1987, p. 605) findings, without a resolution — see Berndt and Field (1981) and Solow (1987). Some argue that time-series econometric studies are likely to find complementarity, whereas cross-section analyses are likely to find substitutability between energy and man-made capital (Griffin 1981, pp. 71–4). This is because relative factor price variations tend to be much more pronounced cross-sectionally than over time within one country. If these relative price differentials have been existent for a long time, cross-section studies are likely to find long-run equilibrium effects and in the long run we would always expect higher substitutability between factors than in the short run.

Looking at Table 3.1 shows, however, that some studies do not fit this explanation. At best, it can therefore only be part of the story. Another explanation offered by Berndt and Wood (1979, p. 349f) is that studies that find substitutability usually tend to include only three factors (labour, man-made capital and energy) in the production function, whereas studies that find complementarity include materials as a fourth factor. But, again, there are some studies using four inputs and still finding substitutability between capital and energy (for example, Turnovsky et al. 1982).

A third reason for the differing results is given by Solow (1987) and Chichilnisky and Heal (1983). They develop models in which different countries can exhibit either substitutability or complementarity between energy and man-made capital in spite of having the same physical production function. These differences can occur because of differences in energy prices and differences in energy demand conditions. Overall, it has to be said that a satisfactory explanation for the variance in results from econometric studies has not been found yet and that we do not have a reliable answer on the question whether energy and man-made capital are substitutes or complements. Most of the evidence points in the direction of substitutability, a verdict that is buttressed by Markandya and Pedroso-Galinato (2007) who come to the conclusion that their estimates of the elasticity of substitution between energy resources and other inputs tend to be generally high in their cross-national study. Nevertheless, we cannot have much confidence that energy and man-made capital are truly easily substitutable.

2. The second objection is that we cannot rule out the possibility that σ becomes smaller than 1 as more and more of the resource is used up. That is, σ is not constant over time, but is itself a function of time, that is, σ = σ(t). Dasgupta and Heal assume a CES production function for simplicity, but there is no reason to expect that in reality the elasticity of substitution between man-made capital and resources is constant over time. As Dasgupta and Heal (1979, p. 207) remark themselves, constancy might be a flawed assumption as the resource is run down and the ratio of man-made capital to resources becomes very high. Especially in that phase even assuming σ = 1 might contradict physical laws since it assumes that *F/R* and ∂F/∂R→ ∞ as *R*→ 0; that is, the average product and the marginal product of the resource tend toward infinity as the resource stock tends to zero.

3. The third objection applies the same kind of argument to the share of man-made capital and the resource share of total income. There is no reason to expect that in reality those shares remain constant as the stock of the resource tends toward depletion (Slade 1987, p. 351). α and β are not constant over time, but themselves functions of time, that is α = α(t) and β = β(t). Hence, even if σ was constantly equal to 1 throughout, the elasticity of output with respect to the resource β(t) might supersede the elasticity of output with respect to man-made capital α(t), after which the resource will become essential.

4. The fourth objection is that the dichotomy of man-made capital versus resources is an artificial and flawed one since man-made capital consists partly of resources. Victor (1991) looks at the properties of a Cobb-Douglas production function if it is assumed that man-made capital is itself produced from man-made capital, resources and labour. Let the production function *F* be of the form[14]

$$F = K^c R^d L^e \text{, with } c, d, e > 0 \text{ and } c + d + e = 1 \tag{3.17}$$

Now let the production function for producing man-made capital be of the form

$$K = K^p R^q L^s \text{, with } p, q, s > 0 \text{ and } p + q + s = 1 \tag{3.18}$$

Solving (3.18) for *K* gives

$$K = R^{\left(\frac{q}{1-p}\right)} L^{\left(\frac{s}{1-p}\right)} \tag{3.19}$$

Substituting (3.19) into (3.17) and re-arranging we arrive at

$$F = R^{\left(\frac{c \cdot q}{1-p} + d\right)} L^{\left(\frac{c \cdot s}{1-p} + e\right)} \tag{3.20}$$

It is obvious that man-made capital can no longer infinitely substitute for an ever-declining resource stock. Of course, resources might still be substituted for by an ever-increasing labour input; but, in contrast to man-made capital, labour is not a factor that can be increased indefinitely since labour is supplied by human beings. That is, in effect, given that resources are needed for the production of man-made capital, resources become essential for production, even for the Cobb–Douglas case: man-made capital cannot infinitely substitute for vanishing resources.

Note, however, that just because substitution possibilities are restricted, this does not imply that R and K are complements as Daly (1995a, p. 51) erroneously suggests when he argues as follows:

> Manmade capital is itself a physical transformation of natural resources which are the flow yield from the stock of natural capital. Therefore, producing more of the alleged substitute (manmade capital), physically requires more of the very thing being substituted for (natural capital) — the defining condition of complementarity.

The first part of this argument is undoubtedly correct because it follows from the first law of thermodynamics (conservation of mass). The problem with the second part of the argument is, however, that the conclusion ('complementarity') does not follow from the correct observation. In economic terms perfect complementarity is defined as a limitational production function of the form $F[K(R), R] = \min(vK, wR)$, with $v > 0$, $w > 0$ being parameters and isoquants that look like rectangles. In words, increasing man-made capital input in the production process for output does not increase output if resource input is not increased at the same time. Daly (1995a, p. 55) accepts this definition. However, the simple fact that one input into the production of man-made capital is natural capital does not imply complementarity thus defined.

One can show this both for the case that the economy is on the production possibility frontier and for the case that it is not. Let us start with the latter case first. Assume an economy with an endowment of five units of man-made capital and 10 units of resources. Assume for simplicity that each unit of capital together with two units of resources produces exactly one unit of the consumption good. Further assume that man-made capital and resources are perfect substitutes in the production of the consumption good; that is, instead of using 10 units of resources and five units of capital to produce five units of the consumption good, one could also use 10 additional units of capital to substitute for the resource. Assume, however, that the production of each capital good itself requires 0.5 units of natural resources. Now, produce 10 additional units of the capital good to substitute for the 10 units of resources in the production of the consumption good. Since the production of each unit of capital requires only 0.5 units of natural resources, total resource input has decreased by five units. These five units could be used to increase production. It follows that $K = K(R)$ does not imply that output cannot be increased without increasing resource input at the same time.

Of course, as soon as all resources have been substituted for in the production of the consumption good, then, in the absence of technical progress, there is no longer leeway for substitution since the resource requirement for the production of the capital good is presumed to be fixed; that is, with $K = K(R)$, it is not possible to increase production indefinitely while at the same time driving resource use down to zero. This is the case of the economy being on the production possibility frontier. By assumption all the available resources are in efficient use and output cannot be increased further. However, for this case as well Daly's argument is not correct: the pure fact that resources are needed for the production of man-made capital ($K = K(R)$) does not imply anything for the shape of the iso-quants in the production function for the consumption good and therefore does not imply that $F[K(R), R] = \min(vK, wR)$. As Pearce (1997, p. 296) points out, if Daly's argument was valid then all forms of capital would be complements to each other since all forms of capital embody to some extent other forms of capital as well.

3.2.4   Technical Progress

Let us finally turn to proposition (d). Technical progress can be divided into what economists call 'resource-augmenting' technical progress and what I call 'augmenting-resource' technical progress for lack of a *terminus technicus*. Resource-augmenting technical progress increases the efficiency of resource use and means that ever-more output can be produced from a given amount of resources or that for a given output ever-less resource input is needed, respectively. 'Augmenting-resource' technical progress reduces resource extraction costs which means that lower-quality ores of a resource become economical to extract. This implies that the economically relevant resource stock *increases*, although the total physical stock of a finite non-renewable resource cannot be increased, of course. It is this what Baumol (1986) had in mind when he spoke of 'the possibility of continuing expansion of finite resources'.

In some sense technical progress is the strongest proposition of the resource optimists. Let us turn to resource-augmenting technical progress first. It is easy to see that if there is permanent resource-augmenting technical progress, that is if a unit of output can be produced with ever-declining resource inputs, then the resource is inessential even if substitution possibilities between man-made capital and resources are nil (Dasgupta and Heal 1979, p. 207). Assume, for example, that there is exponential resource-augmenting technical progress. The production function now looks like

$$F = F\left[K(t), R(t) \cdot e^{kt}\right] \tag{3.21}$$

with k as the rate of technical progress. It is obvious that permanent resource-augmenting technical progress can compensate for an ever-diminishing natural resource stock. The same holds true as Stiglitz (1974) proves for so-called Hicks-neutral technical progress, that is technical progress that cannot be attributed to a production factor, if:

- the production function is Cobb–Douglas, that is $\sigma = 1$,
- and m/β is sufficiently large, where m is the rate of Hicks-neutral technical progress and β is the income share of the resource, so that m/β can be loosely[15] interpreted as the rate of resource-augmenting technical progress (Toman, Pezzey and Krautkraemer 1995, p. 145).

However, whether permanent resource-augmenting technical progress is possible, especially in the limit as resource stocks go down, is unclear. Ayres and Miller (1980) and Gross and Veendorp (1990) suggest that assuming so contradicts the first law of thermodynamics (conservation of mass). Dasgupta (2008) does not go this far, but finds it hard to give credence to the idea that technological progress can substitute for a permanently vanishing natural resource base. There are likely to be limits to increasing efficiency. While it might be possible to reduce the required resource input per unit of output by a factor of, say, 10 or sometimes even 100 for most resources, it is presumably technically not possible to increase efficiency by a factor of 1000 or more.

Unfortunately, it is rather difficult to measure resource-augmenting technical progress. Take energy use as an example. Figure 3.3 shows the time trend in energy intensity for the world and for OECD countries. Energy intensity is the ratio of energy input expressed in physical terms to the inflation-adjusted value of economic output, usually GDP.[16] The problem with this measurement is that it does not directly measure changes in the technical energy efficiency of production which is what we are looking for when we want to measure resource-augmenting technical progress. A decline in the energy intensity of an economy can come about for a number of reasons other than technical progress itself: for example because of a change in the sectoral structure of the economy; because of substitution of labour or man-made capital for energy; because of a change in the energy input mix towards energy sources which can provide more useful work per unit of heat and so on (Patterson 1996, p. 381; Kaufmann 1992).[17]

Another caveat when inferring conclusions from looking at resource-augmenting technical progress is that, even if resource intensities are falling over time, *absolute* resource consumption may well rise if the rate of consumption growth is higher than the rate of resource-augmenting technical progress. Looking again at Figure 3.3 it is clear that while energy intensities have fallen over time both worldwide and for the OECD countries, consumption of primary energy has continuously risen due to tremendous population and output growth.[18]

In fact, falling energy intensity and rising absolute energy consumption are even more closely related: resource-augmenting technical progress reduces

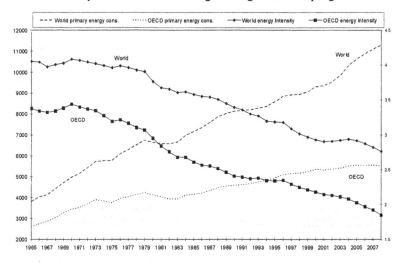

Sources: BP (2009) and World Bank (2009b).

Note: Primary energy consumption in million tonnes oil equivalent on lefthand scale. Energy intensity (consumption/GDP * 10^4) on right-hand scale.

Figure 3.3 Energy consumption and energy intensity (1965 to 2008)

the implicit price of energy, thus making production cheaper, boosting production and favouring the substitution of energy for other factors of production, which in return implies, *ceteris paribus*, an increased demand for energy (Brookes 1990, 1992; Binswanger 2001). Khazzoom (1987) and Brookes (1990, 1992) believe that this 'rebound' effect will in most cases be strong enough to lead to a *net* increase in energy use. Howarth (1997, p. 8) argues, however, that this conjecture will only hold true under the conditions that '(i) energy accounts for a large fraction of the total cost of energy services and (ii) the production of energy services constitutes a substantial fraction of economic activity'. He finds that neither of these conditions is empirically plausible.

Let us now turn to 'augmenting-resource' technical progress. Slade's (1982) and Berck and Roberts' (1996) models show how improvements in the resource-extraction technology can lead to a persistent downward trend in unit extraction costs and real resource prices over quite a long time span although the total resource stock becomes physically smaller.

Using the simple model we introduced in Section 3.2.2, p. 53, we can show how the resource price can fall over time given sufficient progress in resource-extraction technology. Assume that there is exponential technical progress at a constant rate k so that resource-extraction costs develop according to $C(t) = C(0) \cdot e^{-kt}$. The new problem facing the competitive resource-extracting firm is to

$$\underset{R}{\text{Max}}\, \Gamma = \int_0^\infty \left[P(t)R(t) - R(t) \cdot C(0) \cdot e^{-kt} \right] \cdot e^{-rt} \, dt - \lambda R(t) \tag{3.4'}$$

which has the first-order condition

$$P = \lambda e^{rt} + C(0) \cdot e^{-kt} \tag{3.5'}$$

Differentiating (3.5') with respect to time leads to (λ constant)

$$\dot{P} = r\lambda e^{rt} - kC(0) \cdot e^{-kt} \tag{3.6'}$$

Both terms on the right-hand side of (3.6') are positive. The second term is increasing in k (for $0 < k < 1$), hence (3.6') can become negative if k is sufficiently large: resource prices can fall if technical progress is sufficiently strong.

Technical progress can boost the economically relevant resource stock and ease the resource constraint over a significant time span. However, whether there will be and can be permanent and at best exponential technical progress is unclear, of course. That there has been enormous technical progress in the past is beyond doubt, but there is no assurance that there will also be permanent technical progress in the future. As Lecomber (1975, p. 45) has put it: 'The central feature of technical advance is indeed its uncertainty.' It all boils down to whether one believes strongly in technical progress or not. It is worth quoting Beckerman (1972, p. 338) at some length here:

> In fact, given the natural concentrations of the key metals in the Earth's crust as indicated by a large number of random samples the total natural occurrence of most metals in the top mile of the Earth's crust has been estimated to be about a million times as great as present known reserves. Since the latter amount to about a hundred years' supplies this means we have enough to last about one hundred million years. Even though it may be impossible at present to mine to a depth of one mile at every point in the Earth's crust, by the time we reach the year A.D. 100,000,000 I am sure we will think up something. If the idea that actual reserves might be a million times currently proved reserves seems unbelievable it should be borne in mind that existing proved reserves are probably about a million times as big as those known in the days of Pericles.

This is resource optimism in its purest form, but it is also pure speculation. We simply cannot rely on Beckerman's faith holding true.

So far we have only looked at the 'source' side of the economy. Now we take a look at the 'sink' side of the economy and environmental degradation.[19] In reality, of course, there is no such strict dichotomy between both aspects since a renewable resource that becomes exhausted while using it up in production might have provided other environmental amenity functions for human beings as well; or the mining of non-renewable resources produces environmentally detrimental side-effects as is the case in extracting bauxite for the production of aluminium or in drilling oil.

3.3   ENVIRONMENTAL DEGRADATION

First of all, I will analyse whether future generations can be compensated for long-term environmental degradation via increased consumption. Behind the paradigm of WS stands the presumption that rising output can compensate future generations for a degraded environment, whereas SS, as defined in Section 2.3.2, p. 23, denies this possibility.

3.3.1 Can Future Generations be Compensated for Long-Term Environmental Degradation?

The problem with assessing this question is that one has to rely to a great extent on speculation since we cannot know for sure how future generations will value consumption goods relative to environmental services. It seems safe to assume that all individuals independent of the generation they belong to share the same basic needs and wants (such as water, food, shelter, fresh air, basic enjoyments). One might want to argue therefore that ever-rising output cannot compensate for the extinction of all renewable resources and for ever-rising pollution since this would most likely endanger the satisfaction of basic needs and wants. Barry (1991, p. 248) argues that while 'it is true that we do not know what the precise tastes of our remote descendants will be, they are unlikely to include a desire for skin cancer, soil erosion, or the inundation of all low-lying areas as a result of the melting of the ice-caps'.

It does not follow, however, that all environmental damage has to be avoided and that consumption growth cannot compensate for environmental degradation to a certain extent. The problem with Barry's argument is that taken to its logical conclusion it would imply that the current generation must not impose any harm on the future. However, such a prescription carries with it a tremendous opportunity cost. The world we live in is full of trade-offs. As argued in Section 4.5, p. 118, there are no easy answers to how deal with these trade-offs. But, as will be argued in more detail there, ignoring the existence of fundamental trade-offs is not appropriate.

Ideally, one would want to ask future generations which harm they regard as not amenable to compensation. Since this is impossible, one could as a substitute try to find out which forms of harm to the environment the *current* generation regards as undesirable, no matter what the cost of avoiding the harm. More formally, it would have to be investigated whether and to what extent individuals of the current generation exhibit something close to what economists call 'lexicographic preferences' with respect to the environment. Unfortunately, there is hardly any reliable evidence on this point as I shall show now.

It is often claimed that substantial minorities in contingent valuation (CV) studies respond in ways that can be interpreted as being consistent with lexicographic preferences with respect to wildlife and biodiversity protection: 24 per cent of the sample in Stevens et al. (1991), 23 per cent of the sample in Spash and Hanley (1995) and 14 per cent or 19 per cent (depending on the definition) in Hanley and Milne (1996). These studies do not really prove the existence of lexicographic preferences with respect to the environment, however, as a closer inspection makes clear. In Stevens et al. (1991, p 398), for example, the 24 per cent of the sample actually consist both of people who state that wildlife preservation is always more important to them than having more money *and* of people who state that more money is always more important to them than wildlife preservation. Also, their indicated preference is not challenged with a real test. In Spash and Hanley (1995) respondents are counted as exhibiting lexicographic-type preferences for biodiversity protection if they state that biodiversity should be protected irrespective of the costs and refuse to indicate a private willingness-to-pay for biodiversity protection. However, the respondents are not pushed hard with regard to the cost side of protection. Because of the hypothetical character of CV studies, it is all too easy and cheap for individuals to state that they want environmental preservation no matter what the cost. Lexicographic preferences cannot be inferred from these results as long as everything remains hypothetical and the respondents' indicated preferences are not exposed to the acid test of real sacrifices.[20]

In Hanley and Milne (1996, p. 260) respondents are confronted more elaborately with the cost side of preservation. While 99 per cent affirm that 'wildlife and landscape have the right to be protected', this response rate goes down to 49 per cent if protection 'costs jobs/money', down to 38 per cent if it costs 10 per cent of the respondent's income and ends up at 19 per cent if preservation cost was 25 per cent of the respondent's income. As can be seen, the preferences of individuals become 'less lexicographic' as costs increase. And, of course, for a really reliable test respondents would have to be willing to give up almost all their income to keep them just on this side of the bare existence minimum and they would have to do so in reality. Do we really believe there are more than a few individuals who would go so far?

Be that as it may, even if one accepted that about one-fifth of the population exhibited lexicographic preferences with respect to wildlife, biodiversity and landscape protection as indicated by the mentioned studies, would it follow that one should regard environmental harm as non-compensable? The answer is no. First, it would have to be shown that lexicographic preferences are existent in more general terms for environmental amenities and not only for preserving species and landscapes. Do people want to preserve the current climate and reduce carbon dioxide emissions very drastically no matter what the cost? Second, the vast majority quite clearly do *not* exhibit lexicographic preferences, however measured. That only a minority exhibit behaviour that is compatible with lexicographic preferences is also confirmed by a contingent ranking study of Foster and Mourato (2000, p. 18) who find that 'only some 18 per cent of respondents answered *all* their ranking questions lexicographically'. Veisten et al. (2006) show that what appears as lexicographic preferences at first sight often represents nothing else but high valuation for the environmental good, concluding that 'people with lexicographic prefer-

ences for biodiversity are probably less numerous than previously indicated'
(p. 167).

All these qualifications notwithstanding, SS is quite explicit in rejecting
the possibility of compensation for long-term environmental degradation. It
seems fair to say that it rejects compensability mainly for normative reasons.
In other words, consumption growth *should* not be allowed to compensate for
future environmental degradation. The proposition would therefore not be
refuted by the fact that empirical evidence for existing lexicographic preferences is rather weak.

In conclusion, the proposition of SS that natural capital should in principle
be regarded as non-substitutable as a direct provider of utility and that therefore increased consumption cannot compensate for environmental degradation
seems hard to defend if it is taken as a *positive* position and is non-refutable if
it is taken as a *normative* position. On the other hand, presumably not many
people will find the opposite extreme suggestion very attractive, namely that
rising consumption can always compensate coming generations for a deterioration in the environmental conditions. There is the danger, however, that
preferences will accommodate to a changing world. Individuals born into a
world where, for example, 90 per cent of all species are lost might build up
preferences such that they do not feel this as a great loss. Arguably, many
people living in urban areas have already become used to encountering only a
small number of animals and plants personally. The same holds potentially
true for environmental pollution as well. The point is that preferences are
determined partly by the changing outside world; they are not as solid and
unchanging as the Rocky Mountains, as Becker and Stigler (1977, p. 76)
suggest.[21]

However, proponents of WS sincerely believe that in the end economic
growth will be rather beneficial and not harmful for the environment (World
Bank 1992). The paradigm of WS would therefore not have to rely so much
upon the highly questionable substitutability assumption with respect to natural capital as a more direct provider of utility.

I shall take the conjecture that economic growth will improve environmental conditions as the main proposition of WS with respect to
environmental degradation and call it 'environmental optimism'. It is therefore necessary now to analyse the link between economic growth and
environmental degradation.

3.3.2   Economic Growth and the Environment

Before discussing in detail the theoretical arguments concerning the environmental consequences of economic growth and the available evidence which

will fill the rest of this section, let us examine first why it is that the economic activity and especially economic growth pose a problem for the environment. The first law of thermodynamics, that is the law of conservation of mass, implies that no material can be destroyed, it can only be transformed into other goods (bound to become waste some time), and into waste, pollution and so on; in other words, if all other things are equal, then economic activity and the more so economic growth 'is inevitably an entropic process that increases the amount of unavailable (that is, dissipated or high entropy) resources at the expense of available (that is, ordered or low entropy) resources: the stock of wastes increases and environmental quality decreases'[22] (Smulders 1995, p. 165).

Of course, it is the WS proponents' argument that all other things are *not* equal and I start by presenting the case for environmental optimism. After that, the opposite case of environmental pessimism is put forward and it is assessed whether empirical evidence is able to decide between the opposite claims.

3.3.2.1 The case for environmental optimism
There are several reasons suggesting that economic growth might be beneficial for the environment in spite of the first law of thermodynamics:

1. One that is often cited (for example, Beckerman 1992a, 1992b; Baldwin 1995) is that environmental quality is a normal, possibly even a luxury good as economists call it, that is a good with an income elasticity greater than zero, possibly even greater than one: as incomes grow environmental concern rises (normal good) or rises more than proportionally (luxury good). Environmental protection then rises if the political system is responsive to the preferences of its people — and both theory (Olson 1993) and empirical evidence (Rueschemeyer, Stephens and Stephens 1991; Barro 1996) suggest that the political systems in high-income countries are more responsive to the preferences of its citizens than in poor countries. Given that past environmental destruction is not infinitely persistent and irreversible, the rising share of environmental protection in relation to total expenditure implies that environmental quality increases.

   A similar argument is that with rising incomes people become better educated and better able to express their desires and defend their interests. It becomes more difficult with rising incomes to externalise environmental costs upon others, because the latter are better able to fight this degradation of their welfare. Also, richer people are more likely to be aware of environmental hazards due to better education and information. Hence in rich countries more environmental costs are internalised than in poor countries, implying that pollution in poor countries is higher (a similar line of argument is offered by Markandya and Perrings 1991, p. 4).

2. The second reason buttresses the first one in that it suggests that rich countries might not only have higher demand for environmental protection, but also have better means for satisfying this higher demand. Rich countries can better afford spending money on the environment and have the technical equipment for environmental protection. But it is more than that: rich countries also 'have the advanced social, legal and fiscal infrastructures that are essential to enforcing environmental regulations and promoting "green awareness"' (Baldwin 1995, p. 61).

3. The third reason is that with economic growth it becomes more likely that more modern man-made capital is newly installed or replaces the old and Grossman (1995, p. 21) claims that more modern capital by and large tends to be less pollution intensive. Ausubel (1995) suggests that technical progress will vastly reduce the emission of CO_2 in the beginning and middle of the 21st century, thus drastically reducing any need to cut down emissions artificially by introducing taxes. There is some weak support for the claim that more modern capital is less pollution intensive — see, for example, Wheeler and Martin (1992).

4. The fourth reason is that at higher levels of income the share of industry goes down while the share of services goes up and it is often presumed that services are less pollution intensive than industrial manufacturing. Even within industries the share of heavy polluting manufacturing (like chemistry, steel and cement production) decreases in favour of less-polluting high-tech manufacturing. For some weakly supporting evidence, see Jänicke, Mönch and Binder (1992).

5. The fifth reason puts forward a similar, more fundamental argument: economic growth is not logically equivalent to rising output in physical terms but to rising output in value terms (Pezzey 1992a, p. 324). That is, economic growth means a rise in total net value. Resource depletion and environmental destruction as such are not objectives of economic activity, rather they are 'unwanted' side-products of adding value to the inputs of production. Where this value comes from and how pollution intensive it is are logically separate questions from the growth in value. The economic value per unit of pollution can rise or, inversely, the pollution intensity per unit of economic value can fall.

The same argument applies to resource use and resource intensity which would further buttress the optimists' view on resource availability in

Section 3.2, p. 48. Note that this decoupling of economic value from resource input and pollution can stem either from technical improvements or from the changing pattern of output away from resource- and pollution-intensive goods towards goods that are less intensive in resource use and pollution. It can also stem from re-use of goods, recovery and recycling of materials. There is 'no definite upper limit' on the 'service output of a given material' (Ayres 1997, p. 286).

6. The sixth reason takes a closer look at the environmental consequences of poverty. As Beckerman (1992a, 1992b, 1993) and Barbier (1994) observe, poor people are often locked into a trap in which poverty causes environmental degradation which causes poverty in return. Poor people are driven to exploit their environment out of sheer lack of alternatives, which in turn makes them poorer, which in turn raises the pressure on the environment and so on. As Markandya and Pearce (1988, p. 35) observe, the very high time preference rates of poor people which is due to their poverty makes it completely rational for them to destroy the resource their living is dependent upon. Deforestation for the collection of fuelwood seems a good example for this conjecture. Beckerman (1992a, p. 482) concludes that 'in the end the best — and probably the only — way to attain a decent environment in most countries is to become rich'.

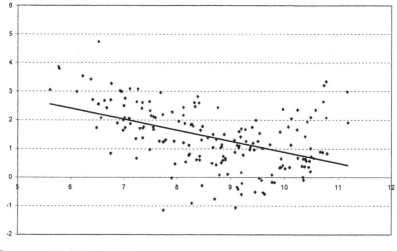

Source: World Bank (2009).
Note: Population growth rate left scale, log of income right scale(2005–07 averages).

Figure 3.4 Population growth rates and per capita income

7. A seventh reason is that with rising incomes the pressure on the environment due to population growth goes down since population growth tends to go down and, all other things equal, more people means more pollution (Cole and Neumayer 2004). Figure 3.4 plots the average population growth rate in 2005–2007 of almost all countries in the world against the natural log of their average 2005–2007 per capita income in US$ of purchasing power parity. There is a weak tendency for lower population growth rates being correlated with higher per capita incomes shown by the linear trend line. Population growth rates are partly influenced by migration. Since people usually migrate towards the richer countries, the negative association between income and population growth would be more pronounced still if one had data on the growth rate of the domestic population only. This is certainly true for Qatar (2.99 per cent and US$70715) and the United Arab Emirates (3.35 per cent and US$47600), which form two of the outliers at the top level of income in figure 3.4.

3.3.2.2 The case for environmental pessimism
There are several objections to the proposition that economic growth might be beneficial to the environment, however, as follows:

1. The first objects to the presumption that the rich care more about the environment than the poor do (see, for example, Martinez-Alier 1995, 2002). The available systematic evidence on this point is far from conclusive (see Kriström and Riera 1996; Flores and Carson 1997). There is some casual evidence, however, suggesting that some societies with very low incomes place a high value on the conservation of species and amenities that are often characterised by common property (Bromley 1989b; Kanbur 1992; Shafik and Bandyopadhyay 1992).

   A similar argument is that although environmental concern might rise with income and perhaps even more than proportionally so, rising incomes lead to an inflation in demand for all kinds of things. More and more goods and more and more new goods need to be produced to satisfy the rich consumer's desire, which in itself means higher pressure on the environment. Poor people do not travel by airplane very much and do not drive a Porsche.

2. The second objection is that while pollution per unit of output might decrease, total pollution might still increase if the rate of growth in output is higher than the rate of decrease in pollution per unit of output. As Lopez (1992, p. 154) observes for technical change, its effect on pollution is in principle ambiguous:

Technical change has two effects: (i) it increases the efficiency of conventional factors of production, and (ii) it may generate biases toward more or toward less environment-intensive technologies. Insofar as (i) is effectively equivalent to conventional factor accumulation, its effect on the environment is negative. The effect of (ii) is to decrease environmental degradation if technical change is environment saving. Given that environmental control costs are a very small fraction of the total cost in developed countries, it is likely that the bulk of the R&D efforts by the private sector are still oriented more toward the development of conventional factors saving techniques rather than to environmental saving techniques. Hence, it is likely that the effect (i) of technical change dominates the effect (ii), implying that growth, even if generated by technical change only, will lead to increased pollution.

On the other hand, Cavendish and Anderson (1994, p. 774) cite evidence that 'in a large number of cases pollution per unit of output can be, and often historically has been, reduced by factors of 10, 100, and sometimes 1000 or more (depending on the case) once the process of substitution is complete'. But there are also limits to this trend of substitution — first, physical limits, but, second, and much more important, economic limits, because often the marginal costs of reducing pollution per unit of output is rising steeply as pollution is tending towards zero. Not everything that is physically possible in theory will ever be put into practice because doing so would be prohibitively costly.

3. A third objection is that in so far as pollution is decreasing because the pattern of output is changing, there are limits as well. This time, however, the limits are not determined by technology or economic cost, but rather by people's preferences and social conventions. While it might be possible to substitute recreational and cultural activities which tend to have rather low pollution intensity for the consumption of high pollution intensive material goods, this substitution cannot go on for ever. As far as we can judge from people's revealed preferences, material goods are rather highly appreciated.

4. The fourth objection acknowledges that structural changes in the economy impact upon environmental quality. This does not work unambiguously in favour of the environment, however. At low levels, with rising incomes the share of agriculture goes down while the share of manufacturing goes up with possibly detrimental effects on the environment, especially if not accompanied by tighter environmental policies. Also, at low levels the share of heavy polluting manufacturing (such as chemicals, steel, cement production and heavy engineering) is usually quite high. The environmental impact of structural change thus very much depends on where a country is

in the process of structural change. Moreover, simply because the share of the manufacturing sector goes down does not imply that the absolute size of a country's manufacturing sector has shrunk. A smaller percentage of a much bigger pie still makes for a larger piece of cake. Take Japan as an example: according to World Bank (2009b) data, Japan's manufacturing share of GDP decreased from 45 per cent in 1971 to just below 30 per cent in 2005. Yet, despite this relative decrease the absolute size of the Japanese manufacturing sector increased from $734 bn to $1552 bn

5. The fifth objection suspects that one important reason why high-income countries could become cleaner was that they exported their most-polluting industries to lower-income countries. In importing goods that are highly resource or pollution intensive but produced elsewhere, developed countries can make their environmental record look cleaner than it actually is if one took account of the international trade linkages and attributed resource use and environmental pollution to the final consuming country (Atkinson and Hamilton 1996; Proops et al. 1999). Of course, when everybody wants to become rich, there eventually will be no poor country 'pollution havens' to take on the dirty industries. Hence becoming 'cleaner' as a consequence of becoming rich no longer will be possible. The available evidence for this argument is rather inconclusive, even though Cole and Neumayer (2005) find evidence that developed countries have increasingly satisfied their demand for pollution-intensive output by imports. For an overview of other studies and more evidence on the pollution haven issue, see Low (1992), Neumayer (2001a, 2001b), Brunnermeier and Levinson (2004), Clapp and Dauvergne (2005), Cole and Elliott (2005), Levinson and Taylor (2008) and Dean, Lovely and Wang (2009).

6. The sixth objection contests that economic growth is a necessary and sufficient condition for reducing population growth.[23] It is argued that investing in female education and providing retirement pension schemes are the best ways to reduce population growth. While these might correlate often with per capita income, economic growth is neither necessary nor sufficient to achieve the goal: there are poor countries like Jamaica with an income of US$6200 and a low population growth rate of 0.44 per cent, there are rich countries like Brunei Darussalam with an income of US$47600 and a high population growth rate of about 2.1 per cent (data from World Bank 2009b). Quite clearly, population growth is determined by many other factors beside the level of a country's income. This can also be seen in referring back to Figure 3.4: while there is a linear trend detectable, there is also considerable variance around the trend.

3.3.2.3 Empirical evidence

From theory no definite answer can be found. Economic growth could be either good or bad for the environment. And quite clearly, the environmental consequences of economic growth are an empirical rather than a theoretical matter. What does the evidence say? Available econometric studies, some time-series, but mostly cross-sectional or time-series cross-sectional, paint a complex picture depending on which indicator for which aspect of environmental quality one chooses to focus on. The empirical literature on the link between economic growth and the environment has literally exploded over the last decade and a half – as a small selection of studies see, for example, Shafik and Bandyopadhyay (1992), Grossman and Krueger (1993, 1995), Grossman (1995), Cropper and Griffiths (1994), Shafik (1994), Selden and Song (1994), Holtz-Eakin and Selden (1995), Baldwin (1995), Stern et al. (1996), Ekins (1997), Moomaw and Unruh (1997), Cole et al. (1997), de Bruyn et al. (1998), Unruh and Moomaw (1998), Agras and Chapman (1999), List and Gallet (1999), Stern and Common (2001), Harbaugh, Levinson and Wilson (2002), Cole (2003) and Cole and Neumayer (2005). One has to be rather cautious in interpreting the generated results: first, the quality of data they rely on is rather poor; second, critics have argued that most of the Environmental Kuznets Curve (EKC) results have been generated with inappropriate econometric methods (Stern and Common 2001; Stern 2004; Wagner 2008; Galeotti et al. 2009); and, third, different studies have come up with different relationships for the same indicator depending on the modelling technique. If, despite these caveats, we take the EKC studies at face value, then one can distinguish three ideal type results (see the stylised graphs in Figure 3.5):

1. Indicators showing an unambiguous improvement as incomes rise. Examples would be access to clean water and adequate sanitation (stylised graph A).

2. Indicators showing a deterioration first until a certain level of income is reached after which an improvement takes place. That is, on a graph with environmental quality on the ordinate and income on the abscissa the graph would show a U-curve. Often in the literature, however, the level of pollution is put on the ordinate so that the graph shows an inverted U-curve (stylised graph B). This curve is called an 'Environmental Kuznets Curve' (EKC), an environmental variant of the much older Kuznets curve named after Kuznets (1955) who hypothesised that income distribution would first become more unequal as development started off in a country and more equal later on. Examples for the EKC would be the emission of suspended particulate matter, sulphur oxides, faecal coliforms, the quality

of ambient air and the rate of (tropical) deforestation. This second case has gained the most attention for reasons I shall discuss later.

3. Indicators showing an unambiguous deterioration in specific aspects of environmental quality as incomes rise (stylised graph C). Examples would be the generation of municipal waste and the emission of CO_2 per capita.[24]

It follows that one has to look carefully at concrete environmental indicators to gauge the environmental consequences of economic growth and no general conclusions can be drawn from the existing evidence. Why are there (at least) three different qualitative cases to distinguish? One possible explanation for the observed variance is that those environmental aspects that are most important in everyday life and that are rather difficult to externalise on others already improve at quite low income levels, whereas those that can easily be externalised onto others, as for example with CO_2 emissions, worsen steadily with economic growth (Shafik 1994, p. 768). Another possible explanation is that some by-products of economic activity such as sulphur and nitrogen oxides (SO_x and NO_x) can rather easily be eliminated — whereas central components of the economy, like CO_2 and solid waste, cannot.

Environmental
Degradation

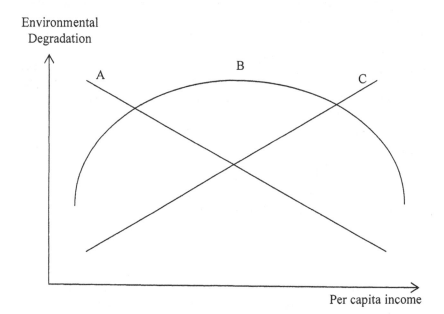

Figure 3.5 Environmental degradation and per capita income

Are environmental improvements policy-induced?

Unfortunately, the reduced-form econometric models that are commonly used in the EKC literature are not able to discriminate between the varying theoretical hypotheses discussed previously to explain the observed data. It is, for example, not possible to tell clearly which part of the effect comes about via quasi-automatic changes during the course of development (for example, by substituting cleaner technologies for dirtier ones or by a change in the structure of the economy) or comes about via deliberate environmental policy efforts (Grossman and Krueger 1995, p. 372). Grossman and Krueger (1996, p. 120), two pioneers of the EKC, suggest that policy, driven by vigilance and advocacy, plays an important mediating role in the observed relationship.

Some studies have examined the causal factors for environmental change on a more detailed level. Selden, Forrest and Lockhart (1999), for example, have tried to decompose changes in US emissions of particulate matter, SO_x, NO_x, non-methane volatile organic compounds, carbon monoxide and lead over the time period 1970 to 1990 into a scale, composition of the economy and various technique effects. They found that the non-energy efficiency technique effect had the largest impact on the reduction of these emissions over time, both absolutely and per capita. What this finding tentatively suggests is that governmental regulation of emissions, that is an induced policy response to growing environmental pollution, and emission abatement technology played a significant role in bringing about these improvements in environmental quality (ibid. p. 28).

This conclusion is supported by an international study of some developed countries for the International Energy Agency (IEA 1997). It finds that increases in economic activity and structural changes within the economy would have increased energy use dramatically if these effects had not been counteracted with improvements in the efficiency of energy use.[25] IEA (ibid.) suggests that energy policies have an important impact on the efficiency of energy use. With respect to CO_2 emissions, IEA (ibid., pp. 254ff) finds that fuel switches from oil to nuclear power and natural gas have played an important role in addition to efficiency improvements in bringing down the carbon intensity of output, if not absolute emissions.

The role of governance, inequality and civil society

Some studies have examined the impact of political freedom and inequality on environmental outcomes. Both Barrett and Graddy (2000) and Torras and Boyce (1998) use the panel data, with which Grossman and Krueger (1993, 1995) established the EKC curve, and add variables measuring the extent of political freedom or democracy with data taken from Freedom House, a US think tank and lobby group.[26] Barrett and Graddy (2000) employ generalized least squares with a random effects estimator and find that countries with high political rights and civil liberties tend to have lower air and water pollution levels. They (ibid., p. 434) suggest that 'a low-freedom country, with an income level near the peak of the inverted-U, can reduce its pollution at least as much by increasing its freedoms as it can by increasing its income per head'. Torras and Boyce (1998) come to similar conclusions using OLS instead. In addition, they find that increased literacy rates tend to reduce pollution levels.[27] Since they define higher political and civil liberties and increased literacy rates as constituting a more 'equitable power distribution', they conclude that 'a more equal distribution of power ... can positively affect environmental quality' (ibid., p. 160).[28]

These findings need to be treated with some care,[29] but more recent studies have corroborated the positive effect of democratic regime type on environmental quality (Li and Reuveny 2006; Farzin and Bond 2006; Bernauer and Koubi 2009). Consistent with such a positive effect on environmental outcomes, Neumayer (2002a) and Neumayer, Gates and Gleditsch (2002) find evidence that democratic countries exhibit stronger environmental commitment, whilst Neumayer (2002b) provides less robust evidence for a positive link between trade openness and environmental commitment. For example, more democratic countries are more likely to sign and ratify multilateral agreements, they are more likely to have a National Council for Sustainable Development and set a larger percentage of their land area under protection status. Bättig and Bernauer (2009) show that while democracies do not yet clearly outperform autocracies in terms of greenhouse gas emission reductions, they are more cooperative in politically and legally committing to climate change policies.

Governance if of course about much more than democracy. Dasgupta et al. (2006) analyse the effect of a World Bank measure of a country's policies and institutional capacity for environmental governance on air pollution levels. This measure is correlated with democracy, but far from perfectly. Finding that environmental governance matters, they conclude from their results that 'policy reform alone is sufficient to reduce air pollution significantly, even in overcroweded, geographically vulnerable cities in countries with very low incomes' (ibid., p. 1609).

As regards the role of civil society, in particular environmental non-governmental organizations (ENGO), Cropper et al. (1992) show that ENGO lobbying had a significant effect on the probability that the United States Environmental Protection Agency (EPA) cancelled a harmful pesticide registration. Riddel (2003) focuses on a different aspect of ENGOs' influence in analyzing their role in election outcomes and finds that the Sierra Club and the League of Conservation Voters had a significant effect on US Senate election outcomes by leveraging campaign contributions channeled through political action committees. Carter (2007, p. 144) concludes from his reading of the available evidence: 'There is little doubt that environmental groups have been the most effective movement for progressive environmental change.' Two quantitative cross-national studies support this conclusion. Fredriksson et al. (2005) find that the number of environmental advocacy groups in a country has a statistically significant negative effect on lead content levels in gasoline, while Binder and Neumayer (2005) estimate the effect of environmental pressure group strength on air pollution levels and conclude that such strength exerts a statistically significant impact on sulfur dioxide, smoke and heavy particulates concentration levels. A few studies have also analysed the effects of party strength. Both Neumayer (2003a) and Bernauer and Koubi (2009) find that countries with stronger green parties have lower air pollution levels.

Unpleasant implications of EKC findings
An important caveat to keep in mind when interpreting the evidence and especially concerning those indicators which appear to follow an EKC is that most less developed countries (LDCs) are just about to enter the level of income where many emissions are still rising and doing so rapidly. The turning point after which pressure on the environment is supposed to diminish varies widely depending on the pollutant looked at as well as the estimation technique and sample used (Cole and Neumayer 2005). Even within single studies the range of turning points can be quite large, for example, from US$1900 for lead to US$11 600 for cadmium in Grossman and Krueger (1993). Cole and Neumayer (2005) examine a large number of EKC studies and estimate when pollution levels are predicted to fall in developing countries, based on a number of economic growth scenarios. Although the estimated EKCs may be overly optimistic, they find that the implications of the EKC for developing countries are still rather bleak: for many pollutants, emissions are predicted to increase for the majority of the developing countries for many years to come, even in an optimistic high growth scenario. These projections thus open up the alarming possibility of *total* pollution rising tremendously with future economic growth. As Ekins (1997, p. 824) has put it, the existing evidence shows 'a stark environmental prospect, unless past growth/environment relationships can be substantially changed'.

Another problem is that practically all studies look at either emission intensity, that is, emissions divided by GDP, or emissions per capita. As concerns the latter, with continued population growth, falling emissions per capita need not translate into falling total emissions. For Baldwin (1995, p. 61) 'the nightmare scenario is that income growth in the poorest LDCs would stall at the point where they are in the high-emission stage, but not quite out of high-growth stage of their demographic transition'. Or even if income growth does not stall and population growth rates fall further, it might be too late since environmental thresholds might have been exceeded, and dramatic and possibly irreversible environmental deterioration will already have taken place. As Panayotou (1993, p. 1) observes, these thresholds are more likely to be relevant in today's low-income fast-growing countries where often 'tropical resources such as forests, fisheries and soils' exist which 'are known to be more fragile and less resilient than temperate resources'. The problem is that nobody knows where those thresholds are, and attempts to measure them must rely on very crude assumptions that can easily be contested by opponents.

One cannot even rely on total pollution decreasing again once high enough levels of income are reached, since econometric evidence does not provide stable causal relationships. There is absolutely no guarantee that the environmental quality of a country that is *now* poor will be equal to the environmental quality of a country that is *now* rich *once* it has become rich itself. This is because external and internal conditions in low-income countries can be quite different from the external and internal conditions of countries with high incomes now at the time of their own development.

3.4 CONCLUSION

Chapter 3 has tried to assess the validity of the opposing claims of WS and SS with respect to the substitutability of natural capital. The conclusion that arises from the analysis is that both paradigms rest on certain assumptions as well as hypotheses and claims about the (distant) future that are non-falsifiable. That does not mean, of course, that either paradigm is nonsensical. Both of them have some theoretical plausibility as well as some empirical evidence in their support.

To see this tension between, on the one hand, the paradigms having some theoretical and empirical plausibility, and, on the other hand, both paradigms resting on non-falsifiable assumptions and hypotheses, take the four propositions from resource optimism as an example. The power of resource optimism stems from the fact that not all four propositions need to hold true in isolation, but that any one of them or some combination thereof is already sufficient to save the economy from running out of resources. Resource optimism is grounded in the belief that any natural resource can be substituted by another resource, *or* by man-made capital, *or* by technical progress, *or* by some combination thereof. The critical assessment of resource optimism in Section 3.2, p. 48, shed some doubt on all of the four propositions in examining them in isolation. But none of the propositions could actually be refuted, and even less so if they are seen together and their interactions are taken into account.

On the other hand, it was also shown that none of the propositions can be relied upon either. Each one of them ultimately rests on basic beliefs about future substitution possibilities or technical progress. As Lecomber (1975, p. 42) has written as long ago as 1975:

> Everything hinges on the rate of technical progress and possibilities of substitution. This is perhaps the main issue that separates resource optimists and resource pessimists. The optimist believes in the power of human inventiveness to solve whatever problems are thrown in its way, as apparently it has done in the past. The pessimist questions the success of these past technical solutions and fears that future problems may be more intractable.

What makes the resource optimism of WS non-refutable is that the optimism is only sound if *at any point of time in the future* at least one of the propositions will hold. The propositions of WS are surely logically conceivable, but whether they are possible in practice or even likely to occur we do not know. The only thing we do know is that they are *not* certain. As Gerlagh and van der Zwaan (2002) point out, substitutability in the long run might be very limited even though there can be very good substitution possibilities in the present and near future. Watkins (2006: 513) is similarly cautious in concluding his otherwise optimistic assessment of resource availability: 'Will supply always be plentiful? That is more than anyone could pretend to know. (...) This degree of uncertainty encourages agnosticism about whether technology and new knowledge will continue to keep the forces of depletion at bay.'

The contest between WS and SS cannot be settled by theoretical inquiry. Nor can it be settled by empirical inquiry since such an inquiry would be dependent on information that is only 'forthcoming in the always receding future', where 'predictions ... are clouded by uncertainty regarding preferences, human ingenuity and existing resource availability' (Castle 1997, p. 305). The call for increased efforts into empirical studies on the potential for substitution of natural capital based on today's technologies, as expressed for example in Victor, Hanna and Kubursi (1995, p. 83), is understandable. As the analysis in this chapter has shown, there has been rather limited actual empirical research on the question of substitutability. But it would be a mistake to believe that such studies could solve the dispute between WS and SS. For as Victor, Hanna and Kubursi (ibid.) observe themselves:

> the question of sustainability is not really one of short term substitution ... based on currently available technologies. Rather it is the potential for new, yet to be invented, technologies to substitute for natural capital. No one can reliably predict what new technologies will be developed, and whether the as-

sumed degree of substitution implicit in weak sustainability will become reality.

This conclusion differs starkly from the apparent self-confidence with which proponents of both paradigms of sustainability advance their position and presume that their assumptions hold in reality. We actually know much less about the substitutability of natural capital in the production of consumption goods than the two paradigms of sustainability want to make us believe.

What is true for resource availability applies to the 'sink' side of the economy as well. Whether natural capital should be regarded as substitutable in the utility function is in principle a matter of speculation as we do not know the preferences of future generations. In as far as future preferences are endogenous and contingent on past levels of environmental degradation, the substitutability hypothesis might be a self-fulfilling prophecy. I also argued that inferring information from the preferences of the current generation does not give an unambiguous picture either. The available evidence that supposedly shows that a substantial minority of individuals exhibit something close to lexicographic preferences with respect to natural capital is rather shaky. Also, the vast majority of individuals seem to exhibit preferences that are compatible with the substitutability assumption. It has to be said, however, that proponents of SS see the non-substitutability of natural capital as a direct provider of utility more normatively than positively. They frame the issue as one of an inviolable right of future generations to be free from long-term environmental degradation. As a normative position it is non-refutable, however.

The next sub-section in this chapter looked at the link between economic growth and the environment. This is because proponents of WS sincerely believe that in the long run the state of the environment improves with economic growth, so that they have to rely less on the controversial assumption that natural capital is substitutable in utility functions as well. The results found on resource optimism apply equally to the environmental optimism of WS. The proposition of WS that economic growth is good for the environment in the long run is logically conceivable, but we do not know whether it will be possible, let alone likely to occur. Ferguson et al. (1996, p. 28) rightly argue that the existing evidence 'cannot be used to justify a view that economic growth ... will automatically be good or bad for the environment. ... The nature of this relationship lies to a large extent in the hands of those responsible for environmental policy and its enforcement'.

There is nothing inevitable about environmental quality deteriorating at early stages of development. Panayotou's (1993, p. 14) claim that the existing evidence 'implies a certain inevitability of environmental degradation along a country's development path, especially during the take-off process of industrialization' seems unfounded in its generality. At the least, as Grossman and Krueger (1995, p. 372) suggest, given the recent increase in environmental awareness and the still expanding development of new cleaner technologies it might be possible for countries with currently low incomes to achieve environmental improvements at lower levels of income than has previously been the case. Equally, Grossman's claim that 'attention to environmental issues is a luxury good poor countries cannot afford' (quoted in Ferguson et al. 1996, p. 6) does not follow from the existing evidence.

On the other hand, there is nothing inevitable about environmental quality improving at high levels of income. Panayotou (1993, p. 14) is again claiming too much when he says in quite general terms that economic growth is 'a powerful way for improving environmental quality in developing countries'. This is because one cannot rely on economic growth curing environmental ills sooner or later. Even Panayotou (ibid., p. 15) admits that following a development path along an environmental Kuznets-curve might be far from optimal because of high environmental damage costs, because it might be extremely costly to raise environmental quality *ex post* (that is, after deterioration has taken place), because of the potential existence of environmental thresholds and because at least some forms of environmental degradation damage human health and economic productivity and are, ironically, themselves impediments to faster economic growth. Hence, there might be a good case for policy makers to prevent environmental degradation at any stage of development.

One has to presume therefore that no general conclusions on the relationship between economic growth and the environment can be drawn. As Common (1995a, p. 103) has put it: 'Definitive "scientific" answers to these questions [of the relationship between economic growth and environmental quality, E.N.] are impossible. They are essentially matters of informed judgement.' We simply do not know whether environmental optimism or pessimism is warranted. While there appear to be some cases historically where improvements in environmental quality coincided with higher incomes, one cannot rely on economic growth curing environmental ills. Economic growth on its own does not seem to be a viable prescription for the solution of environmental problems. A group of distinguished scholars from both economics and ecology came to a similar conclusion in their 'consensus' paper on 'Economic Growth, Carrying Capacity, and the Environment' (Arrow et al. 1995). In the end, whether one thinks economic growth will be beneficial or harmful to the environment in the long run remains a matter of belief.

As Norton (1995, p. 125) observes, a paradigm that is accused of 'insufficient reach' can always answer 'by denying that some phenomena ... are "real"' and argue that they are 'actually bogus entities that are the ontological fallout, the theoretical dross, of failed paradigms'. Norton (1995) argues that it is characteristic for extra-paradigmatic disagreements (as the one between

WS and SS) that there is agreement neither on basic principles nor on the scope of the true subject matter of the discipline or a consensually accepted methodology. Hence, he concludes, these extra-paradigmatic disagreements are not amenable to confirmation or refutation. Also, he suggests, the basic principles of WS and SS are too abstract to be directly supportable, or refutable, by empirical evidence.

Norton's argument conforms with my own conclusion. However, my conclusion was derived from a rather different line of thought than Norton's. The main argument here is that even if there was agreement on the scope of the true subject matter and a consensually accepted methodology, it would still be impossible to confirm or disconfirm either paradigm. My argument thus provides an answer to the puzzling fact, observed by Tilton (1996, p. 92), that as concerns resource availability 'given the many opportunities participants have had to exchange ideas and views, one would expect to find some common core of accepted findings, some general consensus, emerging to which most if not all scholars subscribed'. But one does not find it. Tilton (ibid.) rightly stresses how desirable a resolution of the conflict would be:

> [T]he competing paradigms not only promote contrasting outlooks on the future of humanity, they may influence that future to the extent their proponents are successful in promoting their particular policy prescriptions. This makes the continuing debate between the concerned and unconcerned troubling. The anticipated exploitation of exhaustible resources either does or does not pose a significant threat to sustainable development. Which it is, is important. The policy recommendations of one group cannot be right unless those of the other are wrong.

But if the analysis here is correct, then Tilton's (ibid., p. 96) hope that the 'search for an appropriate and common paradigm' can be 'a first and essential step' to resolve the 'long-standing differences' between resource optimists and pessimists will not and, indeed, cannot be fulfilled.

One problem with the two paradigms of sustainability is that they are quite general in their claims about substitutability of natural capital and allow little distinction for specific cases. They put their arguments forward as generally applicable, apodictic, obvious *a priori* truths rather than as specifically applicable and empirically contingent claims. Pearce (1997, p. 296) is right in saying that it is incorrect 'to caricature the issue as one of total substitutability' versus total non-substitutability. As I argue in the next chapter, the *likelihood* of whether natural capital can be substituted or not crucially depends on which form of natural capital one is looking at and cannot be answered in general terms (for a similar conclusion, see Mikesell 1995). There, I reconsider the importance of natural capital and I argue that if one takes into account the distinctive features of natural capital in a world of risk, uncertainty and ignorance, then, indeed, a *persuasive* case can be made that the preservation of some specific forms of natural capital is a necessary requirement for sustainability. This holds especially true for those forms of natural capital that provide basic life-support functions for mankind.

NOTES

1 For more detail on this, see Barbier (1989, Chapter 1).
2 However, the rise in oil prices was clearly linked to the exercise of market power by OPEC and not to dramatically rising natural resource scarcity, although there is some evidence that prices had started rising before 1973 (Slade 1982, p. 136).
3 Throughout the book technical progress is to be interpreted broadly as encompassing everything from the *invention* of a new technique to *innovation* and *diffusion*, that is, to the widespread incorporation of this technique into production processes.
4 Some natural resources are scarce in a physical sense. If they have no productive use, nobody cares about this scarcity, however. Scarcity in an economic sense I define to be excess demand for the resource at a given price.
5 Of course, Georgescu-Roegen was not so naive as to overlook the fact that the earth is not a closed system. He merely claimed that using solar energy needs more non-solar energy input than is gained in energy eventually (Georgescu-Roegen 1986, p. 23). This may have been true of early solar technologies, but isno longer the case (Ayres 2007, p. 116).
6 In a perfectly competitive economy, the interest rate is equal to the marginal product of man-made capital (Dasgupta and Heal 1979, p. 296).
7 In units of weight the German industry, for example, uses 50 times more non-renewable than renewable resources for production (Bringezu and Schütz 1996).
8 It is a partial equilibrium model and used here because it makes understanding the Hotelling rule easier than the formally better suited, but less easy to understand, general equilibrium model that is presented in Appendix 2, p. 198.
9 It also holds for uncertainty if agents form rational expectations and there is a complete set of contingent forward markets. Neither is very realistic. See Graham-Tomasi, Runge and Hyde (1986). On a more elaborate examination of risk, uncertainty and ignorance see Section 4.2, p. 99.
10 A study of Moazzami and Anderson (1994) finds empirical support for Slade's (1982) 'U-shaped' price trend hypothesis, however.
11 An important assumption is that there is no depreciation of man-made capital. As Dasgupta and Heal (1979, p. 226) indicate, the basic results would go through as well with capital depreciation as long as capital depreciates at less than an exponential rate. Note also that technical progress which Dasgupta and Heal exclude could counteract exponential capital depreciation. On this, see the discussion of technical progress in Section 3.2.4, p.70.
12 Note that σ is bounded below by zero. With $\sigma = 0$, capital and resources are already perfect complements. A negative elasticity of substitution ($\sigma < 0$) is not possible. Formally, since both K and R are positive numbers and the absolute value of the MRS between K and R is always positive, σ can never be negative.
13 Slade (1987, p. 351) reports values that suggest that man-made capital's share and the resources' share are approximately equal. However, this is based on a misunderstanding. Berndt and Wood (1975), on which Slade based her values, included intermediate goods in the production function. Those intermediate goods do not fall from heaven and presumably the share of man-made capital in those intermediate goods is higher than the share of resources, so that the ultimate share of man-made capital is still considerably higher than that

of resources, thus reconciling the reported values with those of Solow (1974a), Hartwick (1977) and Dasgupta and Heal (1979).

14 Note that here labour is not assumed to be constant and therefore enters the production function explicitly.

15 'Loosely' because formally it is not possible for the Cobb–Douglas production function to distinguish pure capital- from resource-augmenting technical progress.

16 This is the most often used measure for energy intensity. For other, more contested concepts of measuring energy efficiency, see Patterson (1996).

17 Reliable evidence on this point is hard to get. Kaufmann (1992) claims that his more complex econometric testing approach refutes earlier evidence from simpler regression models. For example, Howarth (1991) found technical progress to be a statistically significant and important contributor to the decline in energy intensity. However, Kaufmann (1992, p. 54) suggests 'that most of the changes are associated with shifts in the types of energies used and the types of goods and services consumed and produced'. Equally inconclusive is the situation for non-energy resources. Slade (1987, p. 351) cites evidence that suggests technical progress has been resource saving in some sectors but resource using in others.

18 Some even suggest that resource intensity might revert to rise again at high levels of income (De Bruyn and Opschoor 1997).

19 Environmental degradation here means a decrease in the stock of (directly utility-relevant) renewable resources or an increase in the stock of pollution.

20 Smith and Mansfield (1998, p. 209) claim that the findings of their CV study show that 'there are no significant differences between people's choices with real and hypothetical offers'.

21 Still more frightening is the emerging possibility of adapting individuals to a world empty of environmental amenities and full of pollution via genetic engineering.

22 Strictly speaking and as mentioned earlier on, this argument does not apply since the earth absorbs a steady, constant energy influx from outside exceeding the current total world energy demand at about three orders of magnitude (Norgaard 1986, p. 326; Hohmeyer 1992, p. 10). It does apply approximately, however, when most of this influx is — as at present — not used.

23 A more extreme position holds that people are the 'ultimate resource' (Simon 1996) and that population growth is not bad for the environment. This, however, is a minority position that is usually, but not always (see, for example, Boserup 1990), held by people who think that economic growth is the best way to protect the environment (see, for example, Simon 1990, 1996).

24 Some studies suggest that possibly at very, very high levels of income there will be a turning point for CO_2 emissions so that it would follow an EKC rather than a continuously rising trend. But this level is much higher than any of the income levels of present countries (Holtz-Eakin and Selden 1995).

25 In addition to overall indicators, IEA (1997) also provides disaggregated indicators for different economic sectors, including households.

26 Political liberties reflect the existence and fairness of elections, the existence of a real opposition and so on. Civil liberties reflect individual civil rights of free speech, demonstration, organisational freedom and the extent of the freedom of the press. See www.freedomhouse.org.

27 Torras and Boyce (1998, p. 155) find that, contrary to their expectation, higher income inequality sometimes tends to improve environmental quality. They reject their own findings on grounds of the 'questionable quality of the income-distribution data'. Somewhat surprisingly and inconsistently, however, they advocate a 'more equitable income distribution' for environmental reasons later on in their paper (p. 158).

28 For a more elaborate theoretical argument along these lines, see Boyce (1994, 2002). Scruggs (1998), on the other hand, using Freedom House data in OLS estimation, finds that democracy is statistically insignificant once one controls for income inequality in the case

of dissolved oxygen, fecal coliform and particulates emissions. Democracy assumes statistical significance only for the case of sulphur dioxide (SO_2) emissions.

29   Barrett and Graddy (2000) group countries into low, medium and high civil and political freedom, using dummy variables, as well as entering civil and political freedoms as continuous variables in separate regressions. A closer look at their results reveals that the study provides only limited evidence for a positive impact of freedom on the environment. First, some of the variables have signs contrary to expectation. Second, practically none of the dummy or continuous variables is statistically significant on its own. It is only in their combination that these variables gain some statistical significance in all air pollution regressions. For the water pollution regressions even the combined explanatory power of the freedom variables is statistically insignificant in the majority of cases. Torras and Boyce (1998) enter freedom only as a continuous variable and estimate separate coefficients for countries above and below $5000 per capita income in purchasing power parity. Out of 14 regressions, the freedom coefficient has six times an unexpected sign, particularly prevalent in the subset of high income countries, and is statistically insignificant in a further three cases. Another weakness of the study is that in spite of using panel data, no time-series for the freedom variable is constructed. Instead the freedom variable is set equal to the 1995 value throughout.

4. Preserving Natural Capital in a World of Risk, Uncertainty and Ignorance

In the last chapter it was shown that both paradigms are non-falsifiable. But the question still open is this: if society is faced with risk, uncertainty and ignorance about the consequences of running down natural capital, which forms, how much and at what cost should it preserve natural capital? This is the major topic of this chapter.

The first aim of this chapter is to indicate which forms of natural capital are more *likely* to be non-substitutable than others and are therefore in need of preservation. Note the emphasis on 'likely': from the analysis in Chapter 3 it follows that the best we can hope for is to make a *persuasive* case for the importance of the preservation of natural capital. The major objective of this chapter lies somewhere else, however. It tries to explore the difficulties in finding the extent to which these forms of capital need to be preserved and how much cost should be incurred for preservation.

Section 4.1 begins by highlighting distinctive features of some forms of natural capital. There are two aspects — basic life-support function and irreversibility of destruction — that distinguish some forms of natural capital from other forms of capital. Section 4.2 discusses in more depth what has hitherto been dealt with rather implicitly: that the real world is plagued by the absence of perfect information and certainty and characterised by risk, uncertainty and ignorance instead.

Section 4.3 presents various approaches towards coping with risk, uncertainty and ignorance. The traditional neoclassical approach is to include option and quasi-option values into standard environmental valuation. Critics argue that this is insufficient for coping with risk and uncertainty, and with ignorance in particular. Two potential alternatives are therefore discussed, namely the precautionary principle and the concept of safe minimum standards (SMSs). Both function as a kind of insurance policy against the uncertain, but potentially very large, costs of running down natural capital.

Section 4.4 brings the threads together and states which forms of natural capital should be preserved in a world of risk, uncertainty and ignorance. It argues that the protection of global life-support resources such as biodiversity, the ozone layer and the global climate as well as the restriction of the accumulation of pollutants and of unsustainable harvesting and soil erosion appear to be sound insurance policies for achieving sustainability.[1] In contrast, no explicit conservation policy for natural resources used in production seems necessary. The latter holds true, if less clearly, for food resources as well. In essence therefore, Section 4.4 argues that available evidence supports WS more strongly with respect to the 'source' side of the economy, but supports SS more strongly with respect to the 'sink' side of the economy.

Section 4.5 discusses the difficulties that the existence of opportunity costs pose for policy makers. One option is to deliberately ignore opportunity costs. The other option is to seek preservation of the forms of natural capital identified in section 4.4 subject to the constraint that the opportunity costs must not be 'unacceptably high'. There are good reasons for both options, but the concluding section 4.6 argues in favour of the second option and against simply ignoring opportunity costs. Such a position takes on the sometimes awkward decisions and dilemmas policy makers face rather than assuming them away. I argue that my position, which has been derived simply from the existence of distinctive features of natural capital in a world of risk, uncertainty and ignorance and without any recourse to a rights-based theory, is nevertheless compatible with a moderate rights-based deontological position.

4.1 DISTINCTIVE FEATURES OF NATURAL CAPITAL

To establish a case for an explicit preservation of certain forms of natural capital, one must start by trying to show that there are some characteristics of these forms of natural capital that distinguish them from other forms of capital. In my view, there are two aspects that can justify such a distinction: the provision of basic life-support functions and irreversibility of destruction.

- Some forms of natural capital provide very basic and fundamental life-support functions that no other capital can provide (Barbier, Burgess and Folke 1994), that is, functions that make human life on earth possible. Ecosystems and the biodiversity they exhibit are multifunctional in a way and to an extent that is not shared by other capital (Ehrlich and Ehrlich 1992). They are the basis of all life, human and non-human: it is the world ecosystem that contains the economy, not the economy that contains the world ecosystem (Daly and Townsend 1993, p. 3). Mankind can exist and indeed has existed in the past without major man-made or other forms of capital, but it cannot live without functioning ecosystems. The outstanding value of natural capital is not that we can use fossil fuels, for example, but that nature enables the very existence of human life: food, water, fresh air and a bearable climate. Ecosystems might be able to cope with piece-meal destruction for a long time, but if a threshold is exceeded, the whole system could break down. There are 'limits to meta-resource depletion' (Ehrlich 1989). Other life-support resources that really are non-substitutable and whose destruction would often lead to catastrophes are the ozone layer and the biogeochemical cycle of the atmosphere.

- Some forms of natural capital are unique in that they cannot be rebuilt once they have been destroyed. That is, destruction of some forms of natural capital is irreversible or at least quasi-irreversible.[2] In general this is not the case for other forms of capital. Man-made capital can always be reconstructed if it has been destroyed. Reconstruction is costly, of course, and it may take some time, but at least it is possible in principle.[3] An example for irreversible natural capital loss is the destruction of biodiversity: it is impossible to bring an extinct species back to life.[4]

While these distinctive features might make a general case for the preservation of natural capital, it does not give an answer on exactly which forms of natural capital should be preserved and to what extent. This is complicated by the presence of risk, uncertainty and ignorance, to which we turn now.

4.2   RISK, UNCERTAINTY AND IGNORANCE

If one is aware of the distinctive features of natural capital, why can one not simply target all those forms of natural capital that provide basic life-support functions and would be irreversibly lost after destruction? If we lived in a world of certainty, there would not be any problem. But unfortunately there is widespread risk, uncertainty and ignorance in the world we live in. Ignorance here means more than risk and more than uncertainty, two notions that are well known in economics.[5] I discuss all three in the order of descending closeness to certainty.

Risk
Risk refers to a situation where the set of all possible states of the world, the probability distribution over the set of possible states and the resulting payoffs can be objectively known. Buying a lottery ticket is a good example of engaging in a 'risky' action, because the odds of winning can be objectively

known as can the costs of buying the ticket and the value of potential prizes — hence the expected gain or loss can be computed without any remaining doubt.

Unfortunately, we are typically not confronted with a situation of risk in trying to judge the validity of running down natural capital because in most cases we do not know either the probability distribution of all possible states or the potential outcomes resulting from the different states of the world. What is worse: often we do not even know the complete set, that is, we are ignorant of the total number of possible states of the world.

Also, even a situation of risk poses fundamental problems for any attempt to ensure sustainability. Consider a situation in which there is a 99.9 per cent chance of winning a big gain, but a 0.1 per cent probability of incurring a tremendous loss. Further assume that both gains and losses affect at least partially coming generations as well. Should society engage in or refrain from this risky action? There is no obvious answer. A possible solution could be to refrain from any risky action since the present is committed to maintaining the capacity to provide non-declining utility into the future and engaging in the action risks a tremendous loss and hence a decline in utility, even if the probability for this drastic loss is rather small. But is this solution plausible? Presumably not, because refraining from *any* action that risks a net loss brings with it an (opportunity) cost both to the current and the future generations. The fundamental problem is this: in a risky world, ensuring sustainability with certainty can — if at all possible — only be achieved at high costs and if those costs are deemed too high to be acceptable, then sustainability can at best mean ensuring expected sustainability.

Economists would resort to inferring the risk preference or risk aversion from the present generation in order to compute the expected utility of the risky action. The decision criterion would be to engage in the action if the expected utility is positive and to refrain from the action if the expected utility is negative.

Of course, if there is a whole range of risky actions at a given time or over a bounded time interval, then due to the law of large numbers unlucky outcomes become compensated by lucky outcomes and a net gain equal to the expected overall value of a whole set of risky actions results. But things are different when potential losses, however unlikely, imply irreversible *and* catastrophic outcomes that cannot be compensated for. An obvious answer would be to refrain from actions that imply such outcomes, however unlikely they might be. But what to do if the outcomes themselves are not known with certainty? This already leaves the context of risk, so I move on to discuss uncertainty next.

Uncertainty

Uncertainty refers to a situation where the probability distribution over a set of possible states of the world and the resulting payoffs cannot be known objectively, but individuals have subjective beliefs about the distribution and the payoffs.[6] Those beliefs can be updated (and in many cases improved) over time, that is, they are not static as in the context of risk, but dynamic.

Uncertainty comes rather close to our present state of knowledge about many rather novel and complex, but most pressing environmental problems such as climate change. We know something about the effects of dumping greenhouse gases in the atmosphere, we know something about the climatic consequences, we can imagine different states of the world following and we have some idea about the probability distribution over these different states of the world. Our knowledge about climate change is still rather poor, however.[7]

One obvious strategy to combat uncertainty is to invest in research in order to gain better information over the set of possible states, their payoffs and the probability distribution over the set of states. However, for cases of uncertainty in general and for climate change in particular it is not possible to convert a setting of uncertainty into a situation of mere risk (Faucheux and Froger 1995). In most cases some doubt about the correctness of beliefs remains, either because the objective values cannot be known in principle, or because the costs of getting the correct values are 'too high' from an information costs perspective, where 'too high' means a region where the marginal costs of information gathering are higher than the marginal benefits.

Ignorance

Ignorance refers to a situation where we have no idea whatsoever about the set of possible states of the world, about the probability distribution over the set or about the resulting payoffs.[8] A weaker definition would allow for subjective beliefs where those beliefs are largely arbitrary, however, and lack a sound scientific foundation.

It seems fair to say that our knowledge about the extent and the likely consequences of biodiversity[9] destruction resembles more a situation of ignorance than of uncertainty. Estimates from UNEP of the number of existing species vary between five and thirty million (Wilson 1988, p. 5) of which about 1.4 million are named by biologists (Brown et al. 1994, p. 4). Even our knowledge about most of the named species is only rudimentary (Norton 1986). We are arguably miles away from knowing anything about the loss in value terms of this destruction of biodiversity. Especially, by their very nature, one cannot know the value of still undiscovered species that become extinct. As Norton (1986, p. 203) rightly argues, 'it is an understatement to refer to this level of ignorance as mere "uncertainty"'.

We are — almost necessarily — so ignorant of the complex interlinkages within ecosystems that we cannot, and could never, know the value of many single species or the whole of biodiversity to any reasonable extent of precision. Randall (1991, p. 64) suggests that there is a 'positive probability that literally any species, known or unknown, will eventually prove useful'. While possibly true, this probability might be vanishingly small or the species could be economically almost irrelevant. Furthermore, as Randall himself (ibid., p. 65) as well as Ehrenfeld (1986, p. 213) observe, whether future genetic engineering will drastically increase or reduce the value of biodiversity is completely unclear.[10] Climate change is another example of ignorance. I have introduced it under the heading of uncertainty above, but IPCC (1996, p. 161) rightly claims that 'when dealing with many of the effects of climate change, ignorance is perhaps a more appropriate concept than uncertainty'. The lesson is that often environmental problems have aspects of both uncertainty and ignorance.

Also, ignorance has in the past been quite common for environmental problems: DDT and CFCs were both thought to be benign for the environment before their detrimental effect was discovered (Bodansky 1991, p. 43). And ignorance is arguably a pretty good description of the quality of our knowledge about the consequences of human activity on the state of the environment in the long run.

4.3 COPING WITH RISK, UNCERTAINTY AND IGNORANCE

How can policy makers cope with the existence of risk, uncertainty and ignorance? This question will now be examined, where I illustrate the discussion mostly with reference to biodiversity and climate change.

4.3.1 Option and Quasi-option Values

The neoclassical economic approach towards coping with risk, uncertainty and (if less so) ignorance has been to extend the traditional techniques of environmental valuation. In order to cope with risk, economists have included so-called option values.[11] In the environmental context, option value is the expected value of refraining from an action that leads with some given probability to irreversible environmental destruction in order to keep the option open of using the environmental resource in the future. Option value can thus be interpreted as a kind of risk premium: it lowers the net benefit of the considered action; it reflects an additional opportunity cost and the 'price' someone is ready to pay in order to keep open the option of future use of the environmental resource. The more risk averse the individual is, the higher will be the option value. On the other hand, if the individual is risk preferring, he or she will be more inclined to take the action and risk the irreversible environmental destruction.

Option values can be used in a context of uncertainty as well, except that this time it is the *subjectively* expected value that counts. Additionally, economists have included so-called quasi-option values in environmental valuation to cope with uncertainty. In the environmental context, quasi-option value is the value of delaying an irreversible environmental destruction in order to acquire improved information and to make a better informed future decision.[12] For quasi-option values to make sense, we have to *expect* either that future information will tend to favour environmental preservation for given preferences or that the preference for environmental resources will increase over time. Only then is there a positive value, otherwise there would be a cost in keeping the environmental option open (Beltratti, Chichilnisky and Heal 1998; Chichilnisky and Heal 1993).[13] Note that quasi-option value, contrary to option value, does not depend on the valuer being risk averse; even a risk-loving valuer can exhibit a positive quasi-option value for preserving an environmental resource.

Taking option and quasi-option values into account changes the costs and benefits of a considered activity. As an example, see Albers, Fisher and Hanemann (1996) who argue convincingly from both a theoretical analysis and a case study of tropical forest management in Thailand that environmental destruction would be less if foresighted resource managers fully took into account option and quasi-option values.

Critics have argued, however, that the traditional economic approach is insufficient for coping with risk, uncertainty, and ignorance in particular. First, there is a fierce debate over whether option and quasi-option values can be reliably measured — see, for example, Turner (1995), Gren et al. (1994) and Cummings and Harrison (1995). Second, while the validity of the travel cost method and the hedonic pricing method is generally accepted, the contingent valuation method is highly disputed even within neoclassical economics.[14] The problems with the contingent valuation method are many, including the following: how to deal with the fact that respondents typically state a much lower willingsness-to-pay than willingness-to-accept, even though theoretically the two should be close to each other, separated only by a typically small income effect (Knetsch 2007)? Does the valuation of a specific good once valued on its own and another time valued as an embedded part of a more inclusive whole differ only so much that the difference can be explained by income and substitution effects, as Carson and Mitchell (1995) claim? Or does it differ so much that 'the assessed value of a public good is demonstrably arbitrary', as Kahneman and Knetsch (1992, p. 58) claim? Do individuals have well-specified preferences over environmental goods that can be inferred for each specific good or do they merely express a general sense of moral satisfaction (known as the 'warm glow of giving') in answering how much their WTP for the preservation of an environmental good is? If the latter is the case, then it makes no sense to ask people for their valuation of a specific environmental good since what they really want to express is their valuation of general environmental protection or maybe even their valuation of a more general public policy to do some 'good'. Undertaking individual studies one after the other might suggest that people would simultaneously be willing to pay for the preservation of almost every environmental good (Willis and Garrod 1995, p. 194). As a consequence, the sum of all WTP might well exceed their total income and is likely to be much higher than when the individuals were asked to state their valuation for each specific good as part of a whole range of other goods (for evidence on this see, for example, Boyle et al. 1994; Diamond and Hausman 1994; Bateman et al. 1997). The question is what the appropriate valuation *context* should be which has no easy answer (see Hoevenagel 1996). Third, ecological economists are more radical in their critique doubting more fundamentally the ability of economic valuation techniques to provide reliable estimates of the value of environmental changes — see, for example, Vatn and Bromley (1994), Vadnjal and O'Connor (1994), O'Hara (1996), Jacobs (1997b) and Spash (2000, 2008). A range of alternatives to the traditional neoclassical approach have therefore been developed and it is these alternatives I will discuss now.

4.3.2 The Precautionary Principle

The most basic alternative to the traditional neoclassical approach for coping with risk, uncertainty and ignorance is the so-called 'precautionary principle'. O'Riordan and Jordan (1995) list a whole range of core elements of the precautionary principle, but there are two elements that are arguably the most important ones. First, *preventive* measures should be undertaken before there is *definite* scientific evidence 'proving' that a certain human activity causes environmental degradation. The motivation is to avoid regretting environmental inaction after unacceptable irreversible environmental destruction has already taken place. As environmentalists emphasise: it is better to be vaguely right in time than precisely right too late. Second and related to the first point, the burden of proof should shift to those who believe that an economic activity has only negligible detrimental consequences on the environment; that is the new default position should favour environmental preservation, whereas current practice by and large favours economic activity over environmental preservation. The precautionary principle can thus be interpreted as an insurance scheme against uncertain future environmental catastrophes.

The precautionary principle was first integrated into official policy statements in the 1970s in former Western Germany in the form of the so-called *Vorsorgeprinzip* (Boehmer-Christiansen 1994). It soon found its way into virtually every official document on the environment and appeared in countless international environmental treaties (Cameron and Wade-Grey 1995). Some of this seeming 'success' of the precautionary principle was due to the fact that very often its application was merely rhetorical and did not change anything substantial. As Bodansky (1991) observes, part of the reason for this might be due to the fact that the precautionary principle is not able to give a clear answer on when it should be applied; that is what are acceptable and unacceptable environmental dangers, at what costs it should be applied and what types of precautionary actions should be undertaken?

4.3.3 Safe Minimum Standards (SMSs)

Propositions to introduce safe minimum standards (SMSs) date back to Ciriacy-Wantrup (1952) and were originally reserved for issues of species preservation and biodiversity protection. Recently, however, the notion of SMSs has been used increasingly for other environmental topics as well. IPCC (1996, p. 159), for example, speaks of an 'affordable safe minimum standard' for the reduction of greenhouse gases. For reasons of space, I shall only look at SMSs for the protection of species in this section, however.

SMSs call for granting a species some minimally viable standard. As originally introduced by Ciriacy-Wantrup (1952), no explicit qualification was made with respect to an upper limit of preservation costs. Later on, however, SMSs were interpreted as calling for imposing a safe standard, as long as the economic costs of doing so are not 'unacceptably high'. Note that the costs of protection are net of (expected) preservation benefits, where in the case of uncertainty and ignorance some best guess of the size of benefits has to be made.

The concept of SMSs has been officially embraced by UNEP's Global Biodiversity Programme (Crowards 1998). The Endangered Species Act in the US has many characteristics of an SMS (Castle and Berrens 1993, p. 122). This Act has been described as the 'most ambitious piece of species-protection legislation ever enacted by a single nation' (Ando 1998, p. 7). The US Fish and Wildlife Service has considerable leeway to intrude into property rights and impose conservation of endangered species on private agents. Economic actions that threaten the existence of endangered species are only allowed if 'the benefits of such action clearly outweigh the benefits of alterna-tive courses of action consistent with conserving the species in its critical habitat' (US Congress 1978, p. 49).

SMSs have originally been intended for the protection of single species. However, it has now been recognised that the major threat for species derives more from a general destruction of habitats than from direct exploitation of individual species. Consequently, it was acknowledged that only the sustain-able management of habitat areas is able to ensure the long-term survival of species (Barbier, Burgess and Folke 1994, pp. 60, 62). Also, due to the com-plexity of ecosystems and our ignorance about their capacity for resilience as described above, it is increasingly recognised that a sustainable management that safeguards ecological thresholds must be flexible and cannot apply fixed rules like a fixed maximum (seemingly) sustainable yield (Holling 1995, p. 49). Strictly speaking, for many species there are 'no definite ecological–biological safe minimum standards' (Hohl and Tisdell 1993, p. 177) at all. Hence, SMSs now tend more and more to mean the establishing of a viable standard for whole ecosystems where the standard is set well above some supposed minimum level. Protecting ecosystems is also a rather difficult and most likely an expensive task since misguided human manipulation of natural environments that reduces the resilience of ecosystems has to be avoided (Holling 1995). It is far from clear whether sustainable management of eco-systems is feasible and how it is to be carried out (Carpenter 1994). Human protection of species might run counter to natural forces displacing one spe-cies by another emerging species which might or might not be good for ecosystem stability (d'Arge 1994).

There have been some attempts in the literature to base SMS on a solid theoretical foundation by deriving it from a game-theoretic decision model (see Bishop 1978, 1979; Smith and Krutilla 1979).[15] Ready and Bishop (1991) modelled a so-called insurance game where the 'minimax decision criterion' led to preferring preservation over extinction (as a consequence of economic 'development') as long as the expected loss following from extinc-tion is higher than the expected net benefit of development.

To see this, look at the following insurance game (Table 4.1).[16] Let SMS be the strategy to protect a species via a safe minimum standard. Let EXT be the strategy not to protect the species and economically develop the inhabited in the course of which the species becomes extinct. Let the state DISEASE and NO DISEASE mean two possible states of the world: either a disease which causes human suffering breaks out or it does not break out. If it breaks out it can be cured with certainty by using the species, but not if the species is extinct. Let C be the cost to society due to the outbreak of the disease if it cannot be cured, that is, if the species became extinct in the past. Let B be the net economic development benefits to society and further assume that the absolute value of C is bigger than B; that is, the potential costs due to the disease are bigger than the benefits from development.

Table 4.1 Payoff matrix for the insurance game

	DISEASE	NO DISEASE	Min Gain
SMS	0	0	0
EXT	B – C	B	B – C (< 0)

Table 4.1 provides the payoff matrix for this insurance game for each strategy/state of the world combination. The baseline is arbitrarily chosen as a situation where there is no disease and no development in the relevant area so far.

Let us proceed clockwise starting from the upper-left corner. If society chooses SMS, then no matter what happens its payoff will be 0, for there will be no development and the disease will be cured if the state of the world is DISEASE or the disease does not break out anyway if the state of the world is NO DISEASE, so nothing has changed relative to the baseline. If society chooses EXT and the state of the world is NO DISEASE, that is preserving the species would have been useless anyway, then the payoff is B. If instead the state of the world turns out to be DISEASE, that is using the species would have cured the disease in future time if it had not become extinct, then the payoff is B – C which is negative since we assumed C > B.

What are the minimum gains to society for each strategy? In choosing SMS, society gets 0 in any case, so the minimum gain is 0. In choosing EXT, society gets B in case the disease does not break out, but it gets B – C (< 0) if it breaks out, so the minimum gain is B – C. The maximin criterion reflects extreme risk aversion by choosing that strategy that makes the deciding agent best off *in case the most unfavourable* state of the world occurs. Applying the maximin-criterion therefore requires adopting that strategy which *maximises* the *minimum* gain — therefore its name. Preservation is the optimal choice as long as the costs of the SMS, that is the direct cost of protecting the species, that were not included yet are not 'too high' — where 'too high' in this simple game can be computed as higher than C – B.

However, as Ready and Bishop (1991) have shown, this conclusion is highly reliant on the exact specification of the underlying game. In the insurance game it is assumed that a catastrophe, say a disease, has some probability of arising in the future and that preserving the species will cure the disease with certainty. By contrast, if one assumes that it is not the outbreak of the disease that is uncertain, but whether preserving the species will or will not cure the certain disease then the underlying game becomes a so-called lottery game. Arguably, the lottery game is the more realistic set-up and conforms with the argument of many environmentalists that biodiversity should be protected because it *might* bring about a cure for a disease that has been incurable so far (think of AIDS or cancer). The problem now is that the maximin criterion in the lottery game invariably opts for extinction and development as the preferred choice. 'Thus, a seemingly innocuous modification of the motivation of the problem has completely reversed the conclusion (Ready and Bishop 1991, p. 311)'.

To see this, look at the following lottery game. Let the strategies of the game and B and C be defined as before; only this time the states of the world are different. Let the state CURE and NO CURE mean two possible states of the world: either the certain disease can be cured or it cannot be cured. Table 4.2 provides the payoff matrix for this lottery game for each strategy/state of the world combination. The baseline is arbitrarily chosen as a situation where there is no cure for the existing disease and no development in the relevant area so far.

Table 4.2 Payoff matrix for the lottery game

	CURE	NO CURE	Min Gain
SMS	C	0	0
EXT	B	B	B

If society chooses SMS and the state of the world is CURE, then society gets the payoff C (a gain) relative to the baseline. If instead the state of the world turns out to be NO CURE, then the payoff to society choosing SMS will be 0 since nothing has changed. If society chooses EXT and the state of the world is NO CURE, that is, preserving the species would have been useless anyway, then the payoff is B. If instead the state of the world turns out to be CURE, that is using the species would have cured the disease in future time if it had not become extinct, then the payoff is B again since development is the only thing that has changed relative to the baseline.

In choosing SMS society gets either the gain of C or 0, so the minimum gain is 0. In choosing EXT society gets B in any case, so the minimum gain is B. Applying the maximin criterion requires taking that strategy which maximises the minimum gain. Since $B > 0$, the optimal choice is to extinguish the species in order to get the development benefits for sure and to forgo the possibility of curing the disease.

The preference for preservation given that the expected loss from extinction is higher than the expected net benefit from development is restored in the lottery game if one applies the so-called 'minimax *regret* decision criterion' (developed independently by Loomes and Sugden (1982) and Bell (1982)) instead of the maximin criterion. According to this criterion the decision is influenced by a desire to avoid post-decision regret, that is regretting the negative actual consequences of an action that appeared to be the correct one given the information about expected future outcomes at the time of decision.

To see this, let us now compute the maximum regret to society for each strategy. Table 4.3 provides the regret matrix derived from the payoff matrix of the lottery game in Table 4.2 for each strategy/state of the world combination.

Table 4.3 Regret matrix for the lottery game

	CURE	NO CURE	Max Regret
SMS	0	B	B
EXT	C – B	0	C – B

If the state of the world turns out to be CURE, then in choosing SMS society gets C and in choosing EXT society gets B. Since C > B by assumption, the regret in choosing SMS is 0 and the regret in choosing EXT is C – B. If the state of the world turns out to be NO CURE, then in choosing SMS society gets 0 and in choosing EXT society gets B. Since B > 0, the regret in choosing EXT is 0 and the regret in choosing SMS is B – 0 = B. Hence the maximum regret in choosing SMS is max(0, B) = B and the maximum regret in choosing EXT is max(C – B, 0) = C – B. Applying the regret decision criterion requires taking the strategy which minimises the maximum regret. If C is at least twice as large as B, then it will be true that B < C – B and the optimal choice is again to preserve the species in order to prevent the regret of not being able to cure the disease in the case that the disease turns out to be curable.

However, whether public policy decisions should be based on regret is rather dubious, hence Hohl and Tisdell's (1993, p. 177) conclusion is correct that there is 'currently no solid theoretical foundation for the use of SMS'. What is worse, both the insurance and the lottery games can only cope with situations of risk, not with situations of uncertainty or even ignorance, which as argued above are the more relevant ones. The reason is that when applying game theory at least the possible states of the world and the possible strategies have to be known.

The more general problem is that there is no widely accepted theory of choice under uncertainty and ignorance. This should come as no surprise since it is in the very nature of uncertainty and ignorance that they are not easily amenable to axiomatic analysis.[17] Dasgupta, Barrett and Mäler (1999, p. 52) are right in claiming that 'we do not have a theory, normative or otherwise, that would cover long-term environmental uncertainties in a satisfactory way'. Individuals taking actual decisions tend to violate substantial principles of rationality when faced with risk and uncertainty, especially in contexts with low probability (see Machina 1987; Pearce 1994; Zeckhauser and Viscusi 1995). Equally, they tend to underestimate actual risks from everyday life, but overestimate actual risks from large-scale extraordinary disasters (Royal Society 1992, Section 5.3). As Zeckhauser and Viscusi (1995, p. 631) point out, decisions in these contexts reveal the limits of human rationality and are generally not overcome by providing better information.[18]

The absence of a well-specified game-theoretic foundation does not imply that SMS should not be applied by a society that is committed to sustainability but faced with uncertainty and ignorance. What it does say, however, is that there is no rigorous theory of choice that would unambiguously justify SMS.

After this discussion of the implications of risk, uncertainty and ignorance for the preservation of natural capital, I will now try to identify those forms of natural capital, which are in need of preservation. It is therefore necessary to go one step beyond the abstract notion 'natural capital'.

4.4   WHICH FORMS OF NATURAL CAPITAL SHOULD BE PRESERVED?

The last section has shown that there is no simple and entirely convincing way for coping with risk, uncertainty and ignorance. The combination of the widespread existence of risk, uncertainty and ignorance with the distinctive characteristics of natural capital (basic life-support functions and irreversibility of destruction) has ambiguous effects on the case for preserving natural capital: on the one hand, it provides a justification to be cautious about running down natural capital; on the other hand, it makes it difficult to say which forms of natural capital should be preserved and to what extent. Some forms carry more of the distinctive features than others, some are more prone to uncertainty and ignorance than others.

Biodiversity
I first take a closer look at the most basic form of natural capital: ecosystems and their biodiversity. The current biodiversity on earth is the result of billions of years of evolution. Some, including this author, and many proponents of strong sustainability in particular, believe that large-scale biodiversity loss

and human-induced species extinction is morally wrong, represents human hubris and a crime against our fellow sentient beings. Here, I will concentrate on the value of biodiversity to human welfare independent of ethical reasoning, however. Biodiversity contains valuable information and provides insurance value (Swanson 1997, Chapter 4). With respect to the first aspect, the more biodiversity there is, the wider is the set of options for biological activity. The more biodiversity there is, the more likely it is for the bio-industry to find the necessary information for curing illnesses, developing high-yield and robust agricultural crops and so on. With respect to the insurance value the argument that the more biodiversity there is the better equally applies. It is a well-established fact in ecology that ecosystems are characterised by highly non-linear, discontinuous and discrete changes in their ecological 'resilience', that is in their ability to 'recover from and thus absorb' (Barbier, Burgess and Folke 1994, p. 17) external and internal shocks. Although certain so-called keystone species play a role in maintaining diversity, the stability of ecosystems ultimately depends on the extent of its resilience and not so much on the stability of individual components (Turner 1995). The complexity of ecosystems is still poorly understood. 'Ecosystems do not have single equilibria with functions controlled to remain near it. Rather, destabilising forces far from equilibria, multiple equilibria and the absence of equilibria define functionally different states' (Holling 1995, p. 49). Due to this fact, an ecosystem might be able to cope with piecemeal destruction for quite a long time, but it can break down unexpectedly fast after some (often unknown) threshold has been transgressed (Perrings and Pearce 1994) and it loses its self-organising capacity. In some sense, every small-scale destruction increases the likelihood of unravelling the whole eco-system (Randall 1991, p. 65). While not undisputed (see Perrings, Folke and Mäler 1992), there is a large body of evidence from ecological studies suggesting that 'resilience increases with system complexity, and complexity can be measured by biological diversity. In that way, the more diversity there is, the more resilience there is and hence the more sustainable the system is' (Pearce 1994, p. 148).

Ceteris paribus therefore, the more biodiversity there is, the higher is its evolutionary potential and the bigger is the opportunity-set open to future generations (Perrings 1994). Hence, there is a good case for preventing biodiversity loss. On the other hand, this does not imply that if we do not preserve the totality of ecosystems and their biodiversity, we shall lose their basic life-support functions and make human life on earth impossible. Losing some of the existing biodiversity would mean losing some of its informational and some of its insurance value in exchange for the benefits of depletion, but it would not mean that human life is at risk. Presumably we could survive without the 20 per cent of species that Myers (1993, p. 75) fears will be lost by

2020 or the 50 per cent or more by the end of this century. Maybe mankind could even do without as much as 90 per cent of all living species. However, given uncertainty and ignorance, one needs to be cautious about the destruction of ecosystems and the depletion of biodiversity. Because depletion is a discontinuous process, because thresholds exist and because of the unpredictability of the dynamic process of losses in biological diversity it is hard to establish a safe margin within which no major catastrophic consequences have to be feared (Perrings and Opschoor 1994). Perrings, Folke and Mäler (1992, p. 202) summarise this point very clearly:

> What can be said is that there must exist levels of biodiversity loss which cannot be sustained by human society without inducing catastrophic change/fundamental reorganization. A major task for future research is to fix the boundaries for sustainable levels of biodiversity and ecological services with greater precision than has been possible in the past, and to explicitly state the time and space scales we choose to work with.

Finally, let us turn to why it is that much biodiversity is in danger of becoming depleted if no explicit effort for their protection is undertaken. Policy makers who act in the best interest of the country they represent will allocate the nation's limited resources to those activities that promise the highest net rate of return. That is, they will maximise the profits from a portfolio of different national assets. From this perspective, natural capital and hence biodiversity are but one asset in the portfolio, that is they must compete with other assets for allocation of resources that are necessary for sustenance (Swanson 1994). Because of our uncertainty and ignorance about the real value of biodiversity, natural capital is often (rightly or wrongly) thought of as not being worth conserving and is hence converted into another form of asset that promises to generate a higher net rate of return. Thus, for example, forests are logged and converted into agricultural or grazing land or industrialised. Note that the extinction of species is only rarely the consequence of an intended attempt to (over-)exploit the species, but far more often the rather unintended side-consequence of transforming natural capital into another asset.[19] Actually, that is one of the reasons why we are uncertain about the exact extent of biodiversity loss.

One might want to object that biodiversity loss is often a consequence of failing to define explicit property rights and that biodiversity destruction is, hence, a consequence of open access. While it has been known since Hardin (1968)[20] that open access provides powerful incentives for over-exploitation, this argument does not contradict the more general conclusion. As Swanson (1994, p. 814) rightly argues 'it is more likely that open access regimes are caused by decisions not to invest' in biodiversity than a direct cause for biodiversity loss. That is, ill-defined property rights follow from the decision not to protect biodiversity and not vice versa.[21]

Global environmental resources

There is also, more generally, a good case for protecting the 'global environmental system' (Clark 1995, p. 146) such as the global climate and the ozone layer. These are fundamental life-support resources, the destruction of which would endanger the welfare of coming generations. While the ozone layer is well on its way to recovery, the same cannot be said for the global climate. We continue to dump greenhouse gas emissions into the atmosphere far in excess of the natural regenerative capacity despite the fact that climate change poses a formidable threat to sustainable development, as section 2.4, p. 27, has shown. To repeat briefly the conclusion drawn there, precautionary action should be undertaken to prevent large and unpredictable changes in the global climate. Since we do not know exactly beyond which concentration of CO_2 and other greenhouse gases these changes will occur we should make sure that our emissions stay well below the limit that best available science suggests to be the critical level. This calls for a kind of safe minimum standard for the global climate.

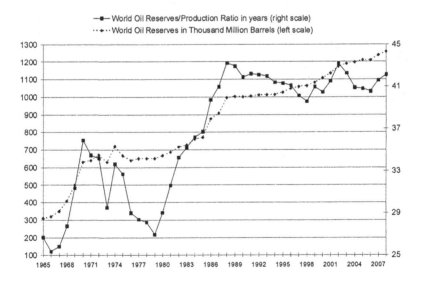

Source: BP (2009).

Figure 4.1 World oil reserves (1965 to 2008)

Accumulating toxic pollutants

A good case can also be made for not letting emissions, especially highly toxic and health-damaging pollutants, accumulate in the environment. The aim should be not to let emissions exceed 'critical loads' after which the capacity of the receiving media to dissipate and diffuse emissions would be damaged. Not following this rule would mean that the stock of pollution is continuously rising over time which is likely to endanger the sustainability goal.

Also ruled out would be the use of nuclear power with its highly damaging by-products on all stages of the nuclear cycle and its accumulation of highly toxic nuclear waste radiating for tens of thousands of years. This is especially because nuclear waste cannot be disposed of, but only more or less safely stored — a permanent burden to future generations. Following this prescription would also rule out the increased use of nuclear power for reducing CO_2 emissions in the atmosphere.

Natural resources for production

One might wonder why so little has been said about resources for production. The reason is that in a context of risk, uncertainty and ignorance it seems likely that the distinctive features of natural capital are especially relevant when it comes to biodiversity, the global environmental system and accumu-

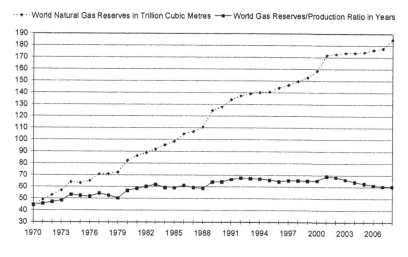

Source: BP (2009).

Figure 4.2 World natural gas reserves (1970 to 2008)

lating toxic pollutants as opposed to the global resource system. Property rights over energy and mineral resources are much better defined and the global environmental system, unlike the global resource system, lacks an 'automatic self-correcting feedback loop' (Clark 1995, p. 146) and especially lacks a functioning price system. Also, the prospects for technical progress appear to be strongest with respect to energy and mineral resources.

In Section 3.2, p. 48, I have discussed how substitution and technical progress can interact powerfully to overcome natural resource constraints. There are good reasons to *presume* therefore that the global resource system will be much better taken care of through existing institutions than the global environmental system. It is the waste-absorbing function of the environment that is most under threat and least protected. That is not to say, that resource availability might never pose a problem, but the frequent falsification of alarms about immediate resource exhaustion presents a case in point.

The world economy has, so far at least, exhibited a most remarkable capability to overcome resource constraints via substitution and technical progress. Reserves of both energy and non-energy resources have by and large persistently increased over time despite many years and decades of large amounts of resource extraction. Figures 4.1 and 4.2, respectively, show the

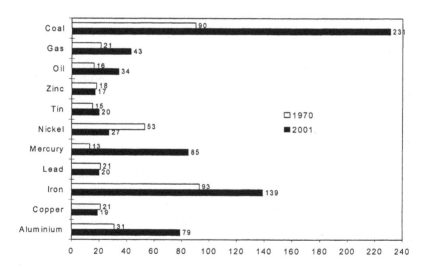

Sources: Meadows et al. (1972), BP (various years), US Bureau of Mines (various years).

Figure 4.3 Exponential reserve index for major resources

trend in world oil and gas reserves from 1965 (oil) or 1970 (gas) to 2008. It also shows their static reserves index, that is the current reserves to current production ratio in years. For both oil and gas, both absolute reserves and the static reserves to production ratio, are much higher in 2008 than in 1965 (oil) or 1970 (gas), respectively. One needs to interpret these figures with a good deal of caution, however. First, there are incentives to over-report reserves (Sauré 2008). Looking in more detail at the reserve figures of oil exporters, particularly of member countries of the Organization of Petroleum Exporting Countries (OPEC), reveals that at times reserves have miraculously shot upwards when it was politically convenient for these countries. Second, reserve indices seemingly suggest that oil wells can be exploited at the same rate until the last drop has been taken out. However, oil extraction from a well typically follows a logistic curve, in which maximum or peak extraction is reached when half of the well has been exhausted. Nevertheless, reserves have kept up with production and past predictions of a peak in global oil production have repeatedly failed to come true (Smil 2006).

Figure 4.3 presents the exponential reserve index for major energy and non-energy resources in 1970 and 2001, respectively. The exponential reserve index states how long current reserves would last if future consumption were to *grow* at current rates of growth.[22] It shows that even the exponential reserve index has increased over three decades in most cases or has decreased only slightly. Surely, there is no guarantee that this fortunate trend will continue into the future, especially as output and possibly resource input might be growing very fast, as the group of nearly industrialised countries becomes larger and larger and continues to catch up with the high-income countries. But despite all the caveats the available evidence so far seems to strongly support the substitutability assumption of WS with respect to natural capital as an input to production.

Food resources
What about food resources? This is a topic where environmental pessimists believe that the limits to growth are close. The classic paper, written by a group of ecologists and often referred to in debates about sustainability — for example, by Myers (1993, p. 75), Rees and Wackernagel (1994, p. 383), Daly (1996, p. 57), and Dasgupta (1997, p. 6) — is Vitousek et al. (1986). They suggest that already almost 40 per cent of the terrestrial net primary productivity (NPP) of the earth is currently absorbed, dominated or destroyed by human activity. 'NPP provides the basis for maintenance, growth, and reproduction of all heterotrophs (consumers and decomposers); it is the total food resource on Earth' (ibid., p. 368). Because human appropriation of NPP cannot increase beyond 100 per cent, Vitousek et al. (1986) believe that substantial growth in food production is impossible. That is, if not the limits

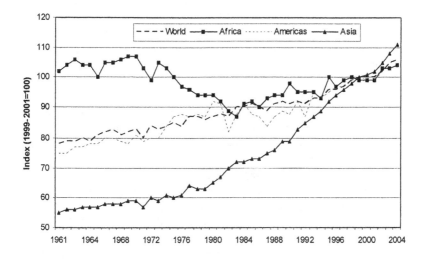

Source: FAO's online statistical database (http://apps.fao.org/).

Figure 4.4 Per capita net food production

to economic growth, then at least the limits to population growth are close according to this view. It is highly contested, however. To start with, the estimate of 40 per cent human appropriation of NNP is at the upper bound of estimates (Imhoff et al. 2004). More importantly, Beckerman (1995, p. 52) attacks Vitousek et al.'s computations as being completely meaningless: 'It simply means that a lot of the photosynthetic product that had previously been produced was of no use to us. It was, in effect, wasted. Now there is less of it. So what?'

To feed more people there are basically two strategies. One is extensification: it is estimated that the amount of land usable for growing crops is three times larger than current usage (Preston 1996, p. 96). Alternatively, land could be used more intensively. In Europe, for example, usage of cropland fell by one-quarter and the total forested area grew by 30 per cent in spite of increased food production (ibid., p. 99). In India enormous gains in cereal production were made through the introduction of modern varieties and the so-called Green Revolution (Lipton 1989). Figure 4.4 shows the trend in per capita world net food production alongside regional net food production in Africa, the Americas and Asia over the period 1961 to 2005. Of course, given the high aggregation of the index and the usually rather poor quality of the underlying data, the indices should be treated with care.

None the less, the figures reveal that while food production has caught up with growing world population and has even increased in per capita terms, particularly so in Asia, it has dramatically declined in Africa over a period of twenty years or so, rising again only from the early 1980s onwards with the levels of per capita food production from the early 1970s only recently regained.[23] What this suggests is that the availability of food is more a problem of intra-generational and, as Smil (1994, p. 257) further claims, even intra-national, distribution than a question of inter-generational sustainability. This finding is supported by those who have studied the political economy of famines and hunger (Drèze and Sen 1989; Drèze, Sen and Hussain 1995; Plümper and Neumayer 2009).

However, Daily et al. (1998, p. 1291) suspect that the increases in food production might have partly come about via 'a "mining" of soil, lowering of water tables, and impairment of other ecosytem services'. Where there are clear signs of over-harvesting, over-fishing, soil erosion, land degradation, salinisation of irrigated fields and similar forms of unsustainable agriculture, a good case can be made to enforce 'sustainable' harvesting, that is harvesting within the limits of natural regeneration, and to maintain soil fertility. The same applies to the protection of drinking water reservoirs. The availability of food and clean water is most basic to ensure the capacity to provide non-declining future welfare and where there are clear signs that danger to food and drinking water security is imminent, protective steps should be undertaken.

Nature as such does not seem to impose limits on increasing food production to feed many more people. Waggoner (1994, p. 1) in a Task Force Report for the American Council for Agricultural Science and Technology comes to the conclusion that 'the global totals of sun on land, CO_2 in the air, fertilizer, and even water could produce far more food than ten billion [people, E.N.] need'. For other cautiously optimistic views on the availability of food for a human population rising up to ten or twelve billion people, see Ruttan (1991), Bongaarts (1994), Smil (1994, 2000) and Dyson (1996, 2001).

So far, I have ignored the problem that following these prescriptions for the preservation of specific forms of natural capital is costly. The discussion therefore now turns to the question of opportunity costs.

4.5   THE PROBLEM OF OPPORTUNITY COST

All choices exclude potential alternative choices and therefore incur opportunity costs. Let us start by having a look at the costs of preserving the remaining biodiversity on earth. The first thing to note is that the protection costs are likely to be high even in terms of direct management costs due to the complexity of safeguarding the resilience of an ecosystem. Agenda 21 estimates the total expenditure needs for global biodiversity protection to be in the range of $8–80 bn per annum (Panayotou 1997, p. 220). Although such figures should always be treated with care, they give some tentative hint on the magnitude of costs for biodiversity protection. The main costs arise in terms of indirect costs, however, due to blocking economic development in a part of a nation's area. Perrings's (1994, p. 93) fear that protecting the current biodiversity 'may very well condemn future generations to progressive impoverishment, especially in the light of the continuing expansion of the global human population' might be overdrawn. But the dilemma of full biodiversity protection is that there are *definite, present, real* costs for *uncertain, future* and perhaps *intangible* benefits from applying SMS. Also, the actual protector will not be able to reap all of the potential future benefits because some of the benefits are positive externalities to other people in other countries, that is the protection of biodiversity has to some extent the characteristics of a global public good. Consequently, there are powerful incentives to free ride on others' effort for biodiversity protection. Since every potential protector has the incentive to free ride, none of them might have sufficient impetus to protect biodiversity.

The dilemma of opportunity costs being definite, present and real whereas the benefits of preservation are uncertain, future and intangible is not exclusive to biodiversity protection. It applies equally to many other environmental issues, most notably climate change. There are basically two possible answers to this dilemma. One is a deliberate decision to ignore the opportunity cost. This is the SMS as originally introduced by Ciriacy-Wantrup: safe minimum standards are established independent of the costs.[24] Because many of the costs of biodiversity depletion are rather speculative, but potentially very high, and because we do not know how much biodiversity is needed to keep up its basic life-support functions, one could decide to refrain from marginal decisions at all and opt for preserving the totality of remaining biodiversity, disregarding the costs of preservation.

Similarly, with respect to environmental pollution, Spash (1993, p. 127) postulates an 'inviolable right of future generations to be free of intergenerational environmental damages', which would imply that 'the current generation would be obliged to identify all activities causing long-term damages and ban them *regardless of the cost*' (ibid., p. 128, my emphasis). Still more generally, Costanza (1994, p. 394), based on uncertainty and ignorance, calls for preserving the complete stock of natural capital without qualification as regards the opportunity costs of preservation:

While a lower stock of natural capital may be sustainable, given our uncertainty and the dire consequences of guessing wrong, it is best to at least provisionally assume that we are at or below the range of sustainable stock levels and allow no further decline in natural capital. This 'constancy of total natural capital' rule can thus be seen as a prudent minimum condition for assuring sustainability, to be abandoned only when solid evidence to the contrary can be offered.

The other possibility is to allow opportunity costs to influence the decision and to explicitly limit the costs society is willing to incur for biodiversity protection and pollution prevention. This is the SMS as it became interpreted over time with the qualification that costs must not be 'unacceptably high'.

Beckerman (1994, pp. 194f) warns against ignoring opportunity costs:

> Given the acute poverty and environmental degradation in which a large part of the world's population live, one could not justify using up vast resources in an attempt to preserve from extinction, say, every one of the several million species of beetles that exist. For the cost of such a task would be partly, if not wholly, resources that could otherwise have been devoted to more urgent environmental concerns, such as increasing access to clean drinking water or sanitation in the Third World.

Jacobs (1995, p. 63) claims that in practice we are not faced with many choices of the 'preserve some obscure species' versus 'improve basic health care' type, but at least they cannot be ruled out in principle. While we might not want to preserve every beetle as such, we might well want to preserve the totality of remaining tropical rainforests and other habitats where beetles reside if we can ignore opportunity cost. Hence there will remain many cases where fundamental ethical conflicts arise. These ethical conflicts are exacerbated by the fact that the vast majority of the world's biological diversity exists in only a few nation-states that belong to the poorest of the world, with the notable exception of Australia (Swanson 1994, p. 806). There is no easy and simple answer on how to solve these difficult choices and trade-offs. I discuss this question further in the concluding section.

If one opts against ignoring opportunity costs, then SMS calls for preservation unless the costs are 'unacceptably high' and costs should be understood as opportunity costs net of the expected benefits of environmental preservation (similarly Crowards 1998). In other words, SMS should be built upon environmental valuation, not replace it. It is not an alternative to valuation efforts, but an extension and qualification to valuation. Stevens et al.'s (1991, p. 399) claim that SMS can do without making estimates of the potential benefits of preservation is not correct if opportunity costs are allowed to enter the decision-making process, because then the expected (if imperfectly measured) benefits of preservation enter the calculation of when preservation costs are deemed 'unacceptably high'.

Some scholars stress the total value that natural capital, and especially natural ecosystems and their biodiversity, has for human beings. Norton (1986, p. 205), for example, argues that this total value is virtually infinite:

> The value of biodiversity is the value of everything there is. It is the summed value of all the GNPs of all countries from now until the end of the world. If biodiversity is reduced sufficiently, and we do not know the disaster point, there will no longer be any conscious beings. With them go all value — economic and otherwise.

Costanza et al. (1997) have provided what they regard as a conservative estimate of the total value of the world's ecosystems. They suggest that this value lies in the range of US$16–54 trillion as a minimum estimate. For comparison, Costanza et al. indicate global GNP to be about US$18 trillion per year, so the estimated value of the world's ecosystems is very large indeed. Also, in Costanza et al. the values for specific items whose magnitude they regard as likely to be infinite have been deliberately truncated to make them finite and to provide a lower bound estimate of the 'real' value.

The specific valuation approach taken in the study of Costanza et al. has been much criticised for methodological reasons (see the contributions in a special symposium published in *Ecological Economics*, **25** (1), 1998). However, for the main question under scrutiny here these criticisms are of no major relevance. This is because the major problem with the study of Costanza et al. is not methodological and it does not matter much whether the numbers they come up with are approximately correct or not. Instead, the major point is that estimates of the *total* value of natural capital, or more concretely ecosystems, are not helpful in judging whether specific SMS decisions lead to costs that are 'unacceptably high'. This is because such decisions are always about marginal values, not total values.

4.6 CONCLUSION

In this chapter, I have shown that the combination of the distinctive features of natural capital with risk, uncertainty and ignorance suggest the conclusion that there are good reasons for the non-substitutability of specific forms of natural capital. They make a persuasive case:

- for preventing large-scale biodiversity losses and for the protection of ecosystems,
- for preserving global environmental life-support resources such as the global climate and the ozone layer,
- for limiting the accumulation of toxic pollutants and
- for restricting over-harvesting and soil erosion.

The case is strengthened by the fact that examples abound of negative interlinkages between environmental problems: deforestation often worsens loss of topsoil and land degradation and contributes to climate change; acid rain not only kills forests but also contaminates freshwater sources; ozone depletion contributes to climate change and some of the substitutes for CFCs have high global warming potentials.

In contrast, there seems to be much less reason for being concerned about natural capital as a provider of resource input for production. What these results imply is that the existing empirical evidence appears to support the non-substitutability assumption of SS more strongly with respect to the role natural capital plays in absorbing pollution and providing direct utility, whereas support is strong for the substitutability assumption of WS with respect to natural capital as a resource input into the production of consumption goods. Essentially, empirical evidence seems to support more WS with respect to the 'source'-side and support more SS with respect to the 'sink'-side of the economy.

Note, however, that for the case that SS seems to be supported by the empirical evidence, it strongly favours the second of the two interpretations SS was given in Section 2.3.2, p. 23. That is, from an SS perspective one would want to keep the physical stocks of certain forms of natural capital intact. In contrast, preserving natural capital in value terms is not a reasonable conclusion from the evidence as it would not preclude that certain forms of natural capital that provide basic life-support functions are endangered. The complete destruction of the ozone layer and the large-scale disruption of the biogeochemical cycle of the atmosphere cannot be compensated for even if other forms of *natural* capital are built up instead. An increase in the number of whales cannot substitute for a bigger hole in the ozone layer, for example. One could of course argue that the depletion value of life-support resources is very large or almost infinite so that preserving natural capital in value terms would necessarily prevent running down these resources. Consequently, the two interpretations of SS would coincide in their policy conclusions. However, it seems more reasonable to target specific forms of natural capital directly if they are regarded as non-substitutable rather than rely on the hope that preserving natural capital in value terms will achieve their preservation indirectly.

An additional problem is posited by the existence of opportunity costs. I have argued in this chapter that there are basically two options. One is to ignore the opportunity costs. Potentially large, but still finite, present and real costs are incurred in order to prevent uncertain and future, but potentially virtually infinite, costs of natural capital depletion. The other option is to allow opportunity costs to play some role and to opt for preservation of the identified forms of natural capital unless the costs are deemed 'unacceptaply' high.

Which option to take? I have argued in favour of the latter option and against ignoring opportunity cost. I readily admit that the latter option does not provide complete insurance against the non-achievement of sustainability and catastrophic outcomes. With the latter option, there is always the possibility of an *ex post* surprise, that is the danger that too much natural capital is depleted in spite of our *ex ante* expectation that this depletion of natural capital would not endanger sustainability. On the other hand, with the first option of preserving natural capital independent of the costs there is also the clear danger of significantly reducing other opportunities for current and future generations. Beckerman and Pasek (1997, p. 72) are correct in suggesting that in certain circumstances it might be better ethically justified to spend scarce resources on health or education rather than on the preservation of natural capital: 'It is difficult to see in what way the environment is in some moral class of its own.' The point is that to ignore opportunity costs is to 'solve' these often awkward trade-off decisions by simply avoiding them or assuming them away.

I have come to this conclusion arguing strictly with reference to risk, uncertainty and ignorance about the substitutability of natural capital. Interestingly, such a conclusion is largely compatible with a moderate deontological ethical position. Such a position would prescribe 'to avoid deliberate [environmental, E.N.] harm except where there are overwhelming beneficial outcomes which go beyond a consequential threshold' (Spash 2002, p. 238). Properly understood, an economic approach conscious of the ubiquitious existence of trade-offs, but also conscious of the equally ubiquitious existence of uncertainty and ignorance therefore need not clash with a more rights-based approach towards sustainability.

If one goes for the second option, then it has to be decided what 'unacceptably high' costs are. This question has no scientific answer. Scientists cannot tell society what it should regard as 'unacceptably high' costs. It is an ethical and political question for which economic or any other science is ill equipped to provide answers. Indeed, the question does not even have a general answer as it will be highly context-specific. Such a position should not be misinterpreted. Research can inform better decisions and environmental valuation can provide better and more comprehensive information as techniques become refined. But it is hubris to believe that natural or social scientists can make the decision on what should be regarded as 'unacceptably high' costs in society's stead.

The next two chapters do not question the validity of either paradigm as the previous two chapters have done. Instead, they take each paradigm for granted and ask whether WS and SS, respectively, can be measured in practice.

NOTES

1 My conclusions are largely compatible with those coming out from a European Union sponsored research project on critical natural capital (CRITINC). See Ekins (2003)
2 Reversibility need not be technically or physically impossible. It is sufficient that reversing a destruction is theoretically possible, but only at prohibitively high costs.
3 Admittedly, this is not true for unique historical buildings which provide non-material value, but certainly for man-made capital used in production.
4 At least so far. There are now efforts to store the DNA of threatened species artificially. One day, genetic engineering might bring 'extinct' species back to life if their DNA has been stored beforehand.
5 There is no consensus on the use of these terms in the literature. Often risk and uncertainty are used interchangeably. What I call uncertainty is often referred to as 'hard uncertainty' or 'Knightean uncertainty' after Knight (1921).
6 Another term often used for uncertainty is ambiguity (Dobbs 1991).
7 For a comprehensive summary of the state of the art, see IPCC (2007a, 2007b, 2007c).
8 Another term for ignorance used by O'Riordan and Jordan (1995, p. 10) is indeterminacy.
9 The term biodiversity is used throughout the book in a rather broad sense encompassing genetic, species and ecosystem diversity.
10 For the case that biodiversity will always remain a highly valuable information input into agriculture and pharmaceutical research, see Swanson (1996).
11 Weisbrod (1964) first introduced the concept of option value.
12 The seminal work on quasi-option values is Arrow and Fisher (1974).
13 Note that the authors speak of option values but mean quasi-option values in the usage of the terms here.
14 See also Mitchell and Carson (1989), Harrison (1992), Freeman (1993), Arrow et al. (1993), the contributions to Hausman (1993), Diamond and Hausman (1994) and Hanemann (1994).
15 To speak of a game-theoretic decision model is misleading since the term 'game theory' is reserved for strategic *interactions* between two or more players. In the 'games' that follow, the first player is 'society' and the second 'player' is nature which is not strategically interacting, but setting different states of the world. Strictly speaking, nature is therefore no player in the game-theoretic sense and one should talk of decision theory rather than game theory. I use the term 'game theory' nevertheless to relate to the relevant literature.
16 Note that the games I construct are different from Ready and Bishop's (1991) games. I use gain matrices instead of loss matrices. Hence I use the maximin criterion, which selects the maximum of the minimum gains, instead of the minimax criterion, which selects the mini-

mum of the maximum losses. Both concepts are equivalent. In my view, the way I set up the games allows for better understanding.

17 For a survey of the issues discussed and of competing theories see, for example, Page and MacLean (1983), Machina (1987, 1989), Kelsey and Quiggin (1992).

18 Note, however, that the often-found aversion against risks of commissions rather than omission, against risks involving involuntary exposure, lack of personal experience and difficulty in imagining risk exposure that characterise many large-scale but small probability risks are not irrational in themselves, as Zeckhauser and Viscusi (1995) seem to suggest, even when their actual incidence is overestimated.

19 Notable exceptions are whales and some highly valued species such as elephants, rhinoceroses and tigers.

20 Note his confusion of open access with common property.

21 Things are somewhat different with the extinction of fish resources where until recently the oceans have been, and still are to a large extent, outside the 200-mile coastal zones and are characterised by open access where no authority exists to allocate and enforce property rights. Even then, one could argue that open access is the consequence of countries' unwillingness to negotiate a multilateral environmental agreement aimed at the preservation of maritime resources.

22 The exponential reserve index is computed as $\ln(uz + 1)/u$, where u is the average rate of consumption growth and z is the static reserve index (see Meadows et al. 1972, p. 68). For 1970, I have computed the average annual growth rate over the time period 1965–70 and for 2001 the average annual growth rate over the time period 1995–2001 in order to average out coincidental annual fluctuations in consumption growth in the years for which the exponential reserve index is computed.

23 For trends in other world regions and for trends in cereal output, see Dyson (1994).

24 It must be said, however, that Ciriacy-Wantrup did not subject SMS to the qualification that costs must not be 'too high', he always argued that the costs of preservation, if properly undertaken, would be relatively small (see Ciriacy-Wantrup 1952, 1971).

5. Measuring Weak Sustainability

In this chapter, I shall discuss whether weak sustainability can be measured in practice. Section 5.1.1 derives genuine savings (GS), a theoretically correct measure of WS, from a dynamic optimisation or optimal growth model. The model is for a closed economy and the following section discusses the necessary amendments for an open economy context. A number of problems in measuring WS in practice are put forward. The examination then turns to the World Bank's efforts at computing GS figures for most countries in the world. I argue that the dismal conclusions of the World Bank (2009a) about the unsustainability of developing countries crucially depend on its method for resource accounting. These conclusions are largely reversed if another method, namely the El Serafy method, is used for computing natural capital depreciation due to resource depletion.

Section 5.2 discusses the Index of Sustainable Econmic Welfare (ISEW), also known under the name Genuine Progress Indicator (GPI), as an alternative indicator of WS. I show that the results generated by the ISEW and GPI methodology depend on problematic assumptions and methodological errors. In sensitivity analyses it is shown that the dismal results of ISEW studies about decreasing 'sustainable economic welfare' in developed countries in the WS sense fail to uphold if more reasonable assumptions are taken and the methodological errors are corrected. Section 5.3 concludes.

5.1 GENUINE SAVINGS (GS)

The purpose of this section is to show that genuine savings (GS) can be used as an indicator of WS. The term 'genuine' was introduced by Hamilton (1994) to distinguish genuine savings, which refers to all utility-relevant stocks of capital including man-made capital, natural capital, human capital as well as (in principle at least) social capital, from traditional net savings, which refers only to man-made or produced capital. Under certain conditions, one can show that an economy cannot be weakly sustainable if its GS rate is persistently below zero (Pezzey 2002; Pezzey and Toman 2002a; Dasgupta

2009). Importantly, the reverse does not hold true: positive GS rates at any moment of time cannot be taken as an indication of weak sustainability, because positive GS rates could be the result of, for example, unsustainable resource management and under-priced natural capital (Asheim 1994, p. 262). GS is thus a one-sided indicator of WS: negative rates indicate weak unsustainability, but positive rates do not necessarily indicate weak sustainability. The policy recommendation of keeping GS above zero can be interpreted as an extension of Hartwick's (1977) famous rule into a more general framework with multiple consumption goods and to various forms of capital: invest into all forms of capital at least as much as there is depreciation of all forms of capitals.[1] GS is built on the assumption of WS about the substitutability of natural capital. The rate of substitutability can change over time as natural capital becomes more scarce relative to the size of the economy and the shadow prices of components of natural capital change over time (Arrow et al. 2007). But substitutability in principle is always assumed.[2]

In order to show what keeping GS above zero means when other forms of capital than man-made capital are included, I now derive GS from a dynamic optimisation model. First, a closed economy is assumed, in Section 5.1.2, p. 135, the analysis is extended to the context of an open economy.

5.1.1   GS in a Closed Economy: A Dynamic Optimisation Model

I start with the following dynamic optimisation or optimal growth model, which is an extended and modified version of the model in Hartwick (1990, 1993). Assume a framework in which population is constant and the social welfare function is a discounted utilitarian function with a constant rate of discount. Further, assume that the productivity of the economy is fully captured by all capital stocks, a condition formally known as stationary technology (Asheim 2003). Also assume that there are no unanticipated future shocks.[3] It is as if all information about the future was available in the present.[4] Finally, assume that the production technology exhibits constant returns to scale and that perfect competition prevails.

In addition to the man-made capital of traditional growth models I also include natural capital and human capital. I subdivide natural capital into the stock of non-renewable resources, the stock of renewable resources and the stock of pollution, which, of course, is a capital 'bad' rather than a capital good. Assume the following dynamics (let a dot above a variable represent the derivative of the variable with respect to time):

- S, the change in the stock of non-renewable resources, is equal to resource discoveries D minus resource depletion R: $\dot{S} = D - R$.

- $\dot{X}$, the change in the stock of accumulated discoveries of non-renewable resources, is equal to current discoveries D: $\dot{X} = D$.

- $\dot{Z}$, the change in the stock of renewable resources, is equal to its natural growth $a(Z)$ plus 'human-induced' growth G minus resource harvest E:
  $\dot{Z} = a(Z) + G - E$.

- $\dot{P}$, the change in the stock of pollution, is equal to $\gamma F(.)$, pollution caused by production, minus natural restoration $b(P)$ minus abatement A:
  $\dot{P} = \gamma F(.) - b(P) - A$.

  Note that γ is a 'conversion factor' converting production into pollution units.[5]

- $\dot{M}$, the change in the stock of human capital, is equal to investment into human capital N: $\dot{M} = N$. Note that for simplicity human capital is treated as if there was no depreciation of its stock over time; that is, knowledge is neither forgotten nor does it become obsolete.[6] Alternatively, one could define N as net investment into human capital.

- Finally, $\dot{K}$, the change in the stock of man-made capital, is defined as a residual and is equal to total output $F(.)$ minus consumption C and other expenditures which consist of expenditures $f(.)$ for mining non-renewable resources, expenditures $g(.)$ for exploring and discovering non-renewable resources, expenditures $h(.)$ for harvesting renewable resources, pollution-abatement expenditures $i(.)$ and finally investment expenditures $j(.)$ into human capital:

$$\dot{K} = F(K, L, R, E, P, M) - C - f(R, S) - g(D, X) - h(E, Z) - i(A) - j(N).$$

Note that $\dot{K}$ is *net* investment into man-made capital. That is, $\dot{K}$ is defined such that depreciation of man-made capital is already netted out.

The arguments of the production function $F(.)$, the growth functions and the expenditure functions together with the signs of their partial derivatives are motivated as follows (let subscripts denote derivatives):

- $F(K, L, R, E, P, M)$: production $F(.)$ depends on the input of man-made capital K, labour L which for simplicity is assumed to be exogenously given as a constant,[7] renewable resources E, non-renewable resources R, but also on P, the *stock* of pollution — for example, the stock of CO_2 or SO_x in the atmosphere. Note that usually it is not the flow of pollution that matters for production, but the accumulated stock. Additionally, production depends on the human capital *stock*. All partial derivatives are positive except for F_P which is negative.

- $f(R,S)$: it is reasonable to assume that the cost of non-renewable resource extraction $f(.)$ increases with the amount of resources extracted ($f_R > 0$) and decreases with the (remaining) stock of non-renewable resources ($f_S < 0$), that is, the smaller is the stock the more expensive is resource extraction.
- $g(D,X)$: it is reasonable to assume that the cost of resource exploration $g(.)$ increases with the amount of resources explored ($g_D > 0$). It also increases with the accumulated stock of discoveries ($g_X > 0$) because the easy-to-find resource deposits are discovered first, so that it becomes more difficult and hence more expensive to find additional deposits.
- $h(E,Z)$: analogous to $f(.)$, only this time for renewable resources.
- $a(Z)$: it is common to assume that renewable resources follow a logistic growth path, in which the growth rate rises with the resource stock initially ($a_Z > 0$ for $Z < Z'$), but falls eventually after the stock has reached a certain size Z' ($a_Z < 0$ for $Z > Z'$).
- $b(P)$: natural restoration is negatively affected by a rising stock of pollution, that is, $b_P < 0$.
- $i(A)$: the cost of abatement $i(A)$ rises with the amount of abatement, hence $i_A > 0$.
- $j(N)$: the cost of building up human capital $j(N)$ rises with the amount of investment into human capital, hence $j_N > 0$.

To complete the model assume a very simple utility function for the 'representative consumer' from equation (2.2) in Section 2.1, p. 7. Assume that the problem of the social planner is to maximise

$$\int_0^\infty U(C,Z,P) \cdot e^{-\rho t} dt \qquad (5.1)$$

that is the discounted utility integrated over infinite time. As before, C is consumption, Z the stock of renewable resources, and P the stock of pollution. ρ is society's pure rate of time preference which is exogenously given and which indicates by how much society discounts utility in the future for the pure reason of being later in time.

Hartwick (1990) included the *flow* of resource harvest and the pollution *flow* into the utility function. In contrast, I include the renewable resource *stock* and the *stock* of pollution into the utility function. If consumers have preferences for environmental quality, it is more reasonable to assume that they care about the whole stock of directly utility-relevant renewable resources and pollution and not just incremental changes to the stock.

The so-called current-value Hamiltonian for this maximisation problem is then given by

$$H = U(C, Z, P) + \lambda \left[F(.) - C - f(R, S) - g(D, X) - h(E, Z) - i(A) - j(N) \right]$$
$$+ \mu[D - R] + \omega[D] + \varphi[a(Z) + G - E] + \psi[\gamma F(.) - b(P) - A] + \xi[N] \quad (5.2)$$

where all the variables are defined as above and are evaluated at time t ($0 \le t \le \infty$) and where all time indices have been suppressed for ease of exposition. The λ, μ, ω, ϕ, ψ, ξ are utility-denominated co-state variables or dynamic Lagrange multipliers (shadow prices) for the state variables: $\lambda > 0$ is the shadow value of man-made capital K, that is the marginal value in utility terms of expanding K by one unit; $\mu > 0$ is the shadow value of the stock of non-renewable resources S; $\omega < 0$ is the shadow cost of the stock of resource discoveries X which is negative because X negatively impacts upon the costs of resource exploration, $\phi > 0$ is the shadow value of the stock of renewable resources Z, $\psi < 0$ is the shadow cost of the stock of pollution P; and $\xi > 0$ is the shadow value of the stock of human capital M. K, S, X, Z, P and M are the state variables of the model.

The terms in square brackets represent the changes in capital stocks as explained and represent the constraints of the maximisation problem. For simplicity, assume all functions to be 'well behaved' and continuously twice differentiable, so that the necessary first-order conditions for maximisation are also sufficient. Further assume that an optimal solution exists (on existence conditions, see Toman 1985). The control variables of the model are C, R, D, E, A and N. The dynamics of the model are given by the canonical equations for optimisation:[8]

i. First-order conditions for maximisation (maximum principle)

$$\frac{\partial H}{\partial C} = 0 \quad \Rightarrow \quad U_C = \lambda \qquad (5.i.1)$$

$$\frac{\partial H}{\partial R} = 0 \quad \Rightarrow \quad \lambda[F_R - f_R] + \psi\gamma F_R = \mu \qquad (5.i.2)$$

$$\frac{\partial H}{\partial D} = 0 \quad \Rightarrow \quad \lambda g_D - \omega = \mu \qquad (5.i.3)$$

$$\frac{\partial H}{\partial E} = 0 \quad \Rightarrow \quad \lambda[F_E - h_E] + \psi\gamma F_E = \varphi \qquad (5.i.4)$$

$$\frac{\partial H}{\partial A} = 0 \quad \Rightarrow \quad -\lambda i_A = \psi \tag{5.i.5}$$

$$\frac{\partial H}{\partial N} = 0 \quad \Rightarrow \quad \lambda j_N = \xi \tag{5.i.6}$$

ii. Dynamic first-order conditions

$$\dot{\lambda} = \rho\lambda - \frac{\partial H}{\partial K} \quad \Rightarrow \quad \dot{\lambda} = \rho\lambda - \lambda F_K - \psi\gamma F_K \tag{5.ii.1}$$

$$\dot{\mu} = \rho\mu - \frac{\partial H}{\partial S} \quad \Rightarrow \quad \dot{\mu} = \rho\mu + \lambda f_S \tag{5.ii.2}$$

$$\dot{\omega} = \rho\omega - \frac{\partial H}{\partial X} \quad \Rightarrow \quad \dot{\omega} = \rho\omega + \lambda g_X \tag{5.ii.3}$$

$$\dot{\varphi} = \rho\varphi - \frac{\partial H}{\partial Z} \quad \Rightarrow \quad \dot{\varphi} = \rho\varphi + \lambda h_Z - \varphi a_Z - U_Z \tag{5.ii.4}$$

$$\dot{\psi} = \rho\psi - \frac{\partial H}{\partial P} \quad \Rightarrow \quad \dot{\psi} = \rho\psi - \lambda F_P - \varphi(\gamma F_P - b_P) - U_P \tag{5.ii.5}$$

$$\dot{\xi} = \rho\xi - \frac{\partial H}{\partial M} \quad \Rightarrow \quad \dot{\xi} = \rho\xi - \lambda F_M - \psi\gamma F_M \tag{5.ii.6}$$

iii. Equations of motion[9]

$$\frac{\partial H}{\partial \lambda} = \dot{K} \quad \Rightarrow \quad \dot{K} = F(.) - C - f(R,S) - g(D,X) - h(E,Z) - i(A) - j(N) \tag{5.iii.1}$$

$$\frac{\partial H}{\partial \mu} = \dot{S} \quad \Rightarrow \quad \dot{S} = D - R \tag{5.iii.2}$$

$$\frac{\partial H}{\partial \omega} = \dot{X} \quad \Rightarrow \quad \dot{X} = D \tag{5.iii.3}$$

$$\frac{\partial H}{\partial \varphi} = \dot{Z} \quad \Rightarrow \quad \dot{Z} = a(Z) + G - E \tag{5.iii.4}$$

$$\frac{\partial H}{\partial \psi} = \dot{P} \quad \Rightarrow \quad \dot{P} = \gamma F(.) - b(P) - A \tag{5.iii.5}$$

$$\frac{\partial H}{\partial \xi} = \dot{M} \quad \Rightarrow \quad \dot{M} = N \tag{5.iii.6}$$

Equations (5.i.1) to (5.i.6) are of primary interest. Plugging (5.i.1) into (5.i.2)–(5.i.5), plugging (5.i.5) into (5.i.2) and (5.i.4), plugging (5.i.2) into (5.i.3) and rearranging terms one arrives at the current value Hamiltonian H^* along an optimal path

$$H^* = U + \lambda\big(F(.) - C - f(.) - g(.) - h(.) - i(.) - j(.)\big)$$

$$-\lambda(F_R - f_R - i_A \cdot \gamma F_R) \cdot R + \lambda g_D D$$

$$+\lambda(F_E - h_E - i_A \cdot \gamma F_E)(a(Z) + G - E)$$

$$-\lambda i_A(\gamma F(.) - b(P) - A) + \lambda j_N N \qquad (5.3)$$

Now, divide the equation by $\lambda = U_C$. Also plug (5.iii.1), (5.iii.4), (5.iii.5) and (5.4) into (5.3). Then one finally arrives at

$$\frac{H^*}{U_C^*} = \frac{U}{U_C^*} + \qquad (5.4)$$

$$+\dot{K}^* - \left[F_R^* - f_R^* - i_A^*\gamma F_R^*\right] \cdot R^* + g_D^* \cdot D^* + \left[F_E^* - h_E^* - i_A^*\gamma F_E^*\right] \cdot \dot{Z}^* - i_A^* \cdot \dot{P}^* + j_N^* \cdot \dot{M}^*$$

$$\underbrace{\hphantom{+\dot{K}^* - \left[F_R^* - f_R^* - i_A^*\gamma F_R^*\right] \cdot R^* + g_D^* \cdot D^* + \left[F_E^* - h_E^* - i_A^*\gamma F_E^*\right] \cdot \dot{Z}^* - i_A^* \cdot \dot{P}^* + j_N^* \cdot \dot{M}^*}}_{Genuine Saving}$$

where the stars indicate optimal values. Appendix 3 shows that, not surprisingly, optimal resource pricing according to Hotelling's rule is implied by this dynamic optimisation model. The same holds true for the so-called Ramsey rule — see Appendix 3, p. 202.

Equation (5.4) defines GS for this model and says that the traditional savings measure, in so far as it does not reflect the corrections yet or does so only imperfectly, has to be amended by the following terms to arrive at GS:

1. $\dot{K}$ (>0 or <0)

This term represents net investment in man-made capital, that is gross investment minus depreciation of man-made capital. Note that it is already included in traditional savings.

2. $\left[F_R - f_R - i_A\gamma F_R\right] \cdot R$ (>0)

This term represents the depletion value of non-renewable resources which has to be *subtracted*. Resource depletion R is valued at the terms in brackets. These are the price for the resource F_R minus its marginal extraction cost f_R which together form the so-called Hotelling rent encountered already in Section 3.2.2, p. 53.[10] $i_A\gamma F_R$ is the marginal pollution effect of extracting one unit of the non-renewable resource valued at marginal abatement costs — for example, emission of CO_2 by using non-renewable energy. Since GS is derived from the current-value Hamiltonian, the economy is assumed to develop along an optimal path such that marginal abatement costs are equal to marginal social costs which in turn are equal to an optimal 'Pigouvian' tax (Hamilton 1996, p. 19).[11] What has to be subtracted, therefore, are what economists call total Hotelling rents (price minus marginal cost times the depleted quantity), but the revenues from an optimal Pigouvian tax have to be added!

The last term in the brackets seems to be counter-intuitive. The formula demands that *for a given amount of depletion* the deduction for non-renewable resource depletion is lower if, in addition, the resource causes pollution, that is, the exact opposite of what one might have expected! The reason is that the existence of pollution makes the resource stock in the ground less valuable in comparison to a situation without resource use causing pollution. Hence the inter-temporal costs of using the resource now instead of preserving it for coming generations are less than without pollution. Note, however, that the total deduction term for the depletion of non-renewable resources need *not* be smaller because the amount of depletion will in general not be the same in an economy where resources cause pollution as in an economy without resource use causing pollution. If one changes the structure of the model, its optimal solution has to be calculated from the start resulting in a completely different time path of the endogenous variables.

Heterogeneous resource deposits of a resource (for example, differing quality deposits of oil with differing extraction costs) should be valued at individual deposit-type market prices and marginal extraction costs. For that reason, Hamilton (1994, p. 160) replaces $F_R - f_R$ (ignoring the pollution effect for a moment) with $\mathit{\Sigma}(F_{Ri} - f_{Ri})R_i$; that is, he values different deposit types separately and sums them up. This is not necessary, however. Strictly speaking, the F_R and f_R terms are row vectors and the R term is a column vector, because there is more than one non-renewable resource in actual economies. Hence different deposit types can be taken care of by expanding the vectors. No change in notation is therefore needed and we can stick to our standard terminology.

Reich (1994) objects to taking depletion of existing resource stocks into account in arguing that human beings have never produced them and their stocks have never entered the national accounting system as an asset. Stahmer (1995, p. 103) argues in response that existing stocks should be regarded as a costless gift of nature. Hartwick and Hageman (1993, p. 229) argue that the *service flows* of resource stocks do enter the GNP, for example in the form of oil used in the economy. This debate misses the point, however. The goal of GS is to measure whether the capacity to provide future welfare is maintained or not. Where this capacity comes from, simply does not matter. As Repetto et al. (1989, p. 2) rightly argue, 'the value of an asset is not its investment cost, but the present-value of its income potential' in the future.

3. $g_D \cdot D$ (>0)

This term represents the value of discoveries of non-renewable resources which has to be added. New discoveries are valued at marginal discovery costs. This term is partly already included in standard national accounting where exploration expenditures are treated as investment (World Bank 1997, p. 28).

4. $\left[F_E - h_E - i_A \gamma F_E \right] \cdot \dot{Z} \begin{Bmatrix} > \\ < \end{Bmatrix} 0$ as $\dot{Z} \begin{Bmatrix} > \\ < \end{Bmatrix} 0$

This term values the net change in the stock of renewable resources. Note that it is negative for a net decrease in the stock and positive vice versa. $i_A \gamma F_E$ is the marginal pollution effect of harvesting one unit of the renewable resource valued at marginal abatement costs — for example, emission of greenhouse gases by clearing rainforests. As with non-renewable resources, the value is calculated as the price for the resource minus its marginal harvesting cost *plus* an optimal Pigouvian tax times the amount of net stock change. Equally, if there is heterogeneity in quality of a renewable resource, individual market prices and marginal extraction costs should enter the correction term.

5. $i_A \cdot \dot{P} \begin{Bmatrix} > \\ < \end{Bmatrix} 0$ as $\dot{P} \begin{Bmatrix} > \\ < \end{Bmatrix} 0$

This term values the net change in the stock of pollution. The value is calculated as marginal abatement cost i_A times the amount of net change in the stock of pollution P. Note that marginal abatement costs are equal to marginal social costs. In turn, both marginal abatement costs and marginal social costs are equal to an optimal Pigouvian tax. Again, this equality only holds because GS is derived from the current-value Hamiltonian, which implies that the economy develops along its optimal path (Hamilton 1996, p. 19). The correction term is necessary because cumulative pollution *flows*, that is a rising pollution *stock*, either decrease the assimilative capacity of the environment for future generations or have caused already environmental damage to future generations. The reverse holds true for a decreasing pollution stock. Parts of abatement expenditures are already netted out of national income as intermediate consumption. Care must be taken to avoid the trap of double counting.

6. $j_N \cdot \dot{M}$ (>0)

This term values the increase in the human capital stock at its marginal investment cost. Educational expenditures on investment goods are already included in standard national accounting. World Bank (1997) proposes to consider current educational expenditures, which make up more than 90 per cent of all educational expenditures (ibid., p. 34), as investment in human capital as well and not as consumption.

The underlying reason for all these corrections is that a degradation in one of the capital stocks reduces the capacity to provide future utility. What is used up today is lost to the economy in the future. Note that, in principle, proponents of SS could espouse this form of measuring sustainability as well. They would simply suggest that because natural capital is nonsubstitutable, its marginal productivity will be infinite as will be any depreciation allowance for natural capital. Hence development that draws down natural capital would be unsustainable. As we will see in the next chapter, p. 169, however, proponents of SS dismiss the possibility of comprehensive monetary valuation of the environment and have therefore developed conceptually different indicators of SS.

Devarajan and Weiner (1995, p. 4) have argued against deriving measures of sustainability from dynamic optimisation models. They have reasoned as follows:

> If the resource is being optimally managed, why worry? Since there is no way we can alter behavior that will lead to a higher welfare, there is little point in trying to adjust national accounts ... The assumption of optimal resource management is simply inconsistent with the phenomenon of environmental deterioration that provided the very motivation for adjustment.

This somewhat misses the point, however. The sustainability criterion imposes an *additional* constraint on the maximisation exercise. Given this constraint the economy will only be on its optimal path after the policy intervention (if that appears to be necessary to fulfil the sustainability requirement), not before. The government can alter behaviour which will lead to a higher welfare *given* the further constraint to ensure WS!

5.1.2 GS in an Open Economy

The model implicitly assumes a closed economy: there is no trade in resources and commodities; there is no transboundary or global pollution. Asheim (1986, 1994), Hartwick (1995), Sefton and Weale (1996) and Vincent, Panayotou and Hartwick (1997) analyse the modifications needed for open economies trading with each other. Because the Hotelling rule must hold in the optimisation model, resource rent is assumed to rise at the interest rate.[12] With marginal extraction costs not falling at a rate higher than the interest rate, future resource prices will be higher than current ones, thus providing the resource exporter with improving terms of trade. Due to that, the exporter of natural resources can make a smaller correction to net savings in comparison to the closed economy and still ensure sustainability. The resource importer, on the other hand, faces a future deterioration in its terms of trade, so it must make a higher correction from net savings than would be the case in a closed economy. That is, it is the resource importer who must make an extra adjustment for the growing scarcity of the resource. Note that this analysis does not follow from any considerations of fairness, but solely from considerations of self-interest in the sense that each country strives to keep the value of its own capital stock at least constant.

If, for some reason, for example unanticipated resource discoveries, future resource prices are declining, the prescriptions would be reversed, of course, and it would be up to the resource exporter to make a higher correction and up to the resource importer to make a lower correction from net savings than would be the case in a closed economy. Vincent, Panayotou and Hartwick (1997, p. 282) suspect that overly optimistic projections of future resource prices have been one reason for the poor economic performance of resource-rich in relation to resource-poor countries (for evidence on this performance, see Sachs and Warner (2001) and Neumayer (2004b) who shows that the poor economic performance holds true not only for growth in GDP, but also for growth in 'genuine' income). Given a 'century-old decline in most resource prices', Vincent, Panayotou and Hartwick (1997, p. 282) suggest that 'under-investment, not overinvestment, is the principal risk facing resource exporters'. That terms-of-trade effects must be taken into account implies that in an open economy context capital gains, that is changes in the value of capital due to changing prices, must not be excluded from the computation of GS as would be appropriate in a closed economy (Asheim 1996).

Transboundary and global pollution present more difficult problems. According to the 'polluter-pays principle' it would be up to the country causing transboundary pollution to include the corresponding correction terms in its GS. Presumably it was this Hamilton and Atkinson (1996, p. 678) had in mind when they reasoned that 'some portion of a given country's saving should, at least notionally, be set aside in order to compensate the recipients of the pollution emitted and transferred across international boundaries'.

On the other hand, if one realistically assumes that sovereign nation-states are unwilling to compensate other nation-states, it might be more reasonable to stick to the presumption that each country should strive to keep the value of its own capital stock at least constant, independent of whether capital deterioration is caused within its own borders or beyond. According to this rule it would be up to the country receiving pollution to include the corresponding correction terms in its accounts or else to try to compensate the emitting country for pollution reductions. One might regard this allocation rule as unfair, but it is not unusual that countries refuse to pay according to the 'polluter-pays principle' if they cause transboundary pollution. The big disadvantage of this allocation rule is that it provides incentives for countries to externalise their pollution on to other countries in order to increase their GS which is not the proper intention of sustainability.

With global pollution it is often rather difficult to say who is the victim, and to what extent, and who is not. In dealing with problems like climate change it might be reasonable to demand that every country is accountable for its own current greenhouse-relevant emissions. This conclusion is not compelling, however, especially not if there is a history of emission accumulation. To give an example: developing countries are likely to resist being accountable for their full current emissions when it is the relatively much higher past emissions of the now-developed countries that are mainly responsible for the *current stock* of greenhouse-relevant emissions (see, for example, Agarwal and Narain 1991). Along these lines, Neumayer (2000a) argues in defence of historical accountability for greenhouse gas emissions. Such a principle, however, is likely to be resisted by developed countries. Hence there is no straightforward allocation rule in this case. The problem is that there has to be some international agreement on allocation rules. If not, double counting as well as no counting at all is likely to occur. This is not a question of mere accounting. It really is about who is responsible for accumulating other forms of capital for environmental deterioration.

So far I have presented the *theory* of measuring WS. Now I turn to practical problems. After that, I shall look at attempts to measure GS in practice, particularly the GS computations undertaken by the World Bank (2009a).

5.1.3 Problems with Measuring GS in Practice

Providing a measure of GS in practice has to tackle the following problems:

1. The framework in which GS is derived as an indicator of WS is very restrictive. The assumption of inter-temporal efficiency implies that all value terms and all quantities have to be optimal since the economy is assumed to develop *along the optimal path*. It is a standard result in economics that optimality can be achieved as a perfect inter-temporal competitive equilibrium; that is, as an equilibrium of a decentralised economy with a complete

set of property rights (that is, no externalities[13]) with competitive households and firms and a full set of forward markets where perfectly rational agents have perfect information and households take full account of the welfare of their actual or prospective descendants (Barro and Sala-i-Martin 1995, pp. 60–71). In reality none of these conditions hold. There is a state which raises income by distortionary taxes, externalities abound and are not internalised via an optimal Pigouvian tax, competition is severely restrained, there is nothing resembling a full set of forward markets, agents are boundedly rational with imperfect information and whether households take full account of the welfare of their descendants is open to debate. The world we live in is full of market failures — especially in an inter-temporal context encompassing future generations. As Aaheim and Nyborg (1995, p. 59) observe, the desire to green the national accounting system was driven by the presumption that natural resource use and environmental degradation are non-optimal. Simply assuming that there are no inefficiencies is therefore utterly unrealistic and is equivalent to solving the problem by assuming it away. Furthermore, efficient shadow prices have to be established via valuation studies for many environmental services. This is because they do not carry prices yet, either because of missing property rights or because the services are not priced in markets.

Contrary to what one might think, it does not even help trying to repair selected inefficiencies in isolation, for example by introducing more competition for firms. The theory of second best tells us that if there is more than one distortion in the economy, then correcting any subset of distortions in isolation does not mean that the resulting prices and quantities are necessarily any closer to the optimal values than before the exercise (Lipsey and Lancaster 1956). The reason is that any still existing distortion will work its way through the economy via general equilibrium effects. Hence what appeared to be an optimal correction of a distortion examined in isolation, might no longer be optimal, taking into account the totality of other distortions. It follows that one has to treat GS as a measure of WS with caution. It is only a valid and reliable measure if one believes that the actual economy develops sufficiently close to its optimal path. If it does not, then the existing institutions and the prices and quantitites they generate may be significantly different from the optimal ones. Sustainability theorists have recently tackled the problem of sustainability accounting in imperfect economies – see, for example, Dasgupta (2001a, 2001b), Arrow et al. (2003b). But many problems and open questions remain (Dasupta 2009).

2. Given that actual economies do not develop along an optimal path, Hamilton, Atkinson and Pearce (1997, p. 3) still assert that *actual* values of GS

point in the right direction at least. They argue that in an over-polluted state relative to the optimum, both the quantity of pollution and its shadow cost measured by marginal social pollution costs are higher than in the optimum. Hence GS will be lower in an over-polluted state than in the optimum. Hence moving from an over-polluted state towards the optimum provides the 'right' signal of increasing GS. The same holds true vice versa for an under-polluted state relative to the optimum (see also Hamilton and Atkinson (1996), where the argument is elaborated upon). In a partial equilibrium analysis the argument of Hamilton, Atkinson and Pearce (1997) is correct. But in dealing with questions of sustainability one is dealing with multiple markets and general equilibria to which the partial analysis results do not apply straightforwardly. There is hence no guarantee that moving to the (presumably unknown) optimum will provide the 'right' signals.

Even if one could safely ignore general equilibrium effects, *actual* values of GS are not guaranteed to point in the right direction for the accounting of resource depletion and resource harvest. In a state of over-depletion and over-harvest relative to the optimum the quantities are higher but the resource prices are likely to be lower than in the optimum. Because of quantities and prices deviating in the opposite direction from their optimal levels, it is unclear whether GS will be lower or higher in a state of over-depletion and over-harvest relative to the optimum. Hence increased GS cannot be trusted to provide the right signal of moving towards the optimal state. Analogous reasoning applies if we start from a state of under-depletion and under-harvest. In the most prominent practical attempt to measure GS (World Bank 2009a), rents from resource depletion and resource harvesting dominate the pollution effect on GS by orders of magnitude for countries with negative rates of GS, see Section 5.1.4, p. 141. Hence, actual changes in GS cannot be trusted to point in the right direction. Arrow et al. (2004, p. 161) make a similar point.

3. If environmental and other externalities are not internalised then existing prices and quantities differ from the optimal ones. In this case, positive GS rates can go hand in hand with unsustainable resource exploitation and environmental degradation. Furthermore, even if efficient, an economy need not be sustainable. If it is not, then shifting towards sustainability will change prices. Pezzey and Toman (2002b, p. 17) therefore suggest that 'sustainability prices and sustainability itself are thus related in a circular fashion: Without sustainability prices, we cannot know whether the economy is currently sustainable; but without knowing whether the economy is currently sustainable, currently observed prices tell us nothing definite about sustainability'.

4. Problems arise if one abandons the unrealistic assumption that there are no future unanticipated shocks. Future unanticipated shocks could be unexpected technical breakthroughs, unexpected resource discoveries, unexpected environmental destruction (as has been the case with climate change and the ozone layer depletion) and the like. If future shocks are not anticipated, as is arguably often the case, then the pre-shock prices are not representative for the post-shock prices and they do not adequately reflect economic scarcities. A regime change occurs and all prices and quantities have to be estimated again (Hartwick 1993, p. 195).

Note that unanticipated future shocks are different from risks. They are cases of uncertainty and ignorance as defined in Section 4.2, p. 99. That is, their probability distribution and contingent payoffs are not known in the present. Hung (1993) has shown that for cases of mere risk, option and existence values (differentiated for each type of risk) have to be included and all prices are to be 'evaluated in terms of contingent (rationally anticipated) values' (ibid., p. 388). This in itself is difficult enough. However, in most cases the probability distribution is presumably unknown, so that future costs or benefits are more or less unanticipated, which means, again, that a regime change occurs, and the computation procedure has to restart again.

As a special case of Hung's (1993) result, Vincent, Panayotou and Hartwick (1997) have shown how the investment rule for resource trading countries has to be augmented by the present-value of anticipated future terms-of-trade shifts, that is the capital gain or loss on the resource stock due to the anticipation of changing future resource prices (see Section 5.1.3, p. 135, on GS in an open economy). However, it is not realistic to assume that changing future resource prices can be fully anticipated. One sufficient condition cited by Vincent, Panayotou and Hartwick (1997, p. 277) — 'a complete set of futures markets' — is nowhere existent.

5. A similar problem as discussed under the previous point arises if one abandons the unrealistic assumption that every determinant of the capacity to provide future welfare becomes embodied in one or the other form of capital (Löfgren 1992; Aronsson and Löfgren 1993; Usher 1994). An example for disembodiment is autonomous or Hicks-neutral technical progress that is independent of the accumulation of man-made capital.[14] If these autonomous trends are correctly anticipated in the present then they can be interpreted as a positive or negative inter-temporal externality and can therefore in principle be taken into account by augmenting GS with the current value of the externality (Aronsson and Löfgren 1993, 1995). If they cannot, then GS will be under- or overestimated.

6. The GS rule also becomes much more complex if the unrealistic assumption of constant population is abandoned. Results depend on whether population growth is assumed to be exponential and whether social welfare only depends on per capita utility as in my own definition in Chapter 2 or also on population size (see Hamilton 2002; Asheim 2004; Arrow et al. 2003a; Hamilton and Atkinson 2006). Not surprisingly, the many developing countries with strong population growth appear to be even less weakly sustainable once population growth is accounted for.

5.1.4 GS in Practice: A Critique of the World Bank's Computations

Several studies have been undertaken providing admittedly crude measures of WS (for example, van Tongeren et al. 1993; Pearce and Atkinson 1993; Hamilton and Atkinson 1996; Proops et al. 1999; Hamilton and Clemens 1999; Dasgupta 2001b; Arrow et al. 2004). I will concentrate here on the GS figures computed by the World Bank (2009a), which is by far the most comprehensive of all studies, both in terms of time and country coverage (see also Hamilton and Clemens 1999). It suggests that the world taken together as well as the high-income countries are not weakly unsustainable due to high investments in man-made and human capital. It also suggests that the Sub-Saharan African region has had negative GS during the 1980s and 1990s, and the North African and Middle East region has had negative GS from the early 1970s onwards. Both regions would hence be detected as unsustainable. The same is true for many countries within these regions as well as for major natural resource extracting countries in other regions.

I will now give a more detailed critique of the World Bank's (2009a) computations of GS. I show that the Bank's rather strong conclusions depend on a method for computing resource rents that is one of at least three competing ones. There are a number of arguments suggesting that the El Serafy method, despite problems of its own, might be preferable to the World Bank method for computing natural capital depreciation. Using this method leads to opposite conclusions for both regions and indeed for most countries that appear unsustainable according to the World Bank's computations. Let us have a closer look at the Bank's study first.

5.1.4.1 The World Bank computations
The data set underlying World Bank (2009a) consists of savings and accompanying data covering most countries in the world from 1970 onwards.[15] The structure of the set is described in detail in Appendix 4, p. 206. GS is computed by the World Bank as follows: net savings is gross domestic saving (including current education expenditures) minus depreciation of man-made

capital; GS is net savings minus depreciation of natural capital from the depletion of natural resources minus damage caused by CO_2 emissions minus, for a few mostly developed countries and more recent years, damage caused by suspended particulate matter emissions. Education expenditures are used as a proxy for the increase in human capital valued at marginal investment costs in equation (5.6). Dasgupta (2001b) has criticised that the World Bank ignores depreciation of human capital and thus overstates investment in human capital. He has a point, but one could also argue that even after including current education expenditures, such expenditures still undervalue the true investment in human capital. The method used for computing depreciation of natural capital from the depletion of resources is discussed in more detail below in the next sub-section. The World Bank values CO_2 emissions at US$20 per metric tonne of carbon, taken from Fankhauser (1995). Whilst this was a median estimate of older studies, by using this somewhat outdated estimate the Bank is likely to underestimate the damage caused by CO_2 emissions in the light of more recent scientific evidence and economic studies – see section 2.4, p. 27.

The World Bank assigns all damage from CO_2 to the emitting country. It counts natural capital depreciation due to resource depletion to the country of resource extraction, not the country of resource consumption. As argued in Section 5.1.3, p. 135, on the open economy case, the allocation rule for CO_2 emissions is not compelling. Damage from climate change is caused by the accumulated stock of CO_2 and other greenhouse gases. Developing countries could make a point in claiming that their incremental CO_2 emissions should count less than those from developed countries considering the already existing stock of CO_2 in the atmosphere mainly due to developed country emissions (see, for example, Agarwal and Narain 1991; Neumayer 2000a). Since damage from CO_2 emissions plays a negligible role in bringing GS rates down below zero, I do not undertake sensitivity analyses for this correction term, however.

As concerns attribution of resource depletion, one could argue that the resources depleted in poor developing countries with high resource exploitation go to rich developed countries for their benefit and that therefore the rich countries are responsible if resource exploitation is unsustainable. Proops et al. (1999) have shown that if natural capital depreciation is attributed to the country of resource consumption, then not surprisingly the GS position of resource-exporting developing countries improves, whereas that of resource-importing developed countries is not so safely positive any longer. There are good arguments why resource exploitation should be attributed to the extracting country itself and not to the consuming country, however. This is because the purpose of resource accounting is to try to measure whether and by how much the natural capital stock of a country is depreciating. It simply does not matter who is 'responsible' or to 'blame' for its depreciation. Furthermore, even in terms of justice one could argue that a resource-rich country is endowed with an extra capital asset by nature. It is up to this country to make sustainable use of it. If it burns all resource rents in consumption instead of investing them into the human capital of its people or in manufactured capital, this is its own fault. It is the responsibility of each country to keep its own capital stock intact.

The countries included in the data set are grouped into regions as shown in Appendix 5, p. 207. Figure 5.1 shows the development of GS relative to GNI (gross national income) for regions over the period 1970 to 2004. The world as a whole, the OECD-countries as well as East Asia and South Asia never have negative GS rates. The highest rates are achieved in East Asia where they usually fluctuate between 10 per cent and 30 per cent. Global, OECD and South Asian GS rates are relatively constant at around 10 per cent. The Latin American and Caribbean region touches zero and slightly below only some time in the early 1980s. The problematic regions are Sub-Saharan Africa, whose GS rates hover around zero and are often slightly negative, and North Africa and the Middle East with GS rates that are negative throughout the whole period with few exceptions. (Gaps in the graphs are due to missing data.) At this level of regional aggregation, it becomes already clear that the regions with the greatest natural resource extraction are the most problematic ones. Indeed, if one looks at individual countries, those with major dependence on natural resource extraction are also the ones which often have negative GS rates. This holds true for such countries in regions other than Sub-Saharan Africa or North Africa and the Middle East as well. The main message from the GS computations is therefore that many developing countries that are dependent on resource exploitation are weakly unsustainable.

5.1.4.2 Competing methods for computing resource rents

Of particular interest is what drives the GS rates below net savings rates. Since net savings minus rents from natural resource depletion minus (negligible) damage from CO_2 emissions equals GS, I discuss in more detail how depreciation of natural capital due to resource extraction should be computed.

This question is controversially debated in the relevant literature (Hartwick 1977, 1990; Hartwick and Hageman 1993; El Serafy 1981, 1989, 1991; Vincent 1997; Santopietro 1998; Davis and Moore 2000). It does have a very simple answer, however, as long as one stays in the framework of a competitive inter-temporally efficient closed economy. In this framework natural capital depreciation is equal to total Hotelling (1931) rent

$$(P - MC) \cdot R \qquad (5.5)$$

where P is the resource price, MC is marginal cost and R is resource extraction. In the case of a renewable resource, R would simply be resource harvesting beyond natural regeneration. Note that equation (5.5) is in principle equivalent to the relevant term in equation (5.4), which is of course not surprising given that this equation is derived from such a model of a competitive inter-temporally efficient economy. The only difference is that the correction term accounting for the pollution effect of non-renewable resource extraction is not included. It is interesting to calculate the overestimation of resource rents due to neglecting pollution. For CO_2 emissions from oil and natural gas consumption the bias can be calculated as follows: each barrel of oil consists of approximately 0.13 tons of carbon (Poterba 1991, p. 75), each thousand cubic feet of natural gas of approximately 0.014 tons of carbon (Carbon Dioxide Information Analysis Center 1998). Taking the World Bank's estimate of US$20 for marginal social cost per tonne of carbon, $i_A \gamma F_R$ would be about US$2.6 per barrel of oil and US$0.32 per thousand cubic feet of natural gas. Hence the correction terms, although still rather small, are not negligible. If one used higher estimates for marginal social costs of CO_2 emissions, then taking the correction term for pollution into account would become more and more warranted.

One of the major difficulties of applying the theoretically correct equation (5.5) in reality is that data on marginal cost are frequently unavailable. Aver-

Genuine Savings rates in % of GNI

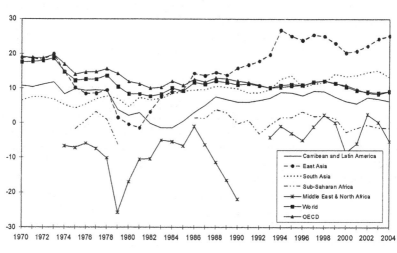

Source: Own computations from World Bank (2009a).

Figure 5.1 Genuine saving rates for regions

age cost (*AC*) are more easily available. The World Bank therefore replaces marginal cost with the more readily available average cost and calculates depreciation as follows

$$(P - AC) \cdot R \qquad (5.6)$$

Another problem is that real economies are not closed, but open. Theory requires to include a correction term for anticipated price changes. However, the Bank does not include such a correction term on either the resource exporter's or importer's side. The reason is presumably that the authors are unsure about the future development of resource prices, so that 'as a default "rule of thumb" for sustainability, simply investing current resource rents is likely to be the prudent course of action' (Atkinson and Hamilton 1996, p. 4) for both importers and exporters.

Resource discoveries do not enter (5.6). The Bank values discoveries at average discovery costs in accordance with the definition of GS in equation (5.4), except that the more readily available average costs are used as a proxy for marginal costs. Since 'exploration expenditures are treated as investment in standard national accounting' (World Bank 1997, p. 28) already anyway, there is no correction term for discoveries.

Two popular alternatives to equation (5.6) are what has become known as the El Serafy method (El Serafy 1981, 1989, 1991, 1993) and the method of Repetto et al. (Repetto et al. 1989, Repetto and Cruz 1991). The method of Repetto et al. calculates natural capital depreciation as follows

$$(P - AC) \cdot (R - D) \qquad (5.7)$$

where *D* is resource discoveries. Note that in this method, resource discoveries are valued at $P - AC$; that is, at net profits and that depreciation can be negative; that is, there will be appreciation if $D > R$ in the accounting period. This method can be derived from another specification of the dynamic optimisation model above: if the expenditure function for resource discoveries is modelled as depending positively on the resource stock *S* instead of depending on the stock of cumulated discoveries *X*, that is $g = g(D, S)$, resource discoveries would also be valued at the (modified) Hotelling rent in line with equation (5.7).[16] Hence, efficient resource pricing according to Hotelling's rule is assumed in the method of Repetto et al. as well. Also note that, strictly speaking, exploration expenditures should be subtracted from net savings if this method is used, in order to avoid partial double counting of resource discoveries.

The El Serafy method values natural capital depreciation as

$$(P - AC) \cdot R \cdot \left[\frac{1}{(1+r)^{n+1}} \right] \tag{5.8}$$

where r is the discount rate and n is the static reserves to production ratio, that is, is the number of years the remaining resource stock would last if production were the same each year as in the current year. If $r > 0$ and $n > 0$, then (5.8) will produce a smaller deduction term for resource depletion than (5.6).

The valuation term in (5.8) is also called the 'user cost' of resource depletion since it indicates the share of resource receipts that should be considered as capital depreciation. Note that no explicit correction term for resource discoveries is needed in this method since discoveries enter (5.8) via changing n and it is computed anew for each year.

The El Serafy method is derived from the following reasoning: receipts from non-renewable resource extraction should not fully count as what El Serafy calls 'sustainable income' in the sense of Hicks (1946) because resource extraction leads to a lowering of the resource stock and thus brings with it an element of depreciation of the resource capital stock.[17] While the receipts from the resource stock will end at some finite time, 'sustainable income' by definition must last for ever. Hence, 'sustainable income' is that part of resource receipts which if received infinitely would have a present-value just equal to the present-value of the finite stream of resource receipts over the life time of the resource.

Define resource receipts RC as:

$$RC \equiv (P - AC) \cdot R \tag{5.9}$$

The present-value of resource receipts RC at the constant discount rate r over the expected life-time n of the resource stock is equal to:

$$\sum_{i=0}^{n} \frac{RC}{(1+r)^i} = \frac{RC \left[1 - \dfrac{1}{(1+r)^{n+1}} \right]}{1 - \dfrac{1}{1+r}} \tag{5.10}$$

The present-value of an infinite stream of 'sustainable income' SI is

$$\sum_{i=0}^{\infty} \frac{SI}{(1+r)^i} = \frac{SI(1+r)}{r} = \frac{SI}{1 - \dfrac{1}{1+r}} \qquad (5.11)$$

Setting (5.10) and (5.11) equal and rearranging expresses SI as a fraction of RC:[18]

$$SI = RC\left[1 - \frac{1}{(1+r)^{n+1}}\right] \qquad (5.12)$$

The correction term, representing user cost or the depreciation of the resource stock, would thus be

$$(RC - SI) = RC\left[\frac{1}{(1+r)^{n+1}}\right] = (P - AC)\cdot R\left[\frac{1}{(1+r)^{n+1}}\right] \qquad (5.13)$$

which is the valuation term in (5.8). The El Serafy method does not presume efficient resource pricing — resource rent growing at the rate of interest according to Hotelling's rule — because it is not dependent on an optimisation model. It is an 'ex post approach, capable of accounting for any entrepreneurial decisions regarding extraction' (El Serafy 1997, p. 222). As a consequence future resource receipts have to be discounted and the El Serafy method requires the selection of a discount rate r. If either the life-time of the resource asset, n, or the discount rate, r, are quite large, the necessary correction term will consequently be rather small (see equation (5.13)). Only in the limit where the discount rate is set to zero will both methods produce the same numbers for resource depletion. This can easily be verified by setting $r = 0$ in (5.13). The reason is that in this limiting case efficient resource pricing is implicitly assumed. Also note that depreciation can never be negative.

Both the El Serafy method and the method of Repetto et al. have been widely used in practice. Presumably the best-known early attempts to measure the value of changes in a nation's resource stock is the World Resources Institute's studies on Indonesia (Repetto et al. 1989) and Costa Rica (Repetto and Cruz 1991) using the method of Repetto et al. Similar studies have been undertaken — using both methods — for Brazil (Serôa da Motta and Young 1995; Serôa da Motta and May 1996); Mexico (Van Tongeren et al. 1993); Papua New Guinea (Bartelmus, Lutz and Schweinfest 1993) and the United Kingdom (Bryant and Cook 1992).

Application of the method of Repetto et al. has produced quite large and volatile results, being very sensitive to new resource discoveries (see Repetto et al. 1989; Repetto and Cruz 1991; Serôa da Motta and May 1996).[19] The El Serafy method, on the other hand, produces less volatility because first it values resource discoveries only indirectly in changing the parameter n and, more importantly, it counts only parts of the total net receipts to be subtracted from net savings whereas the method of Repetto et al. subtracts the total net receipts of resource depletion from net savings.

The method of Repetto et al. also produces more volatility than the World Bank's method. This is because Repetto et al. value resource discoveries at full Hotelling rent, instead of valuing these at marginal or average discovery cost. If resource discoveries were valued at average discovery costs instead, then the method of Repetto et al. would become the same as the one of the World Bank because exploration expenditures are already included in the traditional natural accounts (World Bank 1997, p. 28).

Comparing the World Bank method with the method of Repetto et al., the latter seems to lack direct intuitive appeal. There is no good reason for assuming, as the method of Repetto et al. does, that exploration costs depend on the total stock of a resource. Conversely, it makes much sense to assume that resource discovery costs depend on the stock of past discoveries as the World Bank's method does, because later discoveries should be more expensive than earlier ones if the easy-to-find reserves are discovered first — which one would expect in a dynamic optimisation framework. On the other hand, the two methods are obviously linked since resource discoveries both increase the stock of past discoveries and the resource stock. Overall I would say that on theoretical grounds there are more good reasons in favour of the World Bank's method.

Comparing the World Bank method with the El Serafy method, for a number of reasons it might be better to use the latter method in real-world computations of natural capital depreciation. First, Hartwick and Hageman (1993) show that the El Serafy method can be understood as an approximation to (5.5), which to repeat is the theoretically correct depreciation in a framework of a competitive inter-temporally efficient economy. Its main advantage over the World Bank method in (5.6) is that the El Serafy method can use average cost without apology as it does not depend on marginal cost. The World Bank method, on the other hand, needs to replace marginal cost with average cost as marginal cost is not readily available. Due to the re-placement of marginal with average cost it can also merely represent an approximation to the theoretically correct method. Which of the two methods creates the greater bias is not generally clear. Under certain assumptions about the resource extraction cost function, the two methods can be shown to be two polar cases of the true depreciation value and the bias depends on the elasticity of the marginal cost curve with respect to the quantity extracted (Vincent 1997; Serôa da Motta and Ferraz do Amaral 2000). The upshot of this is that even within a framework of a competitive inter-temporally efficient economy the El Serafy method can be a better approximation to depreciation of natural capital than the World Bank method.

Second, the true appeal of the El Serafy method stems from the fact that it does not depend on the assumption of efficient resource pricing — resource rent growing at the rate of interest according to Hotelling's (1931) rule — because it is not dependent on an optimisation model. In other words, it does not depend on the assumption of a competitive economy developing along the inter-temporally efficient path. The World Bank's method, on the other hand, depends on efficient resource pricing. Now, none of the data the Bank uses are guaranteed to be optimal and the Bank does not use any shadow values other than for damage from CO_2. Hence, for consistency reasons it might be better to use a method such as the El Serafy method, which does not depend on efficient resource pricing either. Interestingly, in Atkinson et al. (1997, pp. 60f) the same authors on whose work the World Bank is built upon admit that since 'there is little evidence for efficient pricing of resources in the ground', it 'may be advisable to value resource depletion as a user cost with a non-zero discount rate' according to the El Serafy method.

Third, the World Bank method leads to implausible results for many resource-dependent countries. Take Saudi Arabia as an example. Figure 5.2 plots the GS rate of Saudi Arabia over the period 1970 to 1999, once as com-

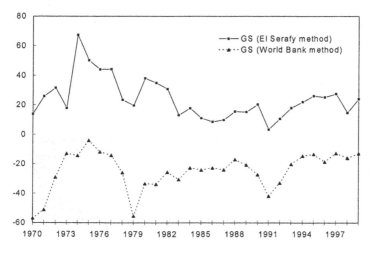

Sources: Own computations from World Bank (2002) and BP (various years).

Figure 5.2 Sensitivity analysis for GS rates of Saudi Arabia

puted with the World Bank method and once with the El Serafy method using a discount rate of four per cent. The message could not be more different: Saudi Arabia is hugely unsustainable if one applies the World Bank method, but has no apparent problems with WS if the El Serafy method is employed. Application of the World Bank method leads to results that are hard to believe. World Bank (2003) estimates the total natural capital wealth of Saudi Arabia in 1994 at about 807 billion US$ as a low estimate and 2.3 trillion US$ as a high estimate. This contrasts with a total value of natural capital depreciation of Saudi Arabia over the period 1970–99 estimated at 1.5 trillion US$. To be fair, it has to be said that the way the World Bank estimates a country's natural capital stock itself is methodologically different from the way it estimates the depreciation of it (see World Bank 1997, pp. 18f and 37f). The natural capital stock is underestimated relative to its depreciation. Still, the World Bank method paints a picture of Saudi Arabia that is hard to believe. The El Serafy method, on the other hand, takes into account the country's enormous oil and natural gas reserves in computing natural capital depreciation and thereby comes to an entirely different conclusion about the weak sustainability of the Saudi Arabian economy. As El Serafy (2001, p. 205) stresses, 'there should clearly be a fundamental difference for national accounting between extracting a given volume out of a large or a small stock. Extracting the same volume amounting to 5 per cent of the stock has different implications for income and sustainability from extracting the same quantity if it amounts to 50 per cent of the stock.'

Of course, the El Serafy method is not without problems either. To start with, one needs to choose a discount rate and it is far from clear what the right discount rate should be. A prudent rule would be to choose a rate of discount that approximates the real rate of return to investing the receipts from resource extraction into other forms of capital. Also, one needs to estimate n, the remaining life time of the resource stock. Given uncertainty about the future, it is not clear what n should be. A simple rule of thumb is to set n equal to the static reserves to production ratio, which becomes updated in every period of accounting as information about the level of extraction and the stock of remaining reserves changes. Since estimates of reserve stocks are sometimes difficult to establish for some resources in some countries, the exact value for n can be contentious and a prudent accountant should use a lower bound estimate. For example, only reserves, which can be economically exploited at current technology, should be included. Moreover, very large values of n should probably be discounted because it is highly uncertain whether the resource in question will still be of economic use over the long run.

The change in results with regards to GS once the El Serafy method is employed is not restricted to Saudi Arabia. The first edition of this book (see pp. 169–177 in Neumayer 1999a) as well as Neumayer (2000b) contain a detailed analysis showing that for most countries, particularly those with substantial reserves, which were detected as weakly unsustainable according to the World Bank method, are no longer weakly unsustainable once the El Serafy method is used. Hamilton (2000, p. 5) admits that the World Bank method 'arguably over-estimates the value of resource depletion, particularly for countries having large reserves to production ratios'. But the GS figures are published by the Bank without any such qualification. On the other hand, using the El Serafy method can lead to upward bias the GS figures, as Hamilton and Ruta (2009) correctly show. At the end of the day, one cannot know with much confidence whether many countries dependent on natural resource exploitation are weakly unsustainable or not. This represents a huge set-back to the measurement of weak sustainability.

5.1.4.4   Other problematic aspects

What are further problematic aspects of the way in which World Bank (2009a) computes GS figures? It is important to further improve the quality of data used for the computations. Sometimes the World Bank has to employ heroic assumptions to arrive at its numbers (see Kunte et al. 1998). Also, the coverage of renewable resources and pollutants needs to be extended if enough data of sufficient quality can be established. Forests are an important renewable resource, but not the only one. If possible, resources like water, soil, wetlands, fish and, more generally, biodiversity should be included. Equally, carbon dioxide emissions and, added more recently for mainly developed countries, particular matter are but two pollutants. Again, if possible, pollutants such as sulphur oxides, nitrogen oxides and fecal coliforms should be included. That the more developed countries by and large do not become identified as potentially unsustainable is for the main part to be explained by their usually quite high net savings rates, but is to a smaller extent also due to the fact that only two pollutants are taken into account so far (compare Atkinson et al. 1997, pp. 85ff). However, even comprehensive accounting for pollution is very unlikely to drive down GS rates in developed countries below zero.

As a final critique, it is not entirely clear what specific policies should be undertaken following the detection of negative GS rates. There are many ways to increase GS. The government could intervene to increase net investment into man-made capital via lowering taxation of man-made capital or reducing government expenditures, for example; it could reduce resource extraction via taxing resource consumption; it could foster resource exploration via subsidising exploration activities; it could lower the stock of pollution via increasing pollution abatement; or it could step up investment in human capital.

5.2   INDEX OF SUSTAINABLE ECONOMIC WELFARE (ISEW) AND GENUINE PROGRESS INDICATOR (GPI)

Independently of the GS, a number of scholars have developed the so-called Index of Sustainable Economic Welfare (ISEW), sometimes also known under the name Genuine Progress Indicator (GPI), which is a competing indicator of GS. The ISEW/GPI is intended to eventually replace a country's gross national product (GNP) or gross domestic product (GDP).[20] ISEWs/GPIs have been developed out of the concern that GNP/GDP is not an adequate indicator for either current welfare or sustainability. From this perspective GNP/GDP is flawed because, among other things, it does not take into account (a) the value of household labour, (b) the welfare effects of income inequality, (c) the effects of environmental degradation on welfare and sustainability and (d) considers 'defensive expenditures' wrongly as contributions to welfare.

The ISEW/GPI stands in a long tradition and indeed partly builds upon earlier attempts to provide a more comprehensive indicator of welfare and to incorporate environmental and/or sustainability aspects into such an indicator — see, for example, Nordhaus and Tobin's (1972) *Measure of Economic Welfare* (MEW), Zolotas' (1981) *Economic Aspects of Welfare* (EAW) and Eisner's (1990) *The Total Incomes System of Accounts* (TISA). The MEW and the EAW take some environmental aspects into account. The MEW adjusts the welfare measure for 'disamenities of urban life' such as 'pollution, litter, congestion, noise' based on hedonic valuation studies.[21] The EAW subtracts air pollution damage costs together with half of the estimated control costs for air and water pollution and the full control costs for solid wastes from the welfare measure. It also deducts the costs of resource depletion. The TISA, on the other hand, does not include any environmental aspects into its measurement, but like the MEW and the EAW seeks to broaden the concept of capital and investment accounted for. For an overview, see Eisner (1988, 1990).

Computation of an ISEW usually starts from the value of personal consumption expenditures which is a sub-component of GNP/GDP. Consumption expenditures are weighted with an index of 'distributional inequality' of income (usually a modified Gini coefficient). Then, certain welfare-relevant contributions are added and certain welfare-relevant losses are subtracted. As an example, take the 2006 GPI for the US as an example. Table 5.1 lists the items that are added to or subtracted from the weighted personal consumption expenditures to arrive at the GPI.

The policy recommendation is to ensure that the ISEW/GPI is not decreasing. One can interpret the ISEW/GPI loosely as a kind of extended or greened

Net National Product (gNNP), which is defined as comprehensive consumption minus GS, where comprehensive means that all utility-relevant items are included in consumption, not just consumption of material goods. It follows that the ISEW/GPI needs to measure more than is required for GS. In addition, the ISEW/GPI covers more utility-relevant factors than are included in our dynamic optimisation model in Section 5.1.2, p. 127, for example, income inequality and the welfare derived from household work. The theoretical sustainability foundation of the ISEW/GPI then follows from the fact that under certain assumptions preventing gNNP from falling is equivalent to preventing GS from becoming negative (Pezzey and Toman 2002a, p. 184; Asheim 2003). See also Lawn (2003) who argues for a theoretical interpretation of ISEW/GPI along the lines of Fisher's (1906) concept of capital and 'psychic income', which is an alternative to Hicks (1946), whose conception of capital and income is usually embraced by sustainability theorists.[22]

Adjustments to weighted personal consumption expenditures, US GPI of 2006

Value of housework and parenting (+)
Value of higher education (+)
Value of volunteer work (+)
Services of consumer durables (+)
Services of highways (+)
Costs of crime (-)
Loss of leisure time (-)
Costs of underemployment (-)
Costs of consumer durables (-)
Cost of commuting (-)
Cost of household pollution abatement (-)
Cost of auto accidents (-)
Cost of water pollution (-)
Cost of air pollution (-)
Cost of noise pollution (-)
Loss of wetlands (-)
Loss of farmland (-)
Loss of primary forests (-)
Resource depletion (-)
Carbon dioxide emissions damage (-)
Cost of ozone depletion (-)
Net capital investment (+/-)
Net foreign borrowing (+/-)

In this section, I shall first of all give a short review of existing ISEW studies. I then discuss methodological problems. I show that their conclusions are highly dependent on certain key and rather problematic assumptions about the weighting of income distribution and the valuing of the depletion of non-renewable resources as well as methodological errors in the computation of long-term environmental damage.

5.2.1   A Review of ISEW and GPI Studies

ISEW/GPI or related studies have been undertaken for, among others, Austria (Stockhammer et al. 1997), Australia (Hamilton 1999; Hamilton and Denniss 2000; Lawn 2008),[23] Belgium (Bleys 2008), Cambodia (Chhinh and Lawn 2007), Chile (Castañeda 1999) China (Lawn 2008), India (Lawn 2008), Germany (Diefenbacher 1994), Israel (Kot 2008), Italy (Guenno and Tiezzi 1998), Japan (Lawn 2008), the Netherlands (Rosenberg, Oegema and Bovy 1995; Bleys 2007), New Zealand (Lawn 2008), Scotland (Moffatt and Wilson 1994), Sweden (Jackson and Stymne 1996), Thailand (Clarke and Islam 2005; Lawn 2008), the US (Daly and Cobb 1989; Cobb and Cobb 1994; Redefining Progress 1999, 2001, 2006), the United Kingdom (Jackson and Marks 1994; updated in Jackson et al. 1997), and Vietnam (Lawn 2008). There also exist some studies for the sub-national level (see, for example, Pulselli et al. 2006). What these studies usually demonstrate is that the ISEW or GPI of a country has been growing much more slowly since 1950 than its GNP/GDP and indeed has either not grown any further or has even fallen since the early 1980s or even 1970s. This result holds true for virtually every country for which a study of ISEW or GPI has been undertaken so far. As an explanation for this widening gap between ISEW or GPI on the one hand and GNP or GDP on the other, Max-Neef (1995, p. 117) has put forward the so-called 'threshold hypothesis': 'for every society there seems to be a period in which economic growth (as conventionally measured) brings about an improvement in the quality of life, but only up to a point — the threshold point — beyond which, if there is more economic growth, quality of life may begin to deteriorate'. This 'threshold hypothesis' is referred to in almost every study of ISEW or GPI and Max-Neef (1995, p. 117) himself regarded the evidence from these studies 'a fine illustration of the Threshold Hypothesis'.

Figure 5.3 provides an example of the so-called threshold effect for the United States. It shows the development of the US GPI per capita in comparison to GDP per capita from 1950 to 2004 in constant US$ of 2000, both indexed to 100 in 1950, at the start of the period, to allow an easy comparison of growth performance. Whilst in the beginning the two graphs roughly move in parallel with each other, from around the 1970s there is an increasing di-

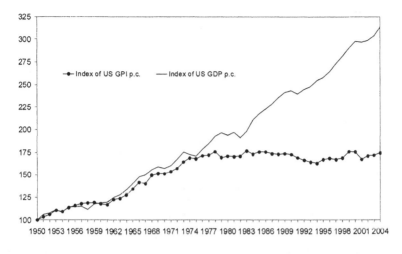

Source: Redefining Progress (2006).

Figure 5.3 United States GDP versus GPI per capita

vergence. Whereas GDP is still increasing, the GPI is no longer increasing. This picture is typical for practically all ISEW or GPI studies. For example, for Germany, Diefenbacher (1994, p. 228) finds after 1980 'ongoing growth of the GNP, but a rather sharp decline of the ISEW'. Also, typically two to three items are largely responsible for causing this increasing divergence between GNP/GDP and ISEW/GPI: resource depletion, long-term environmental damage and, less importantly, a more unequal income distribution.

Take the UK as another example. Jackson and Marks (1994, p. 28) in a pilot study for the UK found that over the period 1950 to 1990 'there is virtually no overall growth' and the 'per capita ISEW in 1990 is just 3 per cent higher than it was in 1950'. This dismal performance is mainly due to the 1980s for which Jackson and Marks (ibid., p. 29) compute a *decline* in ISEW per capita of 4.7 per cent per annum! They cite rising income inequality and environmental degradation as major reasons for this dramatic decline in the last decade of their period of analysis (p. 32).

In the updated study, Jackson et al. (1997), the period up until 1996 is covered. The methodology for the computation of the revised index has somewhat changed from Jackson and Marks (1994). The two main changes are as follows:

- Income inequality is measured via computing a so-called 'Atkinson income' instead of using a modified Gini coefficient. The Atkinson income indicates 'the proportion of the present total income that would be required to achieve the same level of social welfare as at present if incomes were equally distributed' (Atkinson 1983, p. 57) and it varies according to a parameter for aversion to inequality that researchers need to choose. In varying an explicit parameter for aversion to inequality in income distribution, the valuation of income inequality is undertaken explicitly rather than implicitly as is the case with the Gini coefficient.

• Following the methodology of Cobb and Cobb (1994), Jackson and Marks (1994, p. 24) computed accumulating long-term environmental damage by valuing each tonne of coal equivalent of non-renewable fuels consumed in the UK with a constant, rather arbitrary rate of £3.73 (1985 pounds sterling). Jackson et al. (1997) instead use explicit cost estimates for long-term environmental damage from climate change. Starting from an estimate of about £11 marginal costs per tonne of carbon emitted in 1990, they compute the costs per tonne of carbon in retrospect and up to 1996 under the assumption that marginal social costs of carbon emission rise over time. As Cobb and Cobb (1994) did and almost all ISEW/GPI studies do, Jackson et al. (1997) let the costs from long-term damage *accumulate* over time. I will argue that this is incorrect.

In spite of these changes in methodology, Jackson et al. (1997) come to the same basic conclusions as Jackson and Marks (1994). Mayo, MacGillivray and McLaren (1997, p. 1), the short version of Jackson et al. (1997), observe that 'since 1980, according to the ISEW, real well-being has actually fallen by over 20 per cent'. As key reasons for this decline they cite 'environmental degradation (in particular depletion of non-renewable resources and long-term environmental damage) and income inequality' (ibid., p. 5). The decline in welfare shown by the updated ISEW is slightly smaller than the one detected by the pilot ISEW of Jackson and Marks (1994). 'The principal reason for this has been the choice of a relatively low aversion to income inequality' (Jackson et al. 1997, p. 34).

5.2.2   Methodological Problems

I concentrate here on what I regard as the most important methodological problems. For a discussion of other problems of a methodological and conceptual nature, see, for example, Atkinson (1995), Neumayer (1999c, 2000b) and Ziegler (2007). I first discuss defensive expenditures and then have a closer look at the three main determinants of the decline in the ISEWs, namely environmental degradation, resource depletion and more unequal distribution of incomes.

5.2.2.1 Defensive expenditures

The ISEW/GPI can be criticised for being arbitrary in the components it includes or excludes, implicitly or explicitly, as contributors to welfare. One prominent item, defensive expenditures, provides a case in point. The concept of defensive expenditures is dubious and elusive since it is rather arbitrary what should count as defensive (Jacobs 1991, pp. 228–32). Early ISEW/GPI studies often excluded 50 per cent of expenditures for education because their authors believed that education 'contributes little to productivity'. This is clearly at odds with the importance attached by most economists to human capital and education. However, more relevant to this section here is that Cobb and Cobb (1994, p. 54) did not want to count education as consumption either since

> most schooling appears to be defensive. In other words, people attend school because others are in school and the failure to attend would mean falling behind in the competition for diplomas or degrees that confer higher incomes on their recipients.

Proponents of ISEW/GPI have declared many other expenditures as 'defensive', that is, as merely protecting individuals against a decline of welfare caused by some other socio-economic activitiy. For example, Cobb and Cobb (1994) regarded 50 per cent of health expenditures as defensive and therefore not adding to welfare. The problem is that following this line of argument, one could classify many if not most expenditure items as defensive in character. For example, if health expenditures are defensive expenditures against illness, why should food and drinking expenditures not count as defensive expenditures against hunger and thirst? Are holiday and entertainment expenditures to be considered defensive expenditures against boredom? Should they all be subtracted from consumption expenditures?

Daly and Cobb (1989, p. 78) defend their concept of subtracting defensive costs in saying that '"defensive" means a defense against the unwanted side effects of other production, not a defense against normal baseline environmental conditions of cold, rain and so on'. But even accepting Daly and Costanza's definition, one could argue that at least part of food, drink, entertainment and holiday expenditures are caused by the stressful, exhausting and boring modes of modern production that make these expenditures necessary as a defence against their unwanted side effects. As the revised 'System of National Accounts' rightly retorts: 'Pushed to its logical conclusion, scarcely any consumption improves welfare in this line of argument.' (Commission of the European Communities–Eurostat et al. 1993, p. 14).

Responding to criticism, some of the more recent ISEW/GPI studies no longer subtract the most controversial of the so-called defensive expenditures, such as education expenditures – see, for example, Genuine Progress (2006). This is welcome news, but does not solve the problem that it is very hard to tell what should count as defensive expenditures and thus be subtracted from a true measure of welfare.

5.2.2.2 Income inequality

As concerns income inequality, studies differ in the way they value this term. Jackson et al. (1997) use an index, which requires the choice of a parameter representing society's aversion to inequality. Most other studies use an index, mostly the Gini coefficient, which does not offer such a choice of inequality aversion parameter. Jackson et al. use the so-called Atkinson index (Atkinson 1970), which is defined as:

$$1 - \exp\left[\sum \left(Y_i / \bar{Y}\right)^{1/(1-\varepsilon)} f_i\right]^{1/(1-\varepsilon)} \tag{5.14}$$

where Y_i denotes the income of all individuals in the ith income group (n groups altogether), f_i denotes the proportion of the population with incomes in the ith range and $\bar{Y}$ denotes the mean income. The extreme boundary cases are $\varepsilon = 0$, which implies no aversion to inequality whatsoever, and $\varepsilon = \infty$, which implies extreme aversion to income inequality in only taking account of transfers to the very lowest income group.

The great advantage of this approach is that in choosing ε, the researcher makes explicit his or her implicit assumptions on society's aversion to income inequality. Alternatively, the researcher can try to estimate ε from revealed preference studies of consumer behaviour. Pearce and Ulph (1998), for example, provide an estimate of ε for the UK from a survey of the empirical literature with a lower bound of 0.7, an upper bound of 1.5 and a best estimate of 0.8.

If instead, the Gini coefficient is used, then usually one year is set as the base year for the index and by choosing this base year researchers also make an assumptions about the degree of society's aversion to income inequality, but it is an implicit assumption that is usually not clearly communicated to readers. In the 2006 edition of the US GPI, for example, which uses the Gini coefficient, 1968 is set at 100, because in this year 'the Gini index was at its lowest', and the income distribution index 'simply measures the relative change in the Gini index' (Redefining Progress 2006, p. 14). The inequality adjusted consumption expenditures are reached via dividing unadjusted expenditures by this index and multiplying by 100. This approach is very *ad hoc* and the researcher's underlying implicit assumptions about society's aversion to income inequality are not explicated. With the Atkinson index, on the other hand, the researcher is forced to explicate his or her implicit assumptions regarding society's aversion to income inequality, which represents an advantage. The researcher can even attempt to minimise the influence of his or her own value judgements in trying to estimate society's revealed aversion to income inequality.

A more fundamental critique is that the valuation of the distribution of income in a measure of welfare fails to command general agreement. Mishan (1994, p. 172) notes that 'all efforts to adjust the welfare index to accommodate changes in distribution ... must be regarded with misgivings. They are either arbitrary or politically biased and are, therefore, invariably a focus of attack.' Of course, not undertaking any explicit valuation is tantamount to assuming implicitly that the marginal utility of income is constant and the same for the rich and the poor alike — an assumption, which is admittedly no less arbitrary than the one embraced by the proponents of an ISEW/GPI.

5.2.2.3 Long-term environmental damage

As concerns the valuation of long-term environmental damage, or the costs of climate change as this item is sometimes called, the fundamental question is whether this value should accumulate over time or not. With few exceptions (see, for example, Hamilton and Denniss 2000), the authors of ISEW/GPI studies have opted for accumulation. It is the objective of this section to show that accumulation is incorrect.

Most studies follow the approach taken by Daly and Cobb (1989) and Cobb and Cobb (1994). They value each barrel of oil equivalent of annual non-renewable energy resource consumption at 0.50\$ in 1972 dollars. This value is deducted from the ISEW/GPI in this year, but also in all following years. Similarly, in any given year not only the current year's value is deducted, but the values from all past years as well. Cobb and Cobb (1994, p. 74) provide as justification for this accumulation approach that they 'imagined that a tax or rent of \$0.50 per barrel-equivalent had been levied on all non-renewable energy consumed during that period and set aside to accumulate in a non-interest-bearing account ... That account might be thought of as a fund available to compensate future generations for the long-term damage caused by the use of fossil fuels and atomic energy.'

Jackson et al. (1997, p. 23) realise in their computation of the UK ISEW, that 'the major problem with this approach ... is the arbitrary way in which a charge is calculated'. Instead they value each tonne of greenhouse gas emissions with its marginal social cost, which they correctly define as reflecting 'the total (discounted) value of all the future damage arising from that tonne of emissions'. Strangely, however, despite using marginal social cost estimates, they still follow Cobb and Cobb's (1994) lead in letting this damage accumulate over time. Stockhammer et al. (1997) similarly compute marginal social damage costs for the Austrian ISEW — and let the estimated damage accumulate over time. Redefining Progress (2006) does the same for the US GPI.

Accumulation is incorrect. This is easiest to see with studies that value emissions at marginal social cost. In valuing each tonne of emissions with its marginal social cost, the total future damage of this tonne of emissions is already valued, as this is the very definition of marginal social cost. To let this value accumulate over time is self-contradictory and therefore simply wrong as it leads to multiple counting of the total future damage. Jackson et al. (1997) value each tonne of carbon with a marginal social cost of £11.4 in 1990 prices. With accumulation, the present value damage caused by one tonne of carbon is simply infinite without discounting or £11.4/r with discounting, where r is the discount rate. With a discount rate of, say, 5 per cent per annum, the present value damage per tonne of carbon is £228. This present value damage per tonne of carbon of £228 would be nothing else but the marginal social cost per tonne of carbon, which contradicts Jackson et al.'s (1997) earlier assumption of a marginal social cost of £11.4.

That accumulation is incorrect is not as straightforward to show with Cobb and Cobb's (1994) approach, as they do not base their valuation on marginal social costs. Instead, as mentioned, they justify valuing long-term environmental damage from fossil fuel consumption by $0.50 per barrel of oil equivalent with the idea that this would represent the money to be set aside in order to compensate future generations for long-term environmental damage. Lawn (2005: 205) similarly argues that the ISEW/GPI measures 'the sustainable economic welfare being experienced by a nation's citizens in that year' and that 'the impact on the sustainable economic welfare in a given year depends very much on what has happened in the past'. Yet, on such reasoning it would have been wrong to deduct any damage from carbon emissions for most of the period covered by any existing ISEW/GPI study as arguably there has not been much damage that can be linked to climate change in the past decades and even now it is controversial whether any damage can *already* be attributed to climate change. In any case, as before accumulation leads to multiple counting here as well. This is because with accumulation money for the damage caused by each unit of emissions is set aside not only in the year of emission, but for each subsequent year as well, with no limit. Each ton of carbon emitted would thus be assumed to cause an infinite damage, which is clearly an absurdity.

Both Jackson et al. (1997) and Redefining Progress (2006) let the marginal social damage increase over time. This is correct as the marginal social cost per tonne of emitted carbon is a positive function of the accumulated stock of carbon resident in the atmosphere, which has been increasing over time. In other words, the higher the historically accumulated carbon concentration in the atmosphere, the higher the social damage caused by each additional unit of emitted carbon. Climate change is indeed a problem of pollution stock, not of pollution flows, and the marginal social cost increases with the already accumulated stock of carbon in the atmosphere. However, to let the annual damage from carbon emissions accumulate year after year is a clear methodological error and it is very unfortunate that most authors of ISEW/GPI studies continue committing this mistake, despite being aware of the criticism (Redefining Progress 2006). Neumayer (2000b) has shown that if long-term damage from climate change is not assumed to accumulate, then this item no longer contributes to a 'threshold effect', unless the marginal social cost of carbon emissions is assumed to increase strongly over time.

5.2.2.4 Resource depletion

With regards to resource depletion, studies differ in that some use the resource rent method, whereas others use the replacement cost method. Those using the resource rent method, such as Daly and Cobb (1989), Stockhammer et al. (1997), Diefenbacher (1994) and Guenno and Tiezzi (1998) deduct total resource rents from consumption expenditures in the same way that the World Bank computes depreciation of the natural capital stock for its GS rates (see equation (5.8)). As shown in the discussion of GS previously, there are good reasons in this case to employ the El Serafy method instead, which leads to lower estimates of the true depreciation of natural capital caused by resource exploitation.

Cobb and Cobb (1994) were the first to use the replacement cost method instead. Each barrel of oil equivalent was valued at a replacement cost which was assumed to escalate by 3 per cent per annum between 1950 and 1990 and was anchored around an assumed cost of 75$ in 1988. Castañeda (1999), Rosenberg, Oegema and Bovy (1995), Moffatt and Wilson (1994), Jackson and Stymne (1996), Jackson et al. (1997), Hamilton and Denniss (2000) and Redefining Progress (1999, 2001, 2006) have all followed Cobb and Cobb's example with slight modifications, but Bleys (2008) has accepted the criticism put forward in Neumayer (2000b) and abandoned the escalation factor.

It is already questionable to assume that all non-renewable energy resource consumption needs to be replaced fully by renewable resources given that there are still huge reserves of non-renewable resources available for many years to come — see Section 4.4, p. 114. I will concentrate on the 3 per cent escalation factor, however, which clearly gives rise to a threshold effect if resource consumption is not falling and GNP or GDP is not rising too much. As a rationale for this assumption of constantly increasing replacement costs, Cobb and Cobb (1994, p. 267) refer to the costs per foot of oil drilling which they report to have increased by about 6 per cent per annum during the period of high oil prices in the 1970s, which triggered the exploration and drilling of more difficult to exploit oil fields. They reason that 'when the limits of a resource are being reached, the cost of extracting the next unit is more costly than the previous unit' and that 'this principle presumably applies also to renewable fuels, though not as dramatically as to oil and gas', which is why the escalation factor is assumed to be 3 per cent instead of 6 per cent.

Yet, such reasoning is likely to be erroneous. Costs for renewable energy alternatives to non-renewable energy are currently high because the technology is still in the early stages of development, but costs will fall over time as technology improves. Instead of assuming replacement costs to escalate by 3 per cent per year, it might therefore be more appropriate to assume that replacement costs are falling over time.[24] Neumayer (2000b) has shown that if replacement costs are not assumed to escalate, then depletion of energy resources no longer contributes to a 'threshold effect'.

As an example of the severe sensitivity of results with respect to changing the methodology for computing resource depletion and long-term environmental damage, let us have a look at the case of the US again. Figure 5.4 shows the development of GDP per capita, the original GPI per capita, as well as a corrected GPI per capita, all indexed with base year 1950. As seen already in Figure 5.3, there is a widening gap apparent between GDP and the GPI starting from the 1970. If, however, the costs of replacing resource depletion are no longer escalated and long-term environmental damage is not accumulated, then the new, corrected GPI rises in line with or even faster than GDP over the entire time period. Crucially, there is no longer any evidence for the 'threshold effect'. Correcting two problematic methodological assumptions thus completely changes the picture.

This conclusion holds true for countries other than the US as well (Neumayer 2000b). With escalation of the resource replacement costs and the accumulation of long-term environmental damage it is difficult to see how any country could escape the 'threshold effect'. But once these two problematic assumptions are corrected for, the effect no longer holds. The 'threshold effect' is therefore built into the standard ISEW/GPI methodology and not surprisingly these ISEW or GPI studies then seemingly demonstrate this effect.

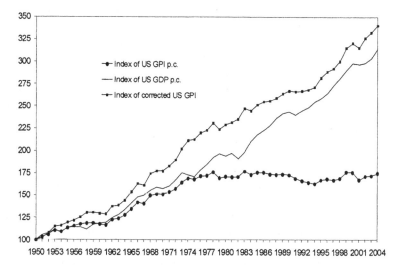

Sources: Redefining progress (2006) and corrections.
Note: 'Corrected' means GPI without 3 per cent escalation factor for resource depletion and without accumulation of carbon dioxide damage (1950 = 100).

Figure 5.4 Index of GDP, GPI and corrected GPI for the United States

5.3 CONCLUSION

Can weak sustainability be measured? Theoretical analysis has come quite a long way now in clarifying the correct adjustments to arrive at a theoretically correct indicator of WS, namely genuine savings (GS). In Section 5.1, it was shown how GS can be derived from a dynamic optimisation model and the necessary adjustments for the open-economy case were discussed. Several reasons have been put forward, however, that render practical estimations of GS and its proper interpretation problematic. A few of these problems have been highlighted in critically assessing the World Bank's (2009a) measurement of GS in a large sample of countries.

Whether reliable indicators of WS are possible in practice is a contested matter. Some clearly reject this possibility, for example Hueting (1991), Common (1993), Faucheux, Muir and O'Connor (1997) and Ekins and Simon (1999, 2001). Others, among them for obvious reasons the main proponents of a GS measure, clearly do believe that GS provides information that is policy relevant and should guide policy decisions. Pearce, Hamilton and

Atkinson (1996, p. 99), for example, state that 'sustainable development can be more than a vague commitment on the part of governments and instead become a measurable concept with wide-ranging policy implications'.

The analysis in this chapter suggests the conclusion that the GS estimates have to be treated with great care and with much caution in interpretation. First, GS cannot be a positive indicator of sustainability, just a negative indicator of unsustainability. Persistently negative rates of GS by and large indicate unsustainability, but positive GS rates do *not* indicate sustainability. In other words, a country that exhibits positive GS rates might well be weakly unsustainable. The claim that 'under most calculations, given the saving rates of all but the lowest-saving countries in the world, most countries now pass this test of sustainability' (IPCC 1996, p. 140) is incorrect as it wrongly suggests that positive GS rates imply weak sustainability.

Second, the World Bank (2009a) data suggest that many Sub-Saharan and North African and Middle East as well as some countries from other regions are weakly unsustainable. The analysis in this chapter has shown that this conclusion depends crucially on the specific method the World Bank uses to compute resource rents. In calculating resource rents with this method the Bank applies an inconsistent methodology; on the one hand, its method for resource accounting assumes efficient resource pricing as it is derived from a dynamic optimisation model. On the other hand, it implicitly rejects efficient resource pricing in ignoring future terms-of-trade effects according to the Hotelling (1931) rule. If for practical reasons one has to abandon the assumption of efficient resource pricing, then it might be better to use a method for resource accounting that does not presume efficient resource pricing either, such as the El Serafy method. Using this method leads to the conclusion that the dismal results about the weak unsustainability of many resource-dependent developing countries become reversed.

Third, the generated numbers have to be treated with care: the quality of the data is often very poor; the assumptions that give rise to the sustainability interpretation of GS are very strong, some of the practical problems are severe; the World Bank method for computing natural capital depreciation is highly contestable, to say the least. Consequently, much caution is warranted in deriving policy conclusions. Following the World Bank's results could sometimes lead to wrong policy implications for the wrong countries. One policy implication Atkinson and Hamilton (1996, pp. 4ff and 14) and Atkinson et al. (1997, p. 114) tentatively suggest, is making aid conditional for developing countries who appear to be unsustainable according to the World Bank's method in order to bring them (back) on a sustainable path. Atkinson et al. (1997, p. 207) propose 'a possible role for *additional* bilateral aid in assisting, where needed, the fulfilment of genuine saving requirements' (my emphasis).

The ISEW/GPI was introduced as a competing indicator of WS. It shares many of the problematic aspects of GS since its sustainability foundation is built upon the fact that the ISEW/GPI can be interpreted as a kind of gNNP derived from a dynamic optimisation model. In addition, it suffers from a number of serious shortcomings specific to the methodology used for the ISEW/GPI. First, whilst it has a basic theoretical foundation as mentioned, the specific adjustments undertaken and their justification are often somewhat *ad hoc*. As shown above, this is the case for defensive expenditures for example. Indeed, with the notable exceptions of Lawn (2003) and Brennan (2008), proponents of the ISEW/GPI and related indicators have devoted comparatively little effort on theoretically justifying their measure.

Second, and connected to the first point, its results depend on a number of problematic assumptions. It has been shown that if no escalation factor is applied to valuing the depletion of non-renewable resources, and if long-term environmental damage is not accumulated, then none of these items contributes any longer to a widening gap between ISEW or GPI on the one hand and GNP or GDP on the other. The other environmentally related items in a typical ISEW/GPI, such as costs of water, air and noise pollution, generally do not contribute to such a gap either (for reasons of space they could not be dealt with here in more detail). One can therefore conclude from the analysis above that variables related to the environment do not provide evidence for the 'threshold hypothesis'. They only do so, if a widening gap between ISEW/GPI and GNP is artificially created via the introduction of the 3 per cent cost escalation factor for non-renewable resource use and the accumulation of long-term environmental damage. With such assumptions built into the ISEW/GPI, it is difficult to see how any country could escape running into the threshold effect sooner or later. In looking at the methodology for the ISEW one is tempted to suspect that they are constructed with the very intention of producing the desired result of decreasing 'sustainable economic welfare'. Some of the problematic assumptions and methodological errors suggest that the proponents really object to WS and want to introduce SS somehow through the backdoor into the ISEW and GPI, which is however an indicator of WS, as readily admitted to by Daly and Cobb (2007: 288), since it assumes that natural capital is substitutable. Indeed, it is rather striking that all the major proponents of ISEW and GPI are also proponents of SS. For example, it is highly ironic that Herman Daly is one of the inventors of the ISEW, whereas in all his other writings he vehemently argues for the non-substitutability of natural capital.

Third, the ISEW/GPI also suffers from the fact that there is no objective answer on what are the factors that determine welfare. It is therefore very subjective. If one includes a correction term for income inequality, why not include a correction term for the degree of political freedom, a correction term for the extent of crime (as some studies have done) or a correction term for the degree of equality between the sexes? A prominent item, which would raise economic welfare over time and is not included in the ISEW/GPI, is improvement in the quality of consumption goods, as this will not necessarily and fully be reflected in the value of personal consumption expenditures. Another very important item is improved life expectancy due to better health care and progress in medical technology. Crafts (2002) estimates the additional welfare gain due to reduced mortality and finds that this raises the growth rate of a welfare measure by about 0.7 to 0.8 percentage points.

Some proponents of the ISEW are aware of the subjectivity of the numbers they produce, as becomes clear in the following quotation from Cobb and Cobb (1994, p. 252): 'The point is rather that when the GNP functions politically as a welfare measure, it should not be allowed to masquerade as a measure that is somehow more objective than alternative ways of determining well-being.' Also, Herman Daly, together with John B. Cobb one of the first proponents of an ISEW, is aware of the many criticisms that can be raised against their measure. At the same time, however, he still sees the ISEW as a better indicator of 'sustainable economic welfare' than GNP and thus justified:

> Of course we had to make many arbitrary judgements, but in our opinion no more arbitrary than those made in standard GNP accounting — in fact less so. ... We have no illusions that our index is really an accurate measure of sustainable economic welfare ... We did not offer the ISEW as the proper goal of economic policy — it too has flaws. If GNP were a cigarette, then the ISEW would be that cigarette with a charcoal filter. (Daly 1996, pp. 97f)

Similarly, Daly (ibid., p. 115) acknowledges the difficulties in constructing a measure of welfare, but sees the ISEW justified by preferring 'even the poorest approximation to the correct concept' to 'an accurate approximation to an irrelevant or erroneous concept'. Yet again, at the same time Daly realises and concedes that 'the mere existence of any numerical index of welfare is a standing invitation to the fallacy of misplaced concreteness' (ibid., p. 98).

NOTES

1   Hartwick (1977) proved the rule for one consumption good and one nonrenewable resource for the Cobb–Douglas production function, Hartwick (1978a) proved the rule for the more general CES production function and Hartwick (1978b) extended the analysis to renewable resources. Dixit, Hammond and Hoel (1980) proved the rule in a more general context, allowing for many types of consumption goods, heterogeneous capital goods and an

endogenous labour supply. Becker (1982) was the first to prove the rule with environmental services as an explicit component of the utility function.

2 Asheim, Buchholz and Withagen (2003) argue that the Hartwick rule and therefore GS as an indicator of WS does not depend on the assumption of substitutability of natural capital. However, their counterexample depends on the assumption that production is based on the extraction of a renewable resource within the limits of the maximum rate of natural regeneration. No actual economy fulfils this criterion, hence one is justified in arguing that the relevance of the Hartwick-rule depends on the assumptions of WS.

3 Shocks are changes in parameters that are exogenous to the model.

4 There is exploration and resource discovery in the model, but all discoveries are anticipated in the sense that their discovery is correctly expected *ex ante*.

5 For simplicity it is assumed that environmental protection takes the form of post-pollution abatement and γ is taken as unchangeably given. This is for convenience only, the results derived later on do not depend on it.

6 For a more complex treatment of human capital, see Aronsson and Löfgren (1996).

7 Labour input is therefore not a control variable of the model.

8 It is disputed whether so-called transversality conditions are necessary for the maximisation over an infinite time horizon (see Chiang 1992, pp. 240ff). However, all cases in which the transversality conditions are unnecessary, involve no time discounting (Barro and Sala-i-Martin 1995, p. 508). In this model there is time discounting, hence the transversality conditions appear to be necessary. I leave them out none the less, however, because they do not illuminate anything of special importance in the model.

9 Note that the equations of motion are just the constraints of the model and are equal to the dynamic changes in the capital stocks as explained further above. The equations of motion together with the dynamic first-order conditions are often called the Euler Equations.

10 Under perfect competition the price for the resource equals its marginal value product.

11 That is, a tax that optimally internalises the environmental externality such that social welfare is maximised (Pigou 1932). Note that in general in order to maximise welfare it will be optimal to allow for some positive level of pollution.

12 In the model this holds true only after some amendments because of resource use and production causing pollution. See Appendix 3, p. 202.

13 If externalities still existed, they would have to be internalised by optimal Pigouvian taxes. The revenue coming from those taxes would have to be redistributed to consumers by lump sum subsidies.

14 To get an impression of its importance, note that about 50 per cent of this century's output growth in developed countries is attributed to disembodied technical progress (Burda and Wyplosz 1997, p. 115). Note as well, however, that these estimates usually do not consider human capital explicitly. Doing so would lower the residual of technical progress that cannot be attributed to one or the other form of capital.

15 Missing are mainly some small countries.

16 This is easy to verify for the reader and is therefore not derived here, but simply stated. 'Modified' here means that it is taken into account that resource use causes pollution. Hamilton (1995, p. 64) shows that the modified Hotelling rent $(F_R - f_R - i_A \gamma F_R)$ must be bigger than g_D so that modelling discovery expenditures as being dependent on the resource stock leads to higher GS than if expenditures depend on the stock of accumulated discoveries.

17 The same reasoning applies to renewable resource stocks if harvesting exceeds natural regeneration.

18 By assumption, RC accrue at the beginning of the accounting period. If RC accrue at the end of the accounting period, then $n + 1$ in equation (5.13) would be replaced by n.

19 In Indonesia, for example, the corrected income measure rises from 929 bn rupiah in 1973 quite dramatically to 3829 bn rupiah in 1974 from which it then falls even more dramatically to 431 bn rupiah in 1975 (Repetto et al. 1989, p. 8).

20   The difference between GNP and GDP is that GDP includes output produced by foreigners within a country and excludes output produced by nationals abroad. The difference for developed countries is usually quite small. Whenever I speak of GNP or GDP in the following, strictly speaking it should read GNP/GDP.

21   Such studies derive the value from environmental disamenities in comparing, for example, house prices from real estate, which is similar in all respects but the environmental disamenity.

22   See Harris (2007) for a critique of Lawn (2003).

23   For Australia there also exists a related measure, which comes under the name of sustainable net benefit index (SNBI) (Lawn and Sanders, 1999).

24   Lawn (2005: 204) defends the escalation factor with reference to price paths of non-renewable resources. But this is a misunderstanding, as the escalation factor must refer to the cost of renewable resources, not the cost of non-renewable resources. In fact, rising non-renewable resources prices are likely to bring down the costs (prices) of renewable resources, as section 3.2 has shown.

6. Measuring Strong Sustainability

In this Chapter, I will discuss several indicators put forward for measuring strong sustainability and explore the problems they encounter. Not all existing indicators of SS can be addressed. However, I will analyse the most important ones. Section 6.1 covers two popular physical indicators, namely ecological footprints and the concept of material flows. It is important to note that these physical indicators are more indicators in the spirit of SS rather than direct measures of SS. This is different with respect to hybrid indicators, looked at in Section 6.2. These try to combine physical standards with monetary valuation and, in setting pre-defined environmental standards, they are more directly and explicitly measures of SS.

6.1 PHYSICAL INDICATORS

These are indicators, which do not undertake any form of monetary valuation. I analyse two physical indicators, namely ecological footprints and material flows. I do not include energy-based indicators called emergy or exergy, which are based on thermodynamics (see Odum 1996; Herendeen 1999; Ferrari, Genoud and Lesourd 2001; Dincer 2002). Neither do I include the concept of Environmental Space (Hille 1997). Some of its basic ideas are taken on board in ecological footprints and material flows, but it is less well known than these two other indicators.

6.1.1 Ecological Footprints: Measuring Sustainability by Land Area

The concept of ecological footprints (EF) focuses on environmental sustainability rather than inter-generational equity more generally. Its objective is to translate all the ecological impact of human economic activity into the 'area required to provide the resources we use and to absorb our waste' (WWF 2008, p. 14), subject to the 'predominant management and production practices in any given year' (Wackernagel et al. 2002, p. 9266). Since the focus is on consumption, the required land area is attributed to the consumer rather than the producer since the consumer rather than the producer is deemed responsible for the impact. That is, for example, resources extracted in a developing country, but exported to a developed country, count towards the ecological footprint of the developed country. This stands in stark contrast to the allocation rule for GS, discussed in section 5.1.2, p. 135. Land rather than money is taken as the unit of accounting since according to its proponents 'monetary analysis is misleading as it suggests substitutability, allows for the discounting of the future and focuses on marginal rather than absolute values' (Wackernagel et al. 1999, pp. 376f). EF is regarded by its proponents as an indicator in the spirit of SS.[1]

If the EF exceeds the bioproductive land area available, then the carrying capacity of the land area is exceeded. This is called an ecological deficit and the economic activity causing the EF is judged to be unsustainable. It is perhaps counter-intuitive that the estimated land area can exceed the actually existing ecologically productive land area on earth. For example, a forest logged down at twice its regeneration rate is accounted for at twice its area (Wackernagel et al. 2002). This is taken as a sign of unsustainability: 'humans are consuming resources at a rate that would require more land than actually exists' (Wackernagel and Yount 2000, p. 26). When is unsustainability apparent? In Moran et al. (2008, p. 470), the proponents of EF state as an explicit test that 'a per capita Ecological Footprint less than the globally available biocapacity per person' represents a minimum requirement 'for sustainable development that is gobally replicable'.

The EF is linked to the somewhat older concept of a sustainable population size. If the EF of a country, for example, exceeds the bioproductive land area available, then this can also be interpreted to the effect that the area's population is bigger than its sustainable size. Ironically, from this perspective there would be unsustainable 'over-population' in the developed countries, which as I will show below typically have ecological deficits, rather than in the developing countries. Proponents of EF usually do not emphasise the link to sustainable population size, however, possibly because they want to stress that consumption levels causing the high EF are unsustainable rather than blaming 'over-population'. Having said that, EF proponents clearly recognise that population and population growth plays an important role in determining the size of current and future ecological footprints (WWF 2008).

The concept of EF builds on earlier measures of the impact of humans on ecosystems such as Vitousek et al.'s (1986) measure of human appropriation of so-called Net Primary Productivity (NPP) and Odum's (1996) accounting of energy flows. The following impacts are included (Wackernagel et al. 2002): (1) crop growing for food, animal feed, fibre, oil and rubber; (2) animal grazing for meat, hides, wool and milk; (3) harvesting of timber for wood, fibre and fuel; (4) fishing in oceans and freshwater; (5) infrastructure for housing, transportation, industrial production and hydro-electric power; and, finally, (6) fossil fuel burning. In addition, 12 per cent of the bioproductive land area is reserved for biodiversity conservation. Due to data problems, neither waste production nor fresh water withdrawal are included. Also, the extraction of non-renewable mineral resources is not included at all, and non-renewable energy resources are taken into account only with respect to the land area required to cope with the environmental damage of fossil fuel burning. The reason is probably that it is difficult to convert non-renewable resource extraction into a required land area.

Obviously, not all bioproductive land is the same. All land area is therefore standardised into one common global measurement unit(global hectare) using yield and equivalence factors. Equivalence factors make different categories of land-use roughly comparable with each other, whereas yield factors make land of the same land-use category, but with differing productivity, comparable. Proponents of EF emphasise that, wherever possible, they use publicly available governmentally approved data and that their calculations are conservative in the sense of under- rather than over-estimating the EF (Wackernagel and Silverstein 2000; Wackernagel and Yount 2000; Wackernagel et al. 2002).

Of all the human impacts, accounting for fossil fuel burning is the most important one, responsible for slightly more than half of the global EF in 2005 (WWF 2008). This so-called energy footprint is the one, which has grown fastest over time and in which the disparity between the developed and developing countries is largest. It is also the most contested component of EF, however. It is calculated as the forest land area required to hypothetically sequester enough carbon from the atmosphere to avoid any increase in the atmospheric concentration of carbon. This is done under the assumption that about 35 per cent of carbon emissions are absorbed by the world's oceans[2] (Wackernagel et al. 2002). Electricity generated from nuclear power plants was first excluded, then included in the energy footprint for some time measured as the land area required to sequester the carbon equivalent if the electricity from nuclear energy were produced with fossil fuels instead, but is now no longer included in order 'to improve methodological consistency' (WWF 2008: 14).

Evidence

The global bioproductive land area is estimated at about one quarter of the earth's surface. The most recent comprehensive study tracking the ecological impact of human activity on a worldwide scale comes to the conclusion that whereas humanity only used up around 54 per cent of global biocapacity in 1961, rising EF started to outgrow in the 1980s the practically constant biocapacity available and in 2005 had exceeded available biocapacity by around

30 per cent. Normalised by population size, an EF of 2.7 global hectares per capita stands in contrast to existing global biocapacity of only 2.1 global hectares per capita (WWF 2008). An EF has also been calculated for nations, regions and even cities (see Chambers, Simmons and Wackernagel 2000, pp. 133–44). Some nations and regions, particularly the developed ones, have a much larger EF than bioproductive land area available and therefore an eco-logical deficit. Not surprisingly, all cities examined also run such a deficit. Table 6.1 lists the ecological footprint and the ecological deficit of a selection of countries in per capita terms. Note that a negative ecological deficit means an ecological surplus.

Critique
A whole range of methodological and other aspects of EF has encountered criticism – see, for example, van den Bergh and Verbruggen (1999), Ayres (2000), IMV (2002), Grazi et al. (2007), Fiala (2008) and Best et al. (2008).

Table 6.1 Ecological footprint and deficit of selected countries and the world

	Ecological Footprint	Ecological Deficit
United Arab Emirates	9.5	8.4
USA	9.4	4.4
Australia	7.8	-7.6
New Zealand	7.7	-6.4
Canada	7.1	-13.0
Ireland	6.3	2.0
UK	5.3	3.7
Belgium	5.1	4.0
Japan	4.9	4.3
Germany	4.2	2.3
Netherlands	4.0	2.9
Russia	3.7	-4.4
World	2.7	0.6
Brazil	2.4	-4.9
China	2.1	1.2
Central African Republic	1.6	-7.8
Gabon	1.3	-23.7
India	0.9	0.5

Note: EF in global hectares per capita in 2005.

Source: WWF (2008)

On a very fundamental level, one could argue that EF adds up apples and oranges in adding such diverse items as actual land use for agricultural products and purely hypothetical land use for the absorption of carbon dioxide emissions.

I will concentrate here on more specific points, however. The first critique addresses the way in which the EF for fossil fuel use is computed. Ayres (2000) argues that there are many more technical possibilities to sequester carbon from the atmosphere than land-intensive forestry. He mentions pumping compressed carbon dioxide into empty oil and gas wells or liquefied carbon dioxide into the deep oceans. One might dismiss these as merely potential future possibilities, which might or might not be possible and might have undesirable environmental side effects. More importantly, however, fossil fuels could be replaced with renewable energy, particularly wind and solar energy.[3] Whilst prohibitively costly to do at current costs, the required land area would be much lower than under the forestry option as renewable resources are far more land-efficient. Wind turbines and photovoltaic generators could even be placed on land that is not bioproductive or already in use, such as at sea or in deserts or on top of buildings. Such land use would not subtract from the bioproductive land available. IMV (2002) has calculated that the energy footprint becomes negligible with little impact on the overall EF if, hypothetically, 50 per cent of world energy demand were satisfied with renewable energy, which IMV (2002) claims to be technically possible, and for the remaining energy demand mainly low carbon fuels such as natural gas were used. To repeat, the economic cost at the current state of technology would be prohibitive, but given that EF is blind towards monetary valuation and therefore costs, its proponents cannot argue against considering renewable energy as a hypothetical solution to the carbon dioxide emission problem. It is also no argument against this alternative computation that the use of renewable energy on such a large scale is purely hypothetical at the moment. The same argument would apply to the forestry option employed by the proponents of EF, which is equally purely hypothetical. If the energy footprint becomes negligible then the global EF is well within the limit of bioproductive land area available. Similarly, many developed countries no longer exhibit an ecological deficit.

The second critique is not directly targeted at EF itself, but at a certain interpretation following from the concept of an ecological deficit, which is derived from an EF. Whereas such a deficit would typically be regarded by economists as a normal exchange of goods, in which trading partners have differing comparative advantages, to the mutual benefit of both partners (van den Bergh and Verbruggen 1999), proponents of EF see ecological deficits as inherently dangerous and undesirable, particularly at the level of nation-states. The main reason for this anti-trade bias is that 'trade reduces the most effective incentive for resource conservation in any import region, the regional population's otherwise dependence on local natural capital' (Rees and Wackernagel 1996, pp. 238f). As a result, a 'restoration of balance away from the present emphasis on global economic integration and interregional dependency toward enhanced ecological independence and greater intraregional self-reliance' is recommended (ibid., p. 241). Willey and Ferguson (1999, pp. 2) are even more explicit in proclaiming that 'all nations should live within their own ecological capacity'. Against this, van den Bergh and Verbruggen (1999, p. 66) maintain that national boundaries are geopolitical and cultural artefacts and therefore have no environmental meaning.

As a last critique, it is doubtful whether EF really represents an indicator of SS. EF does not constrain substitutability within natural capital. This does not conflict with the first definition of SS, which refers to the value of total natural capital, but it does conflict with the second definition of SS, which constrains substitutability within natural capital as well and requires to maintain critical functions of natural capital intact. Furthermore, in making total available bioproductive land area the yardstick against which hypothetical land use is measured, human activities, which are clearly not strongly sustainable, need not be indicated as unsustainable by the EF measure. As seen previously, the land area required to hypothetically absorb carbon dioxide emissions can be much reduced if renewable energy production is taken as the hypothetical option rather than reforestation. Doing so would then suggest that the global EF is well within the global bioproductive land area available, even though carbon dioxide emissions would still be clearly beyond the natural regenerative capacity of the global atmosphere, which violates the SS requirement. Even with the reforestation option, the fact that a global ecological deficit exists and EF therefore indicates a violation of SS is purely coincidental. This is because if only there were more bioproductive land area available globally, then according to current EF methodology the world as a whole need not have an ecological deficit. Global human impact would still be in violation of strong sustainability, however, given climate change caused by excessive carbon and other greenhouse gas emissions, but it would not be so indicated by EF.

6.1.2 Material Flows: Measuring Sustainability by Weight

The concept of material flows (MF) is inspired by early work by Ayres and Kneese (1969) on industrial metabolism. Fischer-Kowalski (1998) and Fischer-Kowalski and Hüttler (1998) provide an intellectual history of matierals flow analysis. Its starting point is a deep dissatisfaction with environmental policies that focus mainly or even exclusively on emissions and waste products. Its proponents maintain that many environmental problems are caused long before pollutants are emitted and waste is produced because MF need to be moved in order to produce products. It is the sheer size of MF, which creates environmental problems, and this size needs to be reduced substantially in order to lower the pressure on the environment. Reduction of MF is suggested as a good candidate for a 'one single long-term goal in environmental policy' (Hinterberger and Wegner 1996, p. 7).

Similar to EF, the concept of MF is regarded by its proponents as an indicator in the spirit of SS (Hinterberger et al. 1997, p. 12). From their perspective, 'a core environmental condition of sustainability is a physical steady-state system, with the smallest-feasible flows of resources at the ... input and output boundaries between the technosphere and the ecosphere' (Spangenberg et al. 1999, p. 492). The concept of MF, first developed by Schmidt-Bleek (1993a, 1993b), is inspired by Herman Daly (1992a) and his emphasis on the growing scale or material throughput of the economy as the main cause of environmental degradation. It therefore shares Daly's emphasis on optimal scale and a limit to or reduction of throughput in a 'steady-state' economy as the priority for environmental policy making. The emphasis on scale rather than efficiency also partly explains why weight is used as the unit of accounting rather than money. The other reason has to do with the perceived difficulties of monetary valuation of environmental degradation, on which more below.

From the perspective of MF, the focus needs to shift from the 'sink'-side of the economy to the 'source'-side. This is due to a number of reasons. First, the pre-occupation with emissions and waste tends to ignore that all consumption goods come with a hidden 'ecological rucksack', which is defined as 'the sum of all the materials that are not physically included in the economic output under consideration, but have been necessary for production, use, recycling and disposal' (Spangenberg et al. 1999, p. 498). Substantial ecological rucksacks typically occur at the resource extraction or harvesting stage. Examples would be earth and rock displaced during non-renewable resource extraction and soil erosion in agriculture (Matthews et al. 2000, p. 1). Second, the precautionary principle is invoked to justify giving priority to a reduction of MF (Hinterberger et al. 1997). Given that uncertainty and ignorance render a precise assessment of the ecological impact of pollutants difficult and imply that many forms of environmental damage cannot be known in advance, reducing MF is seen as a promising alternative as it will reduce the pressure on the environment across the board. Third, Spangenberg et al. (1999) also argue that no environmental policy will ever be able to efficiently control the thousands of substances emitted into the environment. Their monetary valuation, which is necessary for finding the efficient level of pollution, is regarded as an impossible task. In comparison, it would be much easier to control mineral and energy materials entering the economic system, the number of which is estimated between 50 and 100 in the case of Germany.

The aim and policy recommendation is to reduce MF by a factor of four (Weizsäcker et al. 1997) or, more ambitiously, by a factor of ten (Factor 10 Club 1994), at least in developed countries, over the next 40 to 50 years, which is regarded as technically feasible (Hinterberger et al. 1997).[4] All material inputs are classified into five main categories: abiotic raw materials (mineral and energy resources), biotic raw materials, moved soil (agriculture and forestry), water and air. MF reduction should be achieved in all categories (Hinterberger et al. 1997). However, in most empirical studies such as Adriaanse et al. (1997) and Matthews et al. (2000) water flows are excluded because they 'are so large that they would completely dominate all other material flows and would obscure the meaning and, thus, the usefulness of the indicators' (Matthews et al. 2000, p. 8).

Evidence

One of the most prominent of empirical studies is that of Adriaanse et al. (1997), which computed MF for Germany, Japan, the Netherlands and the US over the period 1975 to 1994. This study has been updated to 1996 in Matthews et al. (2000) and extended to cover Austria as well. Matthews et al. (2000) also distinguishes between MF from different economic sectors as well as MF into different environmental media, namely air, land and water. It also allows establishing which MF remain in the economy longer than one year and which ones are dissipative and therefore difficult to recover and recycle. In Adriaanse et al. (1997, p. 7) the hidden flows of imported primary natural resources and semi-manufactures are attributed both to the country of final consumption of materials and to the country exporting the materials for further use in another country. In Matthews et al. (2000, p. 43) it is recognised, however, that this would lead to double-counting among trading countries. Hidden flows are therefore attributed solely to the importing country (ibid., p. 14 and 43).

Table 6.2 summarises the main findings from Matthews et al. (2000). Note that in this table MF refers to what they (ibid., p. 7) call domestic process output, that is, materials extracted from the domestic environment plus imported materials used in the domestic economy and flowing to the domestic environment. It does not include domestic hidden flows, which do not themselves enter the domestic economy. In all five countries under study, MF have increased by between 16 (Netherlands) and 28 (US) per cent between 1975 and 1996. These absolute increases in weight have occurred despite substantial reductions in the material flow intensity of GDP, which has fallen between 26 (US) and 42 (Japan) per cent. In other words, the decoupling of MF from GDP has not been strong enough to bring about absolute reductions

Table 6.2 Material flows and material flow intensity, 1975 and 1996

Country		MF	MF/GDP	MF per capita
Austria	1975	85.7	0.059	11.3
	1996	100.8	0.042	12.5
	% change	+18	-29	+10
Germany	1975	865.3	0.47	14.0
	1996	1074.7	0.30	13.1
	% change	+24	-36	-6
Japan	1975	1173.0	4.80	10.5
	1996	1406.5	2.78	11.2
	% change	+20	-42	+7
Netherlands	1975	242.6	0.59	17.8
	1996	281.3	0.42	18.1
	% change	+16	-29	+2
United States	1975	5258.7	1.24	23.9
	1996	6773.8	0.92	25.1
	% change	+28	-26	+5

Note: MF in million metric tons; MF/GDP in metric tons per million constant
monetary units of own currency; MF per capita in metric tons per capita.

Source: Matthews et al. (2002, p. 20).

in MF. In cross-country comparison, we are not surprised to find that the Japanese economy has the lowest per capita MF, whereas the US has the highest.

A similar pattern emerges at the aggregate OECD level over the period 1980 to 2005. Total so-called Domestic Material Consumption (DMC), which measures the total amount of material directly used in an economy, has increased by 27 per cent from 16486 million tonnes to 20984 tonnes. Over the same period, DMC per unit of GDP decreased by 36 per cent (OECD 2008a: 40). Here, as well, substantial increases in MF productivity have been insufficient to halt the rise in total MF.

MF have also been computed for 15 European Union countries (Eurostat 2002) and seven world regions (Behrens et al. 2007) over the period 1980 to 2000. The OECD has developed a methodological guide for studies of MF and resource productivity (OECD 2007) and there are major efforts under way to compile MF data on a regular basis by official agencies, particularly in OECD countries, but also in some non-OECD countries (see OECD 2008b for an overview).

Critique

The most important criticism against the concept of MF is that it adds up apples and oranges (Gawel 1998). From an ecological point of view, two forms of material throughput with differing environmental damage impacts cannot be meaningfully added together just because one can express both in weight terms. Without further analysis of what the material throughput consists of and what are its environmental implications, there is no reason to presume that, say, Japan's MF of 11.2 metric tons per capita is any better than the MF of the US at 25.1 tons per capita. Indeed, one could argue that the very statement that the MF of the US were 25.1 tons per capita in 1996 is entirely void of any meaning. Similarly, it is pointless to simply rank countries according to the size of their MF.

In its prescription to reduce general MF across the board, the concept seems to draw the erroneous conclusion from the difficulties of valuing environmental damage that one cannot successfully distinguish according to differences in environmental damage at all. It is simply not true that, as Hinterberger and Luks (1998, p. 7) suggest, 'in most cases it is impossible to distinguish between "good" and "bad" throughput'. In its call for general MF reduction across the board, the concept goes from a rejection of one extreme belief, namely in the possibility of comprehensive environmental valuation, to the other extreme, which is seemingly blind towards admittedly incomplete attempts at valuation. The call for general reductions in MF is not guaranteed to be ecologically effective, but is guaranteed to be highly economically inefficient with respect to whatever reduction in environmental damage might be achieved (Gawel 2000). The failure to appreciate the importance of valuing benefits and opportunity costs unnecessarily renders the concept largely unattractive. Because general reductions in MF are not guaranteed to be ecologically effective, it is also doubtful whether MF can function as an indicator of SS. Following the policy recommendation of reducing general MF by a certain factor need not reduce the stress on critical functions of natural capital if the specific MF, which are threatening these functions, are not directly addressed. Gawel (2000, pp. 165–67) is also right in arguing that proponents of MF need to be clear whether they see general MF reductions as the panacea for most if not all environmental problems, or regard differentiated MF reductions, on which more below, as a policy tool complementary to environmental policies targeting specific pollutants at the 'sink'-side of the economy.

Having made this critique of general MF reductions, there is much more potential in the concept once one abandons the idea of such across-the-board reductions. For example, it is true that an environmental policy that merely focuses on the 'sink'-side of the economy will tend to neglect the many environmental problems that are caused during the entire production process and

MF is to be credited with re-drawing our attention to this. Furthermore, once one starts distinguishing between more and less harmful materials, then reductions in those material flows, which tend to threaten critical functions of natural capital, moves us towards SS.

The proponents of MF have started to take these criticisms more seriously. For example, Matthews et al. (2000, p. 3) states that 'we recognize that it is at the level of sub-accounts – the examination of specific material flows, and categories of like flows – that materials flow analysis will have most relevance to detailed policy-making'. The same document also developed a pilot study for the United States, in which material flows are distinguished according to their physical and chemical properties. Similarly, Hinterberger, Luks and Stewen (1999, pp. 364f) recognise a need for differentiating material flows and suggest that MF reductions need to be regarded as complementary to fine-tuned environmental policies tackling problems at the 'sink'-side of the economy rather than substituting for them. A very promising development in this respect is provided by the so-called Environmentally-weighted Material Consumption (EMC) – see van der Voet et al. (2003, 2005) and Best et al. (2008). The idea is to combine material flow data with environmental impact data derived from life cycle impact assessment methods.

6.2 HYBRID INDICATORS

Hybrid approaches are those, which combine physical indicators with monetary valuation. Typically, no monetary values are placed upon items of natural capital. Rather, only the monetary costs of achieving the standards are computed. Roefie Hueting's (1980, 1991) work is the starting point for a number of hybrid approaches. I will look at the three most important ones: so-called sustainability gaps, the Greened National Statistical and Modelling Procedures (GREENSTAMP) and the 'sustainable national income according to Hueting' (SNI).

6.2.1 The Starting Point: Hueting's Pioneering Work

Hueting's point of departure is the suggestion that human impact on the environment has reached a level that threatens the integrity of environmental functions, which represents a 'new scarcity' unknown before (Hueting 1980). His proposal was to define standards, which maintain vital environmental functions intact in the spirit of SS, to estimate the costs of achieving these sustainability standards and to subtract these costs from national income. Also subtracted should be all those expenditures, which are defensive and, according to Hueting, wrongly counted as value added in the national accounts: compensatory, restoratory and preventive environmental expenditures. The resulting 'sustainable national income' (SNI) is defined as 'the maximum attainable level of production and consumption, using the technology of the year under review, whereby the vital functions, that is possible uses, of the physical surroundings remain available forever' (Hueting and de Boer 2001, p. 24). Hueting is well aware that his is a 'partial equilibrium and static approach' since effects on other sectors of the economy are not taken into account (Hueting 1991, p. 205).

As Hueting (1991, p. 204) points out, his proposal was provoked by the need for a practical indicator in the face of insurmountable problems of creating a theoretically correct indicator:

> In the course of a working visit to Indonesia in 1986, I was provoked by the following remark made by the Indonesian minister for Population and Environment: "In my policy making I need an indicator in money terms for losses in environment and resources, as a counterweight to the indicator for production, namely national income. If a theoretically sound indicator is not possible, then think up one that is rather less theoretically sound."

Hueting therefore regards his proposal as a workable, if second-best, alternative to the theoretically correct, but in his view practically impossible, valuation of environmental functions with the help of shadow prices.[5] As will become clear, all the three hybrid approaches dealt with here share this basic conviction.

6.2.2 Sustainability Gaps

Similar to Hueting, the proponents of the concept of 'sustainability gaps', developed by Ekins and Simon (1999, 2001), reject the idea that one could reliably value natural capital depreciation. Its basic idea is to measure the gap between pre-specified environmental sustainability standards and current violation of these standards in physical terms and to translate this gap into monetary terms. Environmental sustainability is defined as 'the maintenance of important environmental functions' (Ekins and Simon 1999, p. 39). The suggested standards are as follows (ibid., p. 47):

- Stable climate
- Undepleted ozone layer
- Biodiversity at current levels
- No loss of function for non-renewable resources

- Sustainable harvest at desired level for renewable resources
- Limiting emissions to critical loads in order to protect human health
- Maintenance of an unspoilt countryside
- Maintenance of environmental security in restricting environmental risks to low levels

Once the standards are defined, the resulting gap between the standards and current practice can be calculated. One can also calculate the years it would take at current trends to achieve the standards. Going one step further, one can, in principle at least, provide a monetary estimate of the costs necessary to achieve the sustainability standards. First, one needs to establish the necessary measures to achieve the standards. These measures can either be in the form of reducing the output of certain goods and services whose production causes environmental degradation, or in the form of input substitution and pollution abatement in production processes, or finally in the form of direct restoration and preservation. Next, cost curves have to be established for the implementation of each measure. Then all measures are sorted with respect to their marginal cost in order to arrive at an overall cost curve for achieving the sustainability standard. Hypothetically, the measure with the least cost is undertaken first, then the measure with the next highest cost and so on. In so far as there might be practical obstacles to following this sequence of least-cost measures, the estimate for the sustainability gap is too low.

Ekins and Simon warn very explicitly against the idea of subtracting the monetised sustainability gap from GNP or GDP and against an interpretation of the gap as the actual amount of money that would need to be spent to achieve sustainability: The calculation of sustainability gaps 'is very much a static, partial equilibrium calculation, representing at a moment in time the aggregation of expenditures that would need to be made to reduce the various dimensions of the physical sustainability gap to zero' (Ekins and Simon 2001, p. 20). If these expenditures were actually undertaken, however, then prices would change, which contradicts the partial equilibrium assumption.

Ekins and Simon (2001) provide empirical estimates of the sustainability gap for the UK and the Netherlands. The one for the UK refers to carbon dioxide and some other air pollutants only, whereas the one for the Netherlands covers more environmental areas due to better data availability. Not surprisingly, their study finds substantial gaps between current practice and the pre-specified environmental standards. In many cases it would take decades to achieve the standards at current trends and for some environmental aspects sustainability standards could never be achieved without reverting current trends. No monetary valuation is attempted due to lack of comprehensive data. Ekins and Simon (2001, p. 21) point out that 'considerable statistical effort is still needed' to derive a monetary value of sustainability gaps 'across all relevant environmental themes'.

6.2.3 Greened National Statistical and Modelling Procedures

The Greened National Statistical and Modelling Procedures (GREENSTAMP) are the result of a research project financed by the European Community. The starting point of GREENSTAMP is also a rejection on mainly practical grounds of the purely monetary approach to the economics of sustainability as represented, for example, by GS (Brouwer et al. 1999). Its proponents believe that it is practically impossible to value depreciation of natural capital reliably and comprehensively as required by this approach. To follow such an approach would be 'largely illusory for providing a meaningful indicator of sustainability' (Brouwer et al. 1999, p. 14).

Instead, proponents of GREENSTAMP want to estimate, with the help of multi-sector national economic input-output models, what the feasible economic output would be if pre-specified environmental standards were to be achieved. In specifying environmental standards, which have to be obeyed, GREENSTAMP is also an indicator of SS. In estimating the opportunity costs of obeying these standards, the approach is inspired by Hueting. However, its proponents deviate from Hueting's original proposal to deduct the costs of achieving the environmental standards from actual national income. They believe that such an approach would estimate a 'sustainable income' that 'is probably lower than the national income that could be obtained, and maintained durably, while respecting the norms' (Brouwer et al. 1999, pp. 15f). Since achieving the pre-specified environmental standards would imply non-marginal changes, for which the partial equilibrium framework becomes untenable, general equilibrium modelling is the preferred alternative. According to GREENSTAMP proponents, the hypothetical national income that could be obtained while obeying the norms can therefore only be estimated if the feasible economic output itself is subject to modelling (O'Connor and Ryan 1999).

The GREENSTAMP methodology has been tested with the help of the so-called M3ED (Modèle Economie Energie Environnement Développement) multi-sectoral dynamic simulation model. Model runs have been undertaken, amongst others, for France (O'Connor and Ryan 1999) and the Czech Republic (Kolar and O'Connor 2000). One of the advantages of the modelling approach is that the model can be run with different assumptions about the environmental standards. The modelling is explicitly dynamic and future oriented (*ex ante* approach). Modelling the transition to the specified environmental standards forms an important part of the analysis. The feasible economic output is therefore estimated over a period of time and projected into the future, which can be done with appropriate assumptions about future values. Accepting that any environmental standards set or assumptions taken about the future are always subjective, GREENSTAMP is defended by its proponents as a valuable exercise to better understand the conditions of achieving sustainability, however defined: 'The information of most value is not found in the aggregate figures themselves – which are always open to alteration through changing assumptions – but in the richness of information and understanding obtained through construction and comparison of the different model outputs and scenarios' (O'Connor and Ryan 1999, p. 130). The model runs for France, for example, have been undertaken for four distinct scenarios ranging from very pessimistic to very optimistic assumptions about technological advances and from very lenient to very stringent environmental standards.

6.2.4 'Sustainable National Income According to Hueting'

The calculations of a 'sustainable national income according to Hueting' (SNI) for the Netherlands, undertaken by a group of researchers at the Free University Amsterdam and the Wageningen University, also build on Hueting's work, which is very explicitly acknowledged. Like GREENSTAMP, the proponents of SNI realise that the adjustments to national income following the observance of externally imposed environmental standards can only be undertaken in a general equilibrium framework.

Contrary to GREENSTAMP's dynamic and future- as well as transition-oriented input-output modelling approach, the SNI explicitly follows a static comparative or *ex post* computable general equilibrium modelling approach. It is defined as 'the situation of the economy after an instantaneous change towards sustainable resource use' (Gerlagh et al. 2001, p. 3). The aim is to establish what the income for a given year would have been if the economy had had to obey the environmental standards. Transition dynamics do not matter as two static situations are compared with each other: once before and once after the sustainability standards are imposed upon economic activity. This follows from a desire that 'the SNI calculations should not be burdened with transition costs' (Gerlagh et al. 2001, p. 3).

In the process of calculation, a range of simplifying assumptions are made (Gerlagh et al. 2001, 2002). For example:

• As already mentioned, all transition or adaptation costs are ignored as 'in a way of speaking, it is assumed that the change to a sustainable economy is foreseen in advance, long enough that economic agents are able to integrate this transition in the planning of their investment decisions' (Gerlagh et al. 2002, p. 164).

- Abatement costs are assumed to be the same for all sectors as no sector-specific data are available.
- 'Defensive expenditures', that is expenditures whose aim is environmental restoration, prevention of environmental degradation or compensation for such degradation are subtracted from national income if they enter the national accounts as value added. This follows from the consideration that actual and potential expenditures to reach the specified sustainability standards are essentially substitutes.
- Costs for remedying environmental problems, which have accumulated over a long time, are also distributed over a long time period instead of attributed to one year only.
- The labour supply is supposed to be inelastic and the labour market clears through an adjusting wage rate, thus ensuring employment neutrality.
- The income and price elasticities of various goods need to be specified.
- The trade balance is assumed to be equal to the national savings balance, which is in turn assumed to constitute a constant share of national income.
- With respect to price changes in world markets, two variants are calculated: one in which prices on the world market do not change, whereas in the other price changes on the world market are presumed to be proportional to price changes in the Netherlands.
- Similarly, because prices will change following the imposition of environmental standards, the SNI can be compared with national income either based on the initial prices or on the new prices. Together with the two scenarios about price changes on the world market, this creates a total of four variants for the general equilibrium model.

Gerlagh et al. (2002) calculate different variants of a Dutch SNI for the year 1990 in an applied general equilibrium model with 27 production sectors. Nine environmental themes are covered: climate change, ozone depletion, acidification, eutrophication, particulate matter and volatile organic compound emissions, heavy metal dispersion into water, dehydration of land and soil contamination. The specific themes chosen are somewhat reflective of the specific environmental problems faced by the Netherlands. For all these themes, environmental sustainability standards are set such that emissions stay within the natural regenerative capacity of the environment. For the last two themes, this rule translates into a standard of zero dehydration and zero soil contamination. Then abatement cost data based on currently available technologies are collected to estimate the costs of reaching the specified standards. Abatement costs consist of operation and maintenance costs for technical abatement measures in the first place and value added from output losses otherwise where these technical measures have been exhausted and output reductions are the only way left to reduce emissions.

In their calculations, Gerlagh et al. (2002) find that the costs of reducing greenhouse gas emissions represent the highest share of the costs of achieving the sustainability standards. They estimate that to reach less than 70 per cent of the sustainability standards is relatively cheap, reducing national income only by about 10 per cent. Further improvements quickly become very expensive, however. Whereas the conventional net national income is estimated at about 450 billion guilders, the SNI, that is, the income where 100 per cent of the sustainability standards are obeyed, is calculated at about 250 billion guilders.

In Hofkes et al. (2002) the calculations are repeated for the year 1995 and a comparison is drawn to the calculations for 1990. They find that 'SNI improves substantially from 1990 to 1995. Growth rates in sustainable income levels exceed growth rates in national income. ... Over the period 1990–95 an absolute delinking of economic growth and environmental pressure has taken place' (Hofkes et al. 2002, p. 21). Hofkes, Gerlagh and Linderhof (2004) provide a trend analysis of SNI for the Netherlands over the period 1990 to 2000.

6.2.5 Critical Assessment

Similar to Hueting's original proposal, the monetary valuation of the sustainability gaps suffers from its partial equilibrium approach for establishing the cost curves. The costs for the implementation of each measure are estimated under the *ceteris paribus* assumption. However, if all those measures that are necessary to achieve the sustainability standards were effectively undertaken, then the *ceteris paribus* assumption would become fictitious. The relative prices of consumption goods and input factors would change as would the extent and structure of environmental degradation. Economic restructuring, feedbacks and interlinkages would have to be considered in a total equilibrium analysis of the economy. This task can only be achieved with comprehensive modelling as undertaken by the other two hybrid indicators.

It is also unclear what the appropriate timeframe is for achieving certain sustainability standards. This holds especially true with respect to standards for non-renewable resources. Simon and Ekins postulate that the use of non-renewable resources must not diminish their 'function' which can be achieved via more efficient use, repair, re-use, recycling and substitution with renewable substitutes. However, it is unclear whether the maintenance of function-ality must be achieved instantaneously or over a long time period. The latter would be more sensible as there is no immediate danger of a running out of non-renewable resources.

With respect to GREENSTAMP and SNI, the modelling approach is their chief advantage as it avoids the implausible partial equilibrium assumptions. At the same time, the hypothetical character of the estimated feasible eco-nomic output as the result of a modelling exercise also represents the greatest weakness of these indicators. The results and indeed the whole modelling exercise are difficult to understand by non-experts. Moreover, the model dependency of the estimates means that the results crucially depend on the underlying assumptions taken. The section on the SNI has illustrated this point in listing a number of assumptions needed, all of which are contestable of course.

GREENSTAMP and SNI are therefore more valuable with respect to the research they generate on how to construct abatement cost curves, how to deal with environmental defensive expenditures and what is needed in terms of environmental statistics and reporting both at the firm and at the macroeco-nomic level. Another important property is that they help to focus the discussion on which environmental standards are considered sustainable. This is explicitly acknowledged by the proponents of GREENSTAMP, which do not regard their calculations as providing one single all-encompassing indica-tor of sustainability, but rather as a way to improve the many building stones needed for a better informed policy-making towards strong sustainability. The SNI, on the other hand, is more ambitious. Whilst it is not supposed to re-place national income, certainly in the eyes of Roefie Hueting it is meant to provide a real alternative to it.

With all three hybrid indicators, one needs to be careful in interpreting the estimated monetary value of the sustainability gap, the estimated feasible economic output in the case of GREENSTAMP and the estimated SNI, re-spectively. A high value for the sustainability gap, a great difference between actual and estimated feasible output or between national income and the esti-mated SNI can mean either of two things. It can either mean that the actual economy is far away from the sustainability norms or that the economy is close to fulfilling the norms, but doing so would be very costly. The environ-mental implications can therefore be quite different for the same monetary value. Similarly, a given monetary value for the sustainability gap, a given difference between actual and estimated feasible output or between national income and SNI does not tell us anything about the relative achievement of strong sustainability with respect to different norms. It could be that certain norms are drastically violated while others are almost achieved or it could be that the economy is equally far away from achieving all norms. Also, a constant or falling value of the sustainability gap, a closing of the gap between actual and feasible economic output or between national income and the SNI tells us nothing about the state of the environment itself. This is because this could be *either* the consequence of the economy moving closer to fulfilling the sustainability standards *or* the consequence of a lowering of costs for achieving the standards due to, for example, technical progress. Detailed knowledge of the sustainability norms and the economy's distance from these norms is therefore essential and one should never rely on the aggregate monetary calculations alone.

The reader might wonder why I have not said anything critical on the concept and treatment of defensive expenditures in hybrid approaches. The reason is that the main concerns raised in the discussion of the ISEW/GPI in section 5.2.2, p. 156, namely the essential arbitrariness of what constitutes a defensive expenditure, is much less of an issue here. This is because such expenditures refer only to environmental expenditures and have a clear reference point in the form of the environmental standards set. The hybrid indicators are also correct in treating actual and hypothetical defensive expenditures equally. This is because hypothetical and actual defensive expenditures are perfect substitutes for each other with respect to achieving the sustainability standards. If actual expenditures are lower, then hypothetical expenditures must correspondingly be higher. The same would apply vice versa.

NOTES

1   Even from the perspective of their proponents, EF is not fully compatible with SS, however, as it does not directly require compensating future generations for past and current fossil fuel use with an alternative energy resource (Wackernagel and Silverstein 2000, p. 392).
2   Initially, the absorptive capacity of the oceans was not included, which sparked a lot of criticism (for example, by Ayres 2000).
3   It is unclear why some proponents of EF who recognise that 'a more sound basis for the "energy footprint" is the required area of land needed to produce the specified energy renewably', as Ferguson (2002, p. 310) does, want to restrict the alternative computation to biologically grown resources (sugarcane/ethanol), which are much more land-intensive than wind and solar energy.
4   Hinterberger, Luks and Stewen (1999, p. 368) suggest that various countries as well as over 100 companies, which are members of the World Business Council on Sustainable Development (WBCSD), have stated their commitment to reduce material flows.
5   In some sense, the hybrid indicator approach is reminiscent of Baumol and Oates' (1971) standards-price approach in the economics of pollution control, where standards are set somewhat arbitrarily given that the efficient level of pollution is often difficult if not impossible to establish.

7. Conclusions

The objective of this book was to explore the limits of the two opposing paradigms WS and SS. The analysis was based on the economic methodology since both paradigms are essentially economic. In Chapter 2 development was defined as sustainable if it does not decrease the capacity to provide non-declining per capita utility for infinity. The meaning of this definition was explained and different forms of capital were introduced as the items that together form the capacity to provide utility.

In Section 2.1 many simplifying assumptions were introduced to make the analysis in this book possible and the insights that arise from the course of examination have to be seen in the light of these assumptions. In other words, the conclusions I arrive at will not necessarily hold if other assumptions or a broader perspective are taken. To give some examples: it was clearly stated that the analysis is confined to *economic* paradigms of sustainability; the definition of SD is anthropocentric and rules out the deep ecology view that non-human entities have value independent of human valuation; finally, for a large part of the book *intra*-generational as opposed to *inter*-generational equity issues were ignored.

Section 2.2 discussed some ethical issues of SD. As the book takes it for granted that the current generation is committed to SD, some justification was provided that makes this commitment plausible as an ethical choice. For similar reasons two misunderstandings about what SD requires were corrected. In Section 2.3 the paradigms of WS and SS were described. The fundamental divergence between the two paradigms arises from differing assumptions about the substitutability of natural capital. It was pointed out that there exist two differing interpretations of SS in the literature: one calls for maintaining natural capital in value terms, the other for preserving the physical stock of (certain forms of) natural capital. The difference matters, as was argued in Section 4.3 — a point to which I will come back further below.

Section 2.3 stressed the importance of the differing assumptions with respect to the substitutability of natural capital using climate change as a case study. The conflict between those like William Nordhaus who come to the conclusion that only very minor greenhouse gas emission abatement is warranted and those who call for more ambitious abatement is not merely a dispute about the right rate of discount to be employed. It was argued that the main conflict must be about whether and to what extent the expected detrimental effect of climate change on natural capital can be compensated with a rise in other forms of capital. Given substitutability of natural capital, there is no need to lower the rate of discount from which more aggressive greenhouse gas emission abatement would follow. Indeed, lowering the discount rate may well be inefficient as it would lead to channelling scarce resources into emission abatement which is likely to have a rate of return far inferior to other investment opportunities. This conclusion does not become invalid if current and future *intra*-generational inequalities are also taken into account. As long as the substitutability of natural capital is implicitly assumed, large-scale abatement of greenhouse gas emissions to protect the natural capital stock is likely to be inferior to investment in other forms of capital. Demanding aggressive reductions in greenhouse gas emissions can only be warranted if, to some extent at least, natural capital is regarded as non-substitutable. Understanding what matters helps to frame the discussion on climate change in a way that makes clear where the real conflict lies.

Chapter 3 addressed the two opposing paradigms of WS and SS in detail. The question of substitutability of natural capital as an input into the production of consumption goods was analysed first. It was suggested that the resource optimism of WS can be summarised in four propositions that were then critically assessed one after the other. Second came the question of the substitutability of natural capital as a direct provider of utility. It was discussed whether future generations can be compensated for long-term environmental degradation. Finally, the analysis addressed the link between economic growth and environmental degradation. This question had to be addressed because in Section 2.3 the proposition that economic growth will be beneficial to the environment in the long run was considered to be the main proposition of WS, so that this paradigm has to rely less on the assumption that natural capital is substitutable as a direct provider of utility.

Chapter 3 concluded that both paradigms are non-falsifiable. The two paradigms fundamentally differ in basic claims about *future* possibilities for substitution and technical progress. While the future is not completely disconnected from the past and the present in that it is contingent on past and present decisions, we are also fundamentally uncertain and ignorant about future developments. Take resource optimism as an example: it was argued that there are powerful theoretical arguments as well as strong empirical evidence up to now in favour of natural capital being substitutable as an input into production. But WS holds that natural capital will be substitutable at all points of time in the future as well. In making claims about the uncertain future, substitutability really becomes an assumption and stops being a falsifiable conjecture. And there is absolutely no guarantee that substitutability of natural capital, in spite of being logically conceivable and possible in the past, will be possible in practice or likely to occur in the future as well.

The major conclusion from Chapter 3 is an important result because of the almost dogmatic belief of the supporters of WS and SS in the basic assumptions of their paradigm. What is necessary to maintain the capacity to provide non-declining future utility is far less clear than either paradigm would want us to believe. There is, on the one hand, reason to be concerned about the substitutability of natural capital. But, on the other hand, any call for the preservation of natural capital can rest on persuasive arguments at best. This conclusion should remind us of our humility as human beings and should caution us against blindly following either paradigm of sustainability.

In no way should Chapter 3 be misinterpreted as saying that scientific research cannot inform decision-making in a society committed to SD. Chapter 4 therefore took up the discussion where it had stopped in Chapter 3 and the whole first part of Chapter 4 was devoted to elaborating whether and why a persuasive case can be made that certain forms of natural capital are in explicit need of preservation while others are not. To do so, it was necessary to go one step beyond this abstract notion of 'natural capital' and to look at specific forms of natural capital instead. Some of the existing literature all too often does not recognise that a more disaggregated approach towards natural capital is necessary since some forms of natural capital more than others exhibit features that distinguish them from other forms of capital and are more prone to uncertainty and ignorance.

I have argued in Chapter 4 that those forms of natural capital that serve basic life-support functions for human beings, such as the global climate, the ozone layer and biodiversity are non-substitutable in their totality, that the accumulation of persistent and highly toxic pollutants should be prevented, and that soil fertility as well as water reservoirs should be preserved. Conversely, a persuasive case can be made that there is no need for preserving natural resources as an input into the production of consumption goods and, albeit less so, as a food resource. Hence, the substitutability assumption of WS is supported more strongly from the analysis in the first part of Chapter 4 with respect to natural capital as a resource input, whereas the non-substitutability assumption of SS is supported more strongly with respect to natural capital as a provider of pollution absorptive capacity and direct utility. Another consequence is that the second interpretation of SS given in Section 2.3.2, p. 23, is more appropriate than the first one: if certain forms of natural capital seem to be non-substitutable, but not others, and if these non-substitutable forms of natural capital are also not substitutable with other forms of *natural* capital, then it makes much more sense to target these forms directly and demand the preservation of their physical stocks than to maintain the value of the aggregate stock of natural capital.

The traditional economic approach of including option and quasi-option values into environmental valuation is commendable, but likely to be insufficient. The precautionary principle and safe minimum standards (SMS) were introduced and critically assessed as alternatives for coping with risk, uncertainty and ignorance. Some believe that one can simply ignore opportunity costs when applying measures such as SMS. I have argued in Chapter 4, however, that a society that is committed to SD should not ignore opportunity costs. In a world of scarce resources where all choices exclude alternatives it would be unwise to neglect the opportunity costs of preserving critical forms of natural capital. Instead, SMS should be applied to the critical forms of natural capital identified in Section 4.4, p. 110, subject to the condition that the costs must not be 'unacceptably high', where costs are opportunity costs minus expected preservation benefits. Clearly then, in this perspective SMS provides an extension and qualification to the traditional economic approach rather than a replacement. The objective should be to reduce uncertainty and ignorance and to strengthen valuation techniques to enable better informed decisions on preserving natural capital. But what society regards as 'unacceptably high' costs is not a scientific, but an ethical and political question. How this question is to be solved is beyond the scope of this book. Some interesting proposals range from strengthening forms of deliberative democracy and discursive ethics (O'Hara 1996; Jacobs 1997b) to mock referenda (Kopp and Portney 1999).

Chapter 5 was devoted to an examination of whether weak sustainability can be measured. It was shown how a theoretically correct measure of WS, namely GS, is constructed. Section 5.1.4 highlighted important practical problems that are often neglected in the relevant literature. It is crucial to be aware of these problems as they have implications on the validity and the interpretation of practical measures of GS. In a critique of the World Bank's (2009a) computations of GS it was shown that the dismal conclusions about the weak unsustainability of many resource-dependent developing countries are largely reversed if the El Serafy method is used instead of the World Bank's method for computing natural capital depreciation. Of course, neither of the two methods is without problems. Even those critical towards the El Serafy method will have to admit, however, that the validity of a measure of unsustainability is highly questionable if its main conclusions are reverted by using a competing and not obviously inferior method for resource accounting.

Measuring GS faces serious problems and these problems have to be taken seriously in interpreting practical measuring attempts and should make one cautious in deriving policy implications. Much more effort is still needed to improve the scope and the quality of the data from which GS is computed. Furthermore, one should always be aware that any practical measure is likely to be partial in the sense that it cannot encompass every form of capital. Recently, social capital has come into the focus of concern. However, it is most doubtful whether one can measure changes in social capital with a comparable validity and reliability as changes in other forms of capital.[1]

Given severe problems with providing a comprehensive measure of WS in the form of GS, maybe one has to be more modest with respect to what can and what cannot be measured. It is worth quoting El Serafy (1993, p. 248) at some length here:

> I submit that we will never be able to make a complete list of the *physical* stock of natural resources existent at any point of time, let alone attach a *money value* to them in order that we might capture the annual changes of such a value in the flow accounts. Any pretense that we shall be able to do so shortly or even, I assert, eventually, should be dismissed as wishful thinking. What is feasible in this area is to identify in individual country situations those aspects of measurable environmental degradation that are of the most importance, and be content with adjusting the conventional accounts, particularly *income*, to reflect such partial degradation.

There is certainly a clear rationale for natural resource accounting as the stock of marketable resources for many developing countries is a very significant part of their national portfolio and information about which share of the resource receipts should be counted as proper income and which should be counted as capital consumption is extremely important for them. This holds especially true if the government leases the exploitation of its resources to a private firm and wants to compute resource royalties and taxes. As many natural resources are commercially marketed, prices can be established and it is not all that difficult to keep track of changes in their stocks. Without resource accounting, what happens is that the receipts of resource depletion are fully counted as income and no correction is made for the capital loss. This makes little economic sense. A country living off its natural resource endowment might enjoy high 'income' today but will be impoverished as soon as the stock is exhausted. This runs counter to the very idea of sustainability as capital consumption is a 'sure recipe for future economic decline' (El Serafy 1989, p. 10).

In Section 5.2, many of the existing ISEW/GPI studies were found wanting as an indicator of WS because of methodological problems. This should not be misinterpreted as a defence of GDP/GNP in terms of a welfare indicator. GDP/GNP does not and should not measure welfare. Instead, it fulfils quite well the function it was supposed to accomplish when it was established after the Second World War: to provide an indicator for macroeconomic stabilisation policy of the economic activity in a country, that is an indicator of the total output produced by the economy.[2] The revised 'System of National Accounts' states this with unambiguous clarity: 'Neither gross nor net domestic product is a measure of welfare. Domestic product is an indicator of over-all production activity' (Commission of the European Communities–Eurostat 1993, p. 41). And 'total welfare could fall even though GDP could increase in volume terms' (ibid., p. 14).[3] Carson and Young (1994, p. 112) — then Director and Chief Statistician, respectively, of the Bureau of Economic Analysis of the US Department of Commerce — are right in arguing that 'the factors determining welfare cannot be reduced and combined into a single measure that would command widespread agreement and acceptance. In this respect, a measure of welfare differs from the GNP'. I have to admit, how-ever, that I doubt whether one could succeed in preventing policy makers, the media and the general public from misusing GNP as a welfare indicator. Un-fortunately, the welfare interpretation of GNP has become absolute folklore and a commonplace.

As concerns SS, Chapter 6 analysed some physical as well as hybrid indi-cators. In accordance with the major thrust of this book, which is to explore the limits of the two opposing paradigms of sustainability, my analysis has been fairly critical. That is not to say that these indicators have nothing inter-esting to say. For example, ecological footprints and material flows remind us that the environmental impact of the goods and services we consume go far beyond what is contained in them or directly observable from their use. The hybrid indicators such as sustainability gaps, GREENSTAMP and SNI induce us to think about which environmental standards we would want to impose on economic activity and to calculate an approximate estimate of their opportu-nity costs.

Beyond these valid fundamental points, doubts remain with respect to the validity and usefulness of the indicators. I have explained above how the overshoot of the EF beyond the bioproductive land area available crucially depends on its method to translate carbon dioxide emissions into land area. As a matter of fact, carbon dioxide emissions are well beyond the natural absorptive capacity of the atmosphere and are still on the rise. This cannot be strongly sustainable as it will disturb and in some cases destroy the natural functions of the global atmosphere. But we have known this already for some time and we do not need EF to tell us what we have known already with what is arguably the result of a complex methodological artefact. Outspoken critics of the concept maintain that due to methodological flaws, EF does not have 'any value for policy evaluation or planning purposes' (Ayres 2000, p. 349) and is 'unsuitable as a tool for informing policy-making' (van den Bergh and Verbruggen 1999, p. 71). As long as the methodology for computing the land area necessary to bring carbon dioxide emissions within the natural absorptive capacity is unchanged, I have to agree with this judgement. Even if the meth-odology became changed on these aspects, doubts regarding the validity and reliability of the EF computations remain for reasons I had no space to go into here (see the special issue of the journal *Ecological Economics*, Volume 32, Issue 3, 2000).

Proponents of the concept of MF are correct in pointing out the misery of an environmental policy that is obsessed with emissions and waste and ignores the environmental damage created along the whole production and consumption process of goods and services. Also, there is some fundamental truth in the statement that 'unless economic growth can be dramatically decoupled from resource use and waste generation, environmental pressures will increase rapidly' (Matthews et al. 2000, p. v). However, there are certainly more effective and more efficient ways to achieve SS than to reduce MF across the board by a factor of ten (or four or twenty or whatever, for that matter). When material flows are differentiated according to their threat to critical functions of natural capital, then the comprehensive coverage of potential environmental impacts 'from cradle to grave' has much to offer. I fully agree with Hinterberger, Luks and Stewen (1999, p. 371) that the concept of MF is still in its early stages and might well have great potential if future research pushes it forward in the right direction. The general importance of MF is therefore not contested here. What is contested is whether MF can be aggregated by weight into one single figure and whether the recommendation to reduce MF across the board makes either economic or ecological sense.

All hybrid approaches provide interesting information on how far we are away from reaching pre-specified environmental standards. Problems start where monetary valuation begins. The concept of sustainability gaps suffers from the untenable *ceteris paribus* clause. With large-scale abatement undertaken, quantities and prices change, which defeats the partial equilibrium assumption. Only general equilibrium modelling can overcome this problem and both GREENSTAMP and SNI provide interesting exercises in modelling the costs of reaching pre-specified environmental standards. However, because general equilibrium modelling is required many assumptions need to be taken, which by necessity are contentious. As some of their proponents readily admit, hybrid indicators 'whatever concept they engage, are highly sensitive to model calibration, specification of environmental standards, technological change and other assumptions used' (O'Connor, Steurer and Tamborra 2001, p. 16). Still, on the whole I would suggest that the hybrid indicators hold great promise as indicators of SS, their various problems notwithstanding.

The SNI calculations roughly point out that to achieve SS would cost about 50 per cent of national income in the case of the Netherlands. This is a very substantial cost, which would render it extremely doubtful whether any country would be willing to incur such a cost. Fortunately, the SNI provides an upper bound estimate. This is because the comparative static SNI approach necessarily overestimates the true costs of achieving SS as it is based on current technology. SS could only be achieved over a long period of time, however, in which technology would change, which would make the move towards SS much cheaper.

Overall the reader might have the impression that many of the conclusions in this book are somewhat pessimistic. The reader should keep in mind, however, that the analysis here was deliberately biased towards exploring the limits of the two opposing paradigms. Exploring the prospects of both paradigms would likely lead to many insights that give rise to more hope with respect to SD. This is beyond the scope of the analysis here, however.

NOTES

1 The same applies to a potentially further form of capital, namely cultural capital, suggested by Berkes and Folke (1992, 1994).

2 It has to be conceded, however, that it does so rather imperfectly in developing countries where, often, much of the economic activity in the so-called informal sectors is not taken into account. Also, mainly only marketed economic activity is included since domestic and personal services produced and consumed by members of the same household or provided without payment are omitted. In addition, economic activity in the black market is by its very nature not included in GNP/GDP.

3 However, Daly's (1996, p. 112) claim that GNP/GDP bears no closer relation to welfare than the stock of gold bullion did in the age of mercantilism is vastly overdrawn. As Beckerman (1995, pp. 108f.) rightly retorts: if this was true, why do people almost always migrate towards the countries with a higher GNP/GDP and rarely vice versa? Also, as Dasgupta (1990) and Dasgupta and Weale (1992) show, at least in poor countries GNP/GDP is highly correlated with basic indicators of the quality of life such as life expectancy, infant mortality, adult literacy and indices of political and civil rights. However, there is convergence in living standards across countries over time (Neumayer 2003b), whereas it is at least questionable whether there is convergence in per capita income (Cole and Neumayer 2003).

Appendix 1 How Present-value Maximisation Can Lead to Extinction

Here is an example that shows how applying present-value maximisation with a constant discount rate as decision criterion can lead to utmost unsustainability. Imagine that there are two utility paths available. The first one provides an infinite stream of utility at a constant level U_1. The second one provides a stream of utility at a constant level U_2. Assume that U_2 is higher than U_1 ($U_2 > U_1$), but that the second path provides higher utility U_2 only for a finite time T ($T < \infty$) and utility falls to zero for ever after time T. Imagine that there is a social planner who has to choose either of the two paths. The present-value of each utility path, using a constant discount rate r, is

$$PV_1 = \int_0^\infty U_1 e^{-rt} dt, \quad PV_2 = \int_0^T U_2 e^{-rt} dt$$

If the social planner applies present-value maximisation as the decision criterion, he or she will prefer path two to path one if and only if

$$\int_0^T U_2 e^{-rt} dt > \int_0^\infty U_1 e^{-rt} dt$$

$\Leftrightarrow$

$$\left[-\frac{U_2}{r} e^{-rt} \right]_0^T > \frac{U_1}{r}$$

$\Leftrightarrow$

$$-U_2 \left[e^{-rT} - 1 \right] > U_1$$

$\Leftrightarrow$

$$e^{-rT} < \frac{U_2 - U_1}{U_2}$$

$\Leftrightarrow$

$$r > \frac{\ln(U_2) - \ln(U_2 - U_1)}{T}$$

How is this result to be interpreted? Assume U_2 to be 10 per cent higher than U_1 and T to be 50 years.[1] Then r has to be just about 4.8 per cent per annum in order to choose utility path 2, that is to prefer human extinction in 50 years time for the sake of 10 per cent higher utility over the 50 years to an infinite, albeit lower, utility stream! That is, present-value maximisation can lead to utmost unsustainability. This might appear counter-intuitive to the reader, but is a compelling consequence of the logic of discounting which gives negligible weight to the distant future. Note, however, that this result depends on the discount rate being constant throughout. If the discount rate varies with the welfare level of the future (see the discussion of the Ramsey formula in the next appendix), then present-value maximisation need not lead to unsustainability. Clearly, the example is not realistic. No policy maker in his or her right mind would choose U_2 over U_1. Its purpose is merely to illustrate how an automatic and blind application of a constant discount rate can suggest that extinction is optimal.

NOTE

1   Because U_2 and U_1 enter the formula only in the form of arguments of an ln–function, I do not have to specify them further. Any numbers that obey the assumption that U_2 is 10 per cent higher than U_1 will give the same results.

Appendix 2 The Hotelling Rule and Ramsey Rule in a Simple General Equilibrium Model

In a general equilibrium dynamic optimisation context, it no longer makes sense to ask how a representative resource-extracting and resource-harvesting firm would maximise its profits, as in Section 3.2.2, p. 53, since this is only the partial equilibrium approach. Instead, here the question is how a 'social planner' would maximise social utility over infinite time.[1]

Let utility be derived from consumption only and let production be dependent on man-made capital and renewable and non-renewable resources only. There is no disembodied technical progress, that is no technical progress that is not embodied in man-made capital. Labour input is assumed to be constant and is therefore suppressed in the production function. This is the simplest setting possible to derive the two rules.

The problem of the social planner is as follows

$$\text{Max} \int_0^\infty U(C) \cdot e^{-\rho t} dt$$

$$\text{s.t.} \quad \dot{S} = -R$$

$$\dot{Z} = a(Z) - E$$

$$\dot{K} = F(K, R, E) - C - f(R) - h(E)$$

where U is utility, C is consumption, ρ is society's pure rate of time preference, t is a time index, S is the stock of non-renewable resources, R is resource depletion, Z is the stock of renewable resources, $a(.)$ is the natural growth function of the renewable resource, E is resource harvesting, K is the stock of man-made capital, $F(.)$ is the production function, $f(.)$ is the expenditure function for non-renewable resource extraction, $h(.)$ is the expenditure function for renewable resource harvesting. $\dot{K}$ is investment in man-made capital net of depreciation. It is common to assume that renewable resources follow a logistic growth path, in which the growth rate rises with the stock of the resources initially ($a_Z > 0$ for $Z < Z'$), but falls eventually after the stock has reached a certain size Z' ($a_Z < 0$ for $Z > Z'$). A dot above a variable indicates its derivative with respect to time.

The so-called 'current value Hamiltonian' of this maximisation problem is

$$H = U(C) + \lambda\big[F(K,R,E) - C - f(R) - h(E)\big] - \mu R + \varphi\big[a(Z) - E\big]$$

Its optimal solution is characterised by the following set of 'canonical equations':[2]

i. Static first-order conditions

$$\frac{\partial H}{\partial C} = 0 \quad \Rightarrow \quad U_C = \lambda \tag{A2.i.1}$$

$$\frac{\partial H}{\partial R} = 0 \quad \Rightarrow \quad \lambda\big[F_R - f_R\big] = \mu \tag{A2.i.2}$$

$$\frac{\partial H}{\partial E} = 0 \quad \Rightarrow \quad \lambda\big[F_E - h_E\big] = \varphi \tag{A2.i.3}$$

ii. Dynamic first-order conditions

$$\dot{\lambda} = \rho\lambda(t) - \frac{\partial H}{\partial K} \quad \Rightarrow \quad \dot{\lambda} = \rho\lambda - \lambda F_K \tag{A2.ii.1}$$

$$\dot{\mu} = \rho\mu(t) - \frac{\partial H}{\partial S} \quad \Rightarrow \quad \dot{\mu} = \rho\mu \tag{A2.ii.2}$$

$$\dot{\varphi} = \rho\varphi(t) - \frac{\partial H}{\partial Z} \quad \Rightarrow \quad \dot{\varphi} = \rho\varphi - \varphi\, a_Z \tag{A2.ii.3}$$

Plugging (A2.i.2) into (A2.ii.2) and rearranging gives

$$\frac{\overline{\dot{\lambda(F_R - f_R)}}}{\lambda(F_R - f_R)} = \rho \quad \text{or} \quad \frac{\dot{\lambda}}{\lambda} + \frac{\overline{(\dot{F_R - f_R})}}{(F_R - f_R)} = \rho \tag{A2.1}$$

Similarly, plugging (A2.i.3) into (A2.ii.3) and rearranging gives

$$\frac{\overline{\dot{\lambda(F_E - h_E)}}}{\lambda(F_E - h_E)} + a_Z = \rho \quad \text{or} \quad \frac{\dot{\lambda}}{\lambda} + \frac{\overline{(\dot{F_E - h_E})}}{(F_E - h_E)} + a_Z = \rho \tag{A2.2}$$

Rearranging (A2.ii.1) gives

$$\frac{\dot{\lambda}}{\lambda} + F_K = \rho \tag{A2.3}$$

Setting (A2.1) and (A2.3) equal and noting that in a general competitive equilibrium F_K is the interest rate and F_R the price of the non-renewable resource we arrive at the desired result that the rate at which the non-renewable resource rent is rising is equal to the interest rate

$$\frac{\overline{(F_R - f_R)}}{(F_R - f_R)} = F_K \tag{A2.4}$$

(Hotelling rule for non-renewable resources)

Similarly for renewable resources

$$\frac{\overline{(F_E - h_E)}}{(F_E - h_E)} = F_K - a_Z \tag{A2.5}$$

(Hotelling rule for renewable resources)

There is an additional term a_Z to account for the effect resource harvesting has on the stock of renewable resources and thereby on the natural growth rate of the resource. For $Z < Z'$, $a_Z > 0$, so resource rent is rising at less than the rate of interest. For that case resource harvesting has a negative effect on natural growth via reducing the renewable resource stock. For $Z > Z'$, $a_Z < 0$, so resource rent is rising at more than the rate of interest. For that case resource harvesting has a positive effect on natural growth via reducing the renewable resource stock.

If resource harvesting has a negative effect on the resource stock, the resource rent rises at less than the interest rate and therefore starts at a higher initial level. Intuitively, this is because the opportunity cost of current resource harvesting is higher than without the negative effect on the resource stock. Vice versa if resource harvesting exhibits a positive stock effect the resource rent starts rising from a lower initial level because the opportunity cost of current resource harvesting is lower than without the positive effect on the resource stock.

I will use this model now to derive another famous rule as well, the so-called Ramsey rule. Plugging (A2.i.1) in (A2.ii.1) and rearranging gives

$$F_K = \rho - \frac{\dot{U_C}}{U_C} \qquad (A2.6)$$

Noting that $\dot{U_C} = U_{CC} \cdot \dot{C}$ and defining the elasticity of the marginal utility of consumption as

$$\eta(C) \equiv -\frac{U_{CC} \cdot C}{U_C} \qquad (A2.7)$$

equation (A2.6) can be re-expressed as

$$F_K = \rho - \frac{U_{CC} \cdot C}{U_C} \cdot \frac{\dot{C}}{C} = \rho + \eta(C) \cdot \frac{\dot{C}}{C} \quad \text{(Ramsey rule)} \qquad (A2.6')$$

How to interpret this result? If the economy is on a dynamically optimal path then the interest rate (the social discount rate) will be equal to the sum of the pure rate of time preference ρ and the product of the elasticity of the marginal utility of consumption $\eta(C)$ and the growth rate of consumption $\dot{C}/C$.

Setting the pure rate of time preference equal to zero and looking at equation (6') again reveals why discounting, properly undertaken, has some desirable ethical properties as well, as was claimed in Section 2.1, p. 7: future streams of consumption should be discounted if future generations enjoy higher consumption ($\dot{C}/C > 0$), which is ethically desirable from a sustainability point of view because if later generations are 'richer' than the present generation anyway then benefits accruing to the distant future should count less than benefits accruing to the present. (Implicitly, diminishing marginal utility ($U_C > 0$, $U_{CC} < 0$) is assumed.)

NOTES

1   The same outcome would be achieved by a decentralised inter-temporal perfect competitive equilibrium (Barro and Sala-i-Martin 1995, pp. 60–71).
2   To keep the exposition as simple as possible all initial and boundary conditions are suppressed as are the equations of motion. All functions are assumed to be well behaved so the first-order conditions are necessary and sufficient for an optimum.

Appendix 3 The Hotelling Rule and the Ramsey Rule in a More Complex Model

The derivation of GS in Section 5.1.1, p. 127, depends on an already quite complex dynamic optimisation model where both the Hotelling and Ramsey rule are no longer as simple as introduced in Appendix 2. Here it is shown how the rules must be amended and how to interpret the amendments.

The static and dynamic first-order conditions of interest here are

$$\frac{\partial H}{\partial C} = 0 \quad \Rightarrow \quad U_C = \lambda \tag{A3.i.1}$$

$$\frac{\partial H}{\partial R} = 0 \quad \Rightarrow \quad \lambda\big[F_R - f_R\big] + \psi\gamma\, F_R = \mu \tag{A3.i.2}$$

$$\frac{\partial H}{\partial A} = 0 \quad \Rightarrow \quad -\lambda_{iA} = \psi \tag{A3.i.5}$$

$$\dot{\lambda} = \rho\lambda(t) - \frac{\partial H}{\partial K} \quad \Rightarrow \quad \dot{\lambda} = \rho\lambda - \lambda F_K - \psi\gamma\, F_K \tag{A3.ii.1}$$

$$\dot{\mu} = \rho\mu(t) - \frac{\partial H}{\partial S} \quad \Rightarrow \quad \dot{\mu} = \rho\mu + \lambda f_S \tag{A3.ii.2}$$

Plugging (A3.i.2) into (A3.ii.2) and rearranging gives

$$\frac{\overline{\lambda(F_R - f_R - i_A\gamma\, F_R)}}{\lambda(F_R - f_R - i_A\gamma\, F_R)} = \rho + (F_R - f_R - i_A\gamma\, F_R)f_S \tag{A3.1}$$

$$\text{or} \quad \frac{\dot{\lambda}}{\lambda} + \frac{\overline{(F_R - f_R - i_A\gamma\, F_R)}}{(F_R - f_R - i_A\gamma\, F_R)} = \rho + (F_R - f_R - i_A\gamma\, F_R)f_S$$

Plugging (A3.i.5) into (A3.ii.1) and rearranging leads to

$$\frac{\dot{\lambda}}{\lambda} + F_K(1 - i_A\gamma) = \rho \qquad (A3.2)$$

Using (A3.2) and (A3.1) leads to

$$\frac{\overline{(F_R - f_R - i_A\gamma F_R)}}{(F_R - f_R - i_A\gamma F_R)} = F_K(1 - i_A\gamma) + \frac{f_S}{(F_R - f_R - i_A\gamma F_R)} \qquad (A3.3)$$

(modified Hotelling rule)

This is the modified Hotelling rule for non-renewable resources. How to interpret this result? Let us start at the left-hand side of the equation. This represents the rate of change of a modified Hotelling rent in including not only price minus marginal cost but also subtracting the marginal pollution caused by resource extraction valued at marginal abatement cost. This modification is due to resource extraction causing pollution which was not included in the simpler model of Appendix 2. As concerns the right-hand side of the equation, the first term looks familiar to the interest rate. It is corrected by the expression in brackets, however. Since $i_A\gamma$ is positive, the first term on the right-hand side is smaller than the uncorrected interest rate. The interest rate is corrected because it is taken into account that the accumulation of man-made capital to produce output causes pollution which lowers the real rate of return on capital. The second term on the right-hand side is the product of the inverse of the modified Hotelling rent and the decrease in resource-depletion costs due to a marginal increase in S, the stock of non-renewable resources (or equivalently, which might be easier to understand intuitively, the increase in resource-depletion costs due to a marginal decrease in S). This term is negative since f_S is negative; that is, the modified Hotelling rent rises at a rate less than the corrected interest rate. The reason is that resource extraction imposes a negative externality on the costs of resource extraction, that is, it raises resource-extraction costs via diminishing the stock of available resources (resource-depletion effect). Because resource extraction has a negative stock effect, resource rent rises at less than the interest rate and therefore starts at a higher initial level. Intuitively, this is because the opportunity cost of current resource extraction is higher than without the negative effect on the resource stock. Re-arranging (A3.3) into (A3.4) allows for yet another interpretation

$$F_K(1 - i_A\gamma)(F_R - f_R - i_A\gamma F_R) = \overline{(F_R - f_R - i_A\gamma F_R)} - f_S \quad (A3.4)$$

The left-hand side of (4) can be interpreted as the marginal cost of not extracting an additional unit of the resource: it is the net resource price multiplied by the social discount rate (see the derivation of the social discount rate via the modified Ramsey rule, below). Hence it is the utility return forgone of not extracting an additional unit of the resource today, but deferring that extraction to the next period.[1] This is sometimes called the holding cost of the resource stock (Perman, Ma and McGilvray 1996, p. 129). The right-hand side of (A3.4) can be interpreted as the marginal benefit of not extracting an additional unit of the resource: the first term is the appreciation in the price of letting the additional unit of the resource in the ground; the second term is the marginal benefit of postponing an increase in the resource-depletion costs that would have occurred if the additional unit of the resource had been extracted. As was to be expected, therefore, marginal costs equal marginal benefits along the efficient resource extraction path.

Let us derive the modified Ramsey rule now. Plugging (A3.i.1) in (A3.ii.1) one arrives at

$$F_K(1 - i_A \gamma) = \rho - \frac{\dot{U_C}}{U_C} \tag{A3.5}$$

Noting again that $\dot{U_C} = U_{CC} \cdot \dot{C}$ and defining the elasticity of the marginal utility of consumption as

$$\eta(C) \equiv - \frac{U_{CC} \cdot C}{U_C} \tag{A3.6}$$

equation (A3.5) can be re-expressed as

$$F_K(1 - i_A \gamma) = \rho - \frac{U_{CC} \cdot C}{U_C} \cdot \frac{\dot{C}}{C} = \rho + \eta(C) \cdot \frac{\dot{C}}{C} \tag{A3.5'}$$

$$\text{(modified Ramsey rule)}$$

which is the modified Ramsey rule. The only difference to the simpler rule in Appendix 2 is the term in brackets on the left-hand side of the equation. Since $i_A \gamma$, expressing the marginal pollution valued at marginal abatement costs, is positive, it says that the modified interest rate (social discount rate), which is lower than the uncorrected version of Appendix 2, should be equal to the sum of the pure rate of time preference and the product of the elasticity of the marginal utility of consumption and the growth rate of consumption. The modified interest rate (social discount rate) is lower since the accumulation of man-made capital to produce output causes pollution which lowers the real rate of return on capital and hence the interest rate. For further interpretation of the Ramsey rule, see Appendix 2.

NOTE

1   The resource owner would have got $\left[F_R - f_R - i_A\gamma\, F_R\right]$ for the extraction of one resource unit which would accumulate to $\left[1 + F_K\,(1 - i_A\gamma)\right]\cdot\left[F_R - f_R - i_A\gamma\, F_R\right]$ in the next period. Since the unit is not extracted, $F_K\,(1 - i_A\gamma)\left[F_R - f_R - i_A\gamma\, F_R\right]$ is just the net cost of deferring extraction.

Appendix 4   The World Bank's Genuine Savings Accounting

The World Bank's genuine savings (GS) accounting is as follows:

- Gross Domestic Saving = Gross Domestic Investment − Net Foreign Borrowing + Net Official Transfers [Net Foreign Borrowing + Net Official Transfers = Current Account Balance After Official Transfers]

- Net Saving = Gross Domestic Saving − Depreciation of Man-made Capital

- Genuine Saving = Net Saving − Resource Rents (Depletion of Natural Resources) − CO_2 Damage − Damage from suspended particulate matter

In the traditional national accounts, current educational spending is considered as consumption. In the calculation of GS current educational spending is instead considered as an investment in human capital and therefore included in Gross Domestic Saving. The difference is relevant, since current expenditures make up more than 90 per cent of all educational expenditures (World Bank 1997, p. 34). All values are in current US$. Saving rates are defined as saving divided by gross national income which is measured at market prices.

For the computation of natural resource rents the following items have been included: oil, natural gas, hard coal, brown coal, bauxite, copper, iron, lead, nickel, zinc, phosphate, tin, gold, silver and forests. Resource rents are computed as price minus average costs times production/harvest. The only pollutant considered so far for all countries are CO_2 emissions, which are valued at US$20 per metric tonne of carbon. This value is taken from Fankhauser (1995) and is often regarded as a consensus estimate. CO_2 emissions are supposed to function as a proxy for other pollutants. For some more, mainly developed, countries damage from suspended particulate matter are also included, but for recent years only. For more information on the data see Bolt, Matete and Clemens (2002), its technical documentation.

Appendix 5 World Bank Regional Grouping of Countries

East Asia and the Pacific
Cambodia
China
Indonesia
Korea, Dem. Rep.
Lao PDR
Malaysia
Mongolia
Myanmar
Papua New Guinea
Philippines
Thailand
Vietnam

Europe and Central Asia
Albania
Armenia
Azerbaijan
Belarus
Bosnia and Herzegovina
Bulgaria
Croatia
Czech Republic
Estonia
Georgia
Hungary
Kazakhstan
Kyrgyz Republic
Latvia
Lithuania
Macedonia, FYR

Europe and Central Asia (cont.)
Moldova
Poland
Romania
Russian Federation
Slovak Republic
Tajikistan
Turkey
Turkmenistan
Ukraine
Uzbekistan
Serbia/Montenegro

High-income OECD
Australia
Austria
Belgium
Canada
Denmark
Finland
France
Germany
Greece
Ireland
Italy
Japan
Korea, Rep.
Netherlands
New Zealand
Norway
Portugal

High-income OECD (cont.)
Spain
Sweden
Switzerland
United Kingdom
United States

Latin America & the Caribbean
Argentina
Barbados
Bolivia
Brazil
Chile
Colombia
Costa Rica
Cuba
Dominican Republic
Ecuador
El Salvador
Guatemala
Haiti
Honduras
Jamaica
Mexico
Nicaragua
Panama
Paraguay
Peru
Puerto Rico
Trinidad and Tobago
Uruguay
Venezuela

Middle East & North Africa
Algeria
Egypt, Arab Rep.
Iran, Islamic Rep.
Iraq
Jordan
Lebanon
Libya

Middle East & North Africa (cont.)
Morocco
Oman
Saudi Arabia
Syrian Arab Republic
Tunisia
West Bank and Gaza
Yemen, Rep.

Other high-income countries
Hong Kong, China
Israel
Kuwait
Singapore
Slovenia
United Arab Emirates

South Asia
Bangladesh
India
Nepal
Pakistan
Sri Lanka

Sub-Saharan Africa
Angola
Benin
Botswana
Burkina Faso
Burundi
Cameroon
Central African Republic
Chad
Congo, Dem. Rep.
Congo, Rep.
Cote d'Ivoire
Eritrea
Ethiopia

Sub-Saharan Africa (cont.)

Gabon
Gambia, The
Ghana
Guinea
Guinea-Bissau
Kenya
Lesotho
Madagascar
Malawi
Mali
Mauritania
Mauritius
Mozambique

Namibia
Niger
Nigeria
Rwanda
Senegal
Sierra Leone
South Africa
Sudan
Tanzania
Togo
Uganda
Zambia
Zimbabwe

Bibliography

Aage, Hans (1984), 'Economic Arguments on the Sufficiency of Natural Resources', *Cambridge Journal of Economics*, **8** (1), 105–13.

Aaheim, Asbjorn and Karine Nyborg (1995), 'On the Interpretation and Applicability of a "Green National Product"', *Review of Income and Wealth*, **41** (1), 57–71.

Adelman, Morris Albert (1990), 'Mineral Depletion, with Special Reference to Petroleum', *Review of Economics and Statistics*, **72** (1), 1–10.

Adelman, Morris Albert (1995), *The Genie out of the Bottle: World Oil since 1970*, Cambridge (MA): MIT Press.

Adriaanse, Albert, Stefan Bringezu, Allen Hammond, Yuichi Moriguchi, Eric Rodenburg, Donald Rogich and Helmut Schütz (1997), *Resource Flows: the Material Basis of Industrial Economies*, Washington DC: World Resources Institute.

Agarwal, Anil and Suita Narain (1991), *Global Warming in an Unequal World*, New Delhi: Centre for Science and Environment.

Agras, Jean and Duane Chapman (1999), 'A Dynamic Approach to the Environmental Kuznets Curve Hypothesis', *Ecological Economics* **28** (2), 267–77.

Albers, Heide J., Anthony C. Fisher and W. Michael Hanemann (1996), 'Valuation and Management of Tropical Forests', *Environmental and Resource Economics*, **8** (1), 39–61.

Allen, Roy G. (1938), *Mathematical Analysis for Economists*, London: Macmillan.

Anand, Sudhir and Amartya Sen (2000), 'Human Development and Economic Sustainability', *World Development* **28** (12): 2029–49.

Ando, Amy W. (1998), 'Ecosystems, Interest Groups, and the Endangered Species Act', *Resources*, **130**, 7–9.

Aronsson, Thomas and Karl-Gustaf Löfgren (1993), 'Welfare Measurement of Technological and Environmental Externalities in the Ramsey Growth Model', *Natural Resource Modeling*, **7** (1), 1–13.

Aronsson, Thomas and Karl-Gustaf Löfgren (1995), 'National Product Related Welfare Measures in the Presence of Technological Change:

Externalities and Uncertainty', *Environmental and Resource Economics*, **5** (4), 321–32.

Aronsson, Thomas and Karl-Gustaf Löfgren (1996), 'Social Accounting and Welfare Measurement in a Growth Model with Human Capital', *Scandinavian Journal of Economics*, **98** (2), 185–201.

Arrow, Kenneth J. and Anthony C. Fisher (1974), 'Environmental Preservation, Uncertainty, and Irreversibility', *Quarterly Journal of Economics*, **88** (2), 312–19.

Arrow, Kenneth J. and Leonid Hurwicz (1972), 'An Optimality Criterion for Decision-making Under Ignorance', in C.F. Carter and J.L. Ford (eds), *Uncertainty and Expectations in Economics: Essays in Honour of G.L.S. Shackle*, Oxford, UK: Basil Blackwell, pp. 1–11.

Arrow, Kenneth J., Bert Bolin, Robert Costanza, Partha Dasgupta, Carl Folke, C.S. Holling, Bengt-Owe Jansson, Simon Levin, Karl-Göran Mäler, Charles Perrings and David Pimental (1995), 'Economic Growth, Carrying Capacity, and the Environment', *Science*, **268**, 520–21, also published in *Ecological Economics*, **15** (2), 91–5.

Arrow, Kenneth J., Partha Dasgupta and Karl-Göran Mäler (2003), 'The Genuine Savings Criterion and the Value of Population', *Economic Theory*, **21** (2–3), 217–25.

Arrow, Kenneth J., Robert Solow, Paul R. Portney, Edward E. Leamer, Roy Radner and Howard Schuman (1993), 'Report of the National Oceanic and Atmospheric Administration (NOAA) Panel on Contingent Valuation', *Federal Register*, **58**, 4601–14.

Arrow, Kenneth, Partha Dasgupta and Karl-Göran Mäler (2003), 'Evaluating Projects and Assessing Sustianable Development in Imperfect Economies', *Environmental Resource Economics*, **21**(2): 217–255.

Arrow, Kenneth, Partha Dasgupta, Lawrence Goulder, Gretchen Daily, Paul Ehrlich, Geoffrey Heal, Simon Levin, Karl-Göran Mäler, Stephen Schneider, Davied Starrett and Brian Walker (2004), 'Are we consuming too much?', *Journal of Economic Perspectives*, **18** (3), 147–172.

Arrow, Kenneth, Partha Dasgupta, Lawrence Goulder, Gretchen Daily, Paul Ehrlich, Geoffrey Heal, Simon Levin, Karl-Göran Mäler, Stephen Schneider, Davied Starrett and Brian Walker (2007), 'Consumption, investment and future well-being: reply to Daly et al.', *Conservation Biology*, **21** (5), 1363–65.

Asheim, Geir B. (1986), 'Hartwick's Rule in Open Economies', *Canadian Journal of Economics*, **19** (3), 395–402.

Asheim, Geir B. (1994), 'Net National Product as an Indicator of Sustainability', *Scandinavian Journal of Economics*, **96** (2), 257–65.

Asheim, Geir B. (1996), 'Capital Gains and Net National Product in Open Economies', *Journal of Public Economics*, **59** (3), 419–34.

Asheim, Geir B. (2003), 'Green National Accounting for Welfare and Sustainability: A Taxonomy of Assumptions and Results', *Scottish Journal of Political Economy*, **50** (2), 113–130.

Asheim, Geir B. (2004), 'Green National Accounting with a Changing Population', *Economic Theory*, **23** (3), 601–19.

Asheim, Geir B., Wolfgang Buchholz and Cees Withagen (2003), 'The Hartwick Rule: Myths and Facts', *Environmental and Resource Economics*, **25** (2), 129–150.

Atkinson, Anthony B. (1970), 'On the Measurement of Inequality',*Journal of Economic Theory*, **2** (3), 244–63.

Atkinson, Anthony B. (1983), *The Economics of Inequality*, Oxford: Oxford University Press.

Atkinson, Giles (1995), 'Measuring Sustainable Economic Welfare: A Critique of the UK ISEW', Working Paper GEC 95-08, Centre for Social and Economic Research on the Global Environment, Norwich and London.

Atkinson, Giles and Kirk Hamilton (1996), 'Sustainable Development and Flows of Assets in International Trade', Working Paper, Centre for Social and Economic Research on the Global Environment, Norwich and London.

Atkinson, Giles, Richard Dubourg, Kirk Hamilton, Mohan Munasinghe, David Pearce and Carlos Young (1997), *Measuring Sustainable Development — Macroeconomics and the Environment*, Cheltenham, UK and Northampton, MA: Edward Elgar.

Ausubel, Jesse H. (1995), 'Technical Progress and Climatic Change', *Energy Policy*, **23** (4/5), 411–16.

Ayres, Robert U. and Jörg Walter (1991), 'The Greenhouse Effect: Damages, Costs and Abatement', *Environmental and Resource Economics*, **1** (3), 237–70.

Ayres, Robert U. (1997), 'Comments on Georgescu-Roegen', *Ecological Economics*, **22** (3), 285–87.

Ayres, Robert U. (2000), 'Commentary on the Utility of the Ecological Footprint Concept', *Ecological Economics*, **32** (3), 347–9.

Ayres, Robert U. (2007), 'On the Practical Limits to Substitution', Ecological Economics, 61 (1), 115-28.

Ayres, Robert U. (2008), 'Sustainability Economics: Where do We Stand?', *Ecological Economics*, **67** (2), 281–310.

Ayres, Robert U. and Allen V. Kneese (1969), 'Production, Consumption, and Externalities', *American Economic Review*, **59** (3), 282–97.

Ayres, Robert U. and Steven M. Miller (1980), 'The Role of Technological Change', *Journal of Environmental Economics and Management*, **7** (4), 353–71.

Azar, Christian and Thomas Sterner (1996), 'Discounting and Distributional Considerations in the Context of Global Warming', *Ecological Economics*, **19** (2), 169–84.

Baldwin, Richard (1995), 'Does Sustainability Require Growth?', in Ian Goldin and L. Alan Winters (eds), *Economics of Sustainable Growth*, Cambridge: Cambridge University Press, pp. 51–77.

Barbier, Edward B. (1989), *Economics, Natural-resource Scarcity and Development*, London: Earthscan.

Barbier, Edward B. (1994), 'Natural Capital and the Economics of Environment and Development', in A. Jansson, M. Hammer, C. Folke and R. Costanza (eds), *Investing in Natural Capital: The Ecological Economics Approach to Sustainability*, Washington DC: Island Press, pp. 291–322.

Barbier, Edward B., David W. Pearce and Anil Markandya (1990), 'Environmental Sustainability and Cost–Benefit Analysis', *Environment and Planning A*, **22** (9), 1259–66.

Barbier, Edward B., Joanne C. Burgess and Carl Folke (1994), *Paradise Lost? — The Ecological Economics of Biodiversity*, London: Earthscan.

Barnett, Harold J. (1979), 'Scarcity and Growth Revisited', in V. Kerry Smith (ed.), *Scarcity and Growth Reconsidered*, Baltimore, MD: Johns Hopkins University Press, pp. 163–217.

Barnett, Harold J. and Chandler Morse (1963), *Scarcity and Growth: The Economics of Natural Resource Availability*, Baltimore, MD: Johns Hopkins University Press.

Barney, Gerald O. (1980), *The Global 2000 Report to the President of the US — Entering the 21st Century*, A Report Prepared by the Council on Environmental Quality and the Department of State, New York: Pergamon Press.

Barrett, Scott (1992), 'Economic Growth and Environmental Preservation', *Journal of Environmental Economics and Management*, **23** (3), 289–300.

Barrett, Scott and Kathryn Graddy (2000), 'Freedom, Growth, and the Environment', *Environment and Development Economics*, **5** (4), 433–56.

Barro, Robert J. (1974), 'Are Government Bonds Net Wealth?', *Journal of Political Economy*, **82** (6), 1095–17.

Barro, Robert J. (1996), 'Democracy and Growth', *Journal of Economic Growth*, **1** (1), 1–27.

Barro, Robert J. and Xavier Sala-i-Martin (1995), *Economic Growth*, New York: McGraw-Hill.

Barry, Brian (1991), *Liberty and Justice: Essays in Political Theory*, Volume 2, Oxford: Clarendon Press.

Bartelmus, Peter, Ernst Lutz and Stefan Schweinfest (1993), 'Integrated Environmental and Economic Accounting: A Case Study of Papua New Guinea', in Ernst Lutz (ed.), *Toward Improved Accounting for the Envi-*

ronment — An UNSTAT–World Bank Symposium, Washington DC: World Bank, pp. 108–43.

Bateman, Ian, Alistair Munro, Bruce Rhodes, Chris Starmer and Robert Sugden (1997), 'Does Part–Whole Bias Exist? An Experimental Investigation', *Economic Journal*, **107** (441), 322–32.

Bättig, Michèle B. and Thomas Bernauer (2009), 'National Institutions and Global Public Goods: Are Democracies More Cooperative in Climate Change Policy?', *International Organization*, **63** (2), 281–308.

Baumol, William J. (1986), 'On the Possibility of Continuing Expansion of Finite Resources', *Kyklos*, **39** (2), 167–79.

Baumol, William J. and Wallace E. Oates (1971), 'The Use of Standards and Prices for Protection of the Environment', *Swedish Journal of Economics*, **73** (1), 42–54.

Becker, Gary S. and George J. Stigler (1977), 'De Gustibus Non Est Disputandum', *American Economic Review*, **67** (1), 76–90.

Becker, Robert A. (1982), 'Intergenerational Equity: The Capital-Environment Trade-Off', *Journal of Environmental Economics and Management*, **9** (2), 165–85.

Beckerman, Wilfred (1972), 'Economists, Scientists, and Environmental Catastrophe', *Oxford Economic Papers*, **24** (3), 327–44.

Beckerman, Wilfred (1974), *In Defence of Economic Growth*, London: Jonathan Cape.

Beckerman, Wilfred (1992a), 'Economic Development and the Environment — Conflict or Complementarity?', Working Paper No. 961, Washington DC: World Bank.

Beckerman, Wilfred (1992b), 'Economic Growth and the Environment: Whose Growth? Whose Environment?', *World Development*, **20** (4), 481–96.

Beckerman, Wilfred (1993), 'The Environmental Limits to Growth: A Fresh Look', in Herbert Giersch (ed.), *Economic Progress and Environmental Concerns*, Berlin: Springer, pp. 3–23.

Beckerman, Wilfred (1994), '"Sustainable Development": Is it a Useful Concept?', *Environmental Values*, **3** (3), 191–209.

Beckerman, Wilfred (1995), *Small is Stupid — Blowing the Whistle on the Greens*, London: Duckworth.

Beckerman, Wilfred and Joanna Pasek (1997), 'Plural Values and Environmental Valuation', *Environmental Values*, **6** (1), 65–86.

Behrens, Arno, Stefan Giljum, Jan Kovanda and Samuel Niza (2007), 'The Material Basis of the Global Economy. Worldwide Patterns of Natural Resource Extraction and their Implications for Sustainable Resource Use Policies', *Ecological Economics*, **64** (2), 444-53.

Bell, David E. (1982), 'Regret in Decision Making under Uncertainty', *Operations Research*, **30** (5), 961–81.

Beltratti, Andrea (1995), 'Sustainable Growth: Models and Policy Implications', in Gianna Boero and Aubrey Silberston (eds), *Environmental Economics*, Basingstoke: Macmillan, pp. 296–315.

Beltratti, Andrea, Graciela Chichilnisky and Geoffrey Heal (1998), 'Uncertain Preferences and Conservation', in Graciela Chichilnisky, Geoffrey Heal and Alessandro Vercelli (eds), *Sustainability: Dynamics and Uncertainty*, Dordrecht: Kluwer Academic, pp. 257–76

Berck, Peter (1995), 'Empirical Consequences of the Hotelling Principle', in Daniel W. Bromley (ed.), *Handbook of Environmental Economics*, Cambridge: Cambridge University Press, pp. 202–21.

Berck, Peter and Michael Roberts (1996), 'Natural Resource Prices: Will They Ever Turn Up?', *Journal of Environmental Economics and Management*, **31** (1), 65–78.

Berkes, Firket and Carl Folke (1992), 'A Systems Perspective on the Interrelations between Natural, Human-made and Cultural Capital', *Ecological Economics*, **5** (1), 1–8.

Berkes, Firket and Carl Folke (1994), 'Investing in Cultural Capital for Sustainable Use of Natural Capital', in A. Jansson, M. Hammer, C. Folke and R. Costanza (eds), *Investing in Natural Capital: The Ecological Economics Approach to Sustainability*, Washington DC: Island Press, pp. 128–49.

Bernauer, Thomas and Vally Koubi (2009), 'Effect of Political Institutions on Air Quality', *Ecological Economics*, **68** (5), 1355-65.

Berndt, Ernst R. and Barry C. Field (eds) (1981), *Modeling and Measuring Natural Resource Substitution*, Cambridge, MA: MIT Press.

Berndt, Ernst R. and David O. Wood (1975), 'Technology, Prices, and the Derived Demand for Energy', *Review of Economics and Statistics*, **57** (3), 259–68.

Berndt, Ernst R. and David O. Wood (1979), 'Engineering and Econometric Interpretations of Energy–Capital Complementarity', *American Economic Review*, **69** (3), 342–54.

Best, Aaron, Stefan Giljum, Craig Simmons, Daniel Blobel, Kevin Lewis, Mark Hammer, Sandra Cavalieri, Stephan Lutter and Cathy Maguire (2008), Potential of the Ecological Footprint for monitoring environmental impacts from natural resource use: Analysis of the potential of the Ecological Footprint and related assessment tools for use in the EU's Thematic Strategy on the Sustainable Use of Natural Resources. Report to the European Commission, DG Environment.

Biancardi, C., E. Tiezzi and S. Ulgiati (1993), 'Complete Recycling of Matter in the Frameworks of Physics, Biology and Ecological Economics', *Ecological Economics*, **8** (3), 1–5.

Biancardi, C., E. Tiezzi and S. Ulgiati (1996), 'The "Recycle of Matter" Debate. Physical Principles versus Practical Impossibility', *Ecological Economics*, **19** (3), 195–96.

Binder, Seth and Eric Neumayer (2005), 'Environmental Pressure Group Strength and Air Pollution: An Empirical Analysis', *Ecological Economics*, **55** (4), 527–38.

Binswanger, Mathias (2001), 'Technological Progress and Sustainable Development: What About the Rebound Effect?', *Ecological Economics*, **36** (1), 119–32.

Bishop, Richard C. (1978), 'Endangered Species and Uncertainty: The Economics of a Safe Minimum Standard', *American Journal of Agricultural Economics*, **60** (1), 10–18.

Bishop, Richard C. (1979), 'Endangered Species, Irreversibility, and Uncertainty: A Reply', *American Journal of Agricultural Economics*, **61** (2), 376–79.

Blanchette, Stephen (2008), 'A Hydrogen Economy and its Impact on the World as We Know it', *Energy Policy*, **36** (2), 522–30.

Bleys, Brent (2007), A Simplified Index of Sustainable Economic Welfare for the Netherlands, 1971–2004. Working Paper. Brussels: Vrije University.

Bleys, Brent (2008), 'Proposed Changes to the Index of Sustainable Economic Welfare: An Application to Belgium', *Ecological Economics*, **64** (4), 741–51.

Bodansky, Daniel (1991), 'Scientific Uncertainty and the Precautionary Principle', *Environment*, **33** (7), 4–5 and 43–4.

Boehmer-Christiansen, Sonja (1994), 'The Precautionary Principle in Germany — Enabling Government', in Timothy O'Riordan and James Cameron (eds), *Interpreting the Precautionary Principle*, London: Earthscan, pp. 31–60.

Bolt, Katharine, Mampite Matete and Michael Clemens (2002), *Manual for Calculating Adjusted Net Savings*, Environment Department, Washington DC: World Bank.

Bongaarts, John (1994), 'Can the Growing Human Population Feed Itself? – As Human Numbers Surge Toward 10 Billion, Some Experts Are Alarmed, Others Optimistic. Who Is Right?', *Scientific American*, **270** (3), 18–24.

Boserup, Ester (1990), *Economic and Demographic Relationships in Development*, Baltimore, MD: The Johns Hopkins University Press.

Bovenberg, A. Lans and Ruud A. de Mooij (1995), 'Do Environmental Taxes Yield a Double-dividend?', in Gianna Boera and Aubrey Silberston (eds), *Environmental Economics: Proceedings of a Conference held by the Confederation of European Economics Association at Oxford 1993*, London: Macmillan, pp. 52–69.

Bovenberg, A. Lans and Sjak Smulders (1995), 'Environmental Quality and Pollution-augmenting Technological Change in a Two-sector Endogenous Growth Model', *Journal of Public Economics*, **57** (3), 369–91.

Boyce, James K. (1994), 'Inequality as a Cause of Environmental Degradation', *Ecological Economics*, **11** (3), 169–78.

Boyce, James K. (2002), *The Political Economy of the Environment*, Cheltenham, UK and Northampton, MA: Edward Elgar.

Boyle, Kevin J., William H. Desvouges, F. Reed Johnson, Richard W. Dunford and Sara P. Hudson (1994), 'An Investigation of Part–Whole Biases in Contingent Valuation Studies', *Journal of Environmental Economics and Management*, **27** (1), 64–83.

BP (various years), *BP Statistical Review of World Energy*, London: BP.

Brekke, Kjell Arne (1997), 'Hicksian Income from Resource Extraction in an Open Economy', *Land Economics*, **73** (4), 516–27.

Brennan, Andrew John (2008), 'Theoretical Foundations of Sustainable Economic Welfare Indicators – ISEW and Political Economy of the Disembedded System', *Ecological Economics*, **67** (1), 1–19.

Bringezu, Stefan and Helmut Schütz (1996), 'Analyse des Stoffverbrauchs der deutschen Wirtschaft — Status quo, Trends und mögliche Prioritäten für Maßnahmen zur Erhöhug der Ressourcenproduktivität', in Jörg Köhn and Maria Welfens (eds), *Neue Ansätze in der Umweltökonomie*, Marburg: Metropolis-Verlag, pp. 230–51.

Bromley, Daniel W. (1989a), 'Entitlements, Missing Markets, and Environmental Uncertainty', *Journal of Environmental Economics and Management*, **17** (2), 181–94.

Bromley, Daniel W. (1989b), 'The Management of Common Property Natural Resources: Some Conceptual and Operational Fallacies', Discussion Paper 57, Washington DC: World Bank.

Brookes, Len (1990), 'The Greenhouse Effect: The Fallacies in the Energy Efficiency Solution', *Energy Policy*, **18** (2), 199–201.

Brookes, Len (1992), 'Energy Efficiency and Economic Fallacies: A Reply', *Energy Policy*, **20** (5), 390–93.

Broome, John (1992), *Counting the Cost of Global Warming*, Cambridge: Cambridge University Press.

Broome, John (1996), 'The Welfare Economics of Population', *Oxford Economic Papers*, **48** (2), 177–93.

Brouwer, Roy, Martin O'Connor and Walter Radermacher (1999), 'GREEned National STAtistical and Modelling Procedures: the GREENSTAMP Approach to the Calculation of Environmentally Adjusted National Income Figures', *International Journal of Sustainable Development*, **2** (1), 7–31.

Brown, Gardner M. and Barry C. Field (1978), 'Implications of Alternative Measures of Natural Resource Scarcity', *Journal of Political Economy*, **86** (2), 229–43.

Brown, Gardner M. and Barry C. Field (1979), 'The Adequacy of Measures for Signalling the Scarcity of Natural Resources', in V. Kerry Smith (ed.), *Scarcity and Growth Reconsidered*, Baltimore, MD: Johns Hopkins University Press, pp. 218–48.

Brown, Katrina, David W. Pearce, Charles Perrings and Timothy Swanson (1994), 'Economics and the Conservation of Global Biological Diversity', Working Paper No. 2, Global Environment Facility, Washington DC.

Brunnermeier, Smita B. and Arik Levinson (2004), 'Examining the Evidence on Environmental Regulations and Industry Location', *Journal of Environment and Development*, **13** (1), 6-41.

Bryant, Chris and Paul Cook (1992), 'Environmental Issues and the National Accounts', *Economic Trends*, **469**, 99–122.

Burda, Michael and Charles Wyplosz (1997), *Macroeconomics — a European Text*, Second Edition, Oxford: Oxford University Press.

Cameron, James and Will Wade-Gery (1995), 'Addressing Uncertainty: Law, Policy and the Development of the Precautionary Principle', in Bruno Dente (ed.), *Environmental Policy in Search of New Instruments*, Dordrecht: Kluwer, pp. 95–142.

Carbon Dioxide Information Analysis Center (1998): *Frequently Asked Questions*, http://cdiac.esd.ornl.gov/cdiac/home.html, Oak Ridge: Carbon Dioxide Information Analysis Center.

Carpenter, Richard A. (1994), 'Limitations in Measuring Ecosystem Sustainability', in Thaddeus C. Trzyna (ed.), *A Sustainable World: Defining and Measuring Sustainable Development*, London: Earthscan, pp. 175–97.

Carraro, Carlo, Marzio Galeotti and Massimo Gallo (1996), 'Environmental Taxation and Unemployment: Some Evidence on the "Double-dividend Hypothesis" in Europe', *Journal of Public Economics*, **62** (2), 141–81.

Carson, Carol S. and Allan H. Young (1994), 'The ISEW from a National Accounting Perspective', in Clifford W. Cobb and John B. Cobb (eds), *The Green National Product: A Proposed Index of Sustainable Economic Welfare*, Lanham: University Press of America, pp. 111–33.

Carson, Rachel (1962), *The Silent Spring*, New York: Fawcett Crest.

Carson, Richard T. and Robert Cameron Mitchell (1995), 'Sequencing and Nesting in Contingent Valuation Surveys', *Journal of Environmental Economics and Management*, **28** (2), 155–73.

Carter, Neal (2007), *The Politics of the Environment*. Second Edition. Cambridge: Cambridge University Press.

Castañeda, Beatriz E. (1999), 'An Index of Sustainable Economic Welfare (ISEW) for Chile', *Ecological Economics*, **28** (2), 231–44.

Castle, Emery N. (1997), 'A Comment on Georgescu-Roegen, Daly, Solow and Stiglitz', *Ecological Economics*, **22** (3), 305–6.

Castle, Emery N. and Robert P. Berrens (1993), 'Endangered Species, Economic Analysis, and the Safe Minimum Standard', *Northwest Environmental Journal*, **9** (1/2), 108–30.

Cavendish, William and Dennis Anderson (1994), 'Efficiency and Substitution in Pollution Abatement', *Oxford Economic Papers*, **46** (5), 774–99.

Chambers, Nicky, Craig Simmons and Mathis Wackernagel (2000), *Sharing Nature's Interest – Ecological Footprints as an Indicator of Sustainability*, London: Earthscan.

Chang, Kuo-Ping (1994), 'Capital-Energy Substitution and the Multi-Level CES Production Funtion', *Energy Economics*, **16** (1), 22–6.

Chapman, Duane, Vivek Suri and Steven G. Hall (1995), 'Rolling DICE for the Future of the Planet', *Contemporary Economic Policy*, **13** (3), 1–9.

Chhinh, Nyda and Philip Lawn (2007), 'The Sustainable Net Domestic Product of Cambodia, 1988-2004', *International Journal of Environment, Workplace and Employment*, **3** (2), 154-74.

Chiang, Alpha C. (1984), *Fundamental Methods of Mathematical Economics*, New York: McGraw-Hill.

Chiang, Alpha C. (1992), *Elements of Dynamic Optimization*, New York: McGraw-Hill.

Chichilnisky, Graciela (1996), 'An Axiomatic Approach to Sustainable Development', *Social Choice and Welfare*, **13** (2), 231–57.

Chichilnisky, Graciela and Geoffrey Heal (1983), 'Energy–Capital Substitution: A General Equilibrium Analysis', Collaborative Paper, International Institute for Applied Systems Analysis Laxenburg, reprinted in Geoffrey Heal (ed.) (1993), *The Economics of Exhaustible Resources*, Aldershot, UK and Brookfield, US: Edward Elgar, pp. 390–401.

Chichilnisky, Graciela and Geoffrey Heal (1993), 'Global Environmental Risks', *Journal of Economic Perspectives*, **7** (4), 65–86.

Ciriacy-Wantrup, S.V. (1952), *Resource Conservation: Economics and Policies*, Berkeley, CA: University of California Press.

Ciriacy-Wantrup, S.V. (1971), 'Conservation of the California Tule Elk: A Socioeconomic Study of a Survival Problem', *Biological Conservation*, **3** (1), 23–32.

Clapp, Jennifer and Peter Dauvergne (2005), *Paths to a Green World: The Political Economy of the Global Environment*. Cambridge, MA: MIT Press.

Clark, Colin W. (1995), 'Scale and the Feedback Mechanism in Market Economics', in Timothy M. Swanson (ed.), *The Economics and Ecology of Biodiversity Decline — The Forces Driving Global Change*, Cambridge: Cambridge University Press, pp. 143–8.

Clarke, Matthew and Sardar M.N. Islam (2005), 'Diminishing and Negative Welfare Returns of Economic Growth: an Index of Sustainable Economic Welfare (ISEW) for Thailand', *Ecological Economics* **54** (1), 81-93.

Cline, William R. (1991), 'Scientific Basis for the Greenhouse Effect', *Economic Journal*, **101** (407), 904–19.

Cline, William R. (1992), *The Economics of Global Warming*, Washington DC: Institute for International Economics.

Cline, William R. (1996), 'The Impact of Global Warming on Agriculture: Comment', *American Economic Review*, **86** (5), 1309–11.

Cobb, Clifford W. and John B. Cobb (1994), *The Green National Product: A Proposed Index of Sustainable Economic Welfare*, Lanham, MD: University Press of America.

Colby, Michael E. (1991), 'Environmental Management in Development: The Evolution of Paradigms', *Ecological Economics*, **3** (3), 193–213.

Cole, H.S.D., Christopher Freeman and Marie Jahoda (eds) (1973), *Thinking About the Future — A Critique of the Limits to Growth*, London: Chatto & Windus.

Cole, Matthew A. (2003), 'Development, Trade and the Environment: How Robust is the Environmental Kuznets Curve?', *Environment and Development Economics*, **8** (4), 557–80.

Cole, Matthew A. and Eric Neumayer (2003), 'The Pitfalls of Convergence Analysis: Is the Income Gap Really Increasing?', *Applied Economics Letters*, **10** (6), 355–7.

Cole, Matthew A. and Eric Neumayer (2004), 'Examining the Impact of Demographic Factors On Air Pollution', *Population and Environment*, **26** (1), 5–21.

Cole, Matthew A. and Eric Neumayer (2005), 'Economic Growth and the Environment in Developing Countries: What are the Implications of the Environmental Kuznets Curve?', in Peter Dauvergne (ed.): *International Handbook of Environmental Politics*, Cheltenham, UK and Northampton, MA: Edward Elgar Publishing, pp. 298–318.

Cole, Matthew A. and Robert J.R. Elliott (2005), 'FDI and the Capital Intensity of "Dirty" Sectors: A Missing Piece of the Pollution Haven Puzzle', *Review of Development Economics*, **9** (4), 530–48.

Cole, Matthew A., A.J. Rayner. and J.M. Bates (1997), 'The Environmental Kuznets Curve: An Empirical Analysis', *Environment and Development Economics* **2** (4), 401–16.

Commission of the European Communities–Eurostat, International Monetary Fund, Organisation of Economic Co-operation and Deeiopment, United Nations and World Bank (1993), *System of National Accounts 1993*, Brussels, Luxembourg, New York, Paris, Washington D.C.

Common, Mick S. (1993), 'A Cost Effective Environmentally Adjusted Economic Performance Indicator', Discussion Paper in Environmental Economics and Management 93-07, University of York, York.

Common, Mick S. (1995a), 'Economists Don't Read Science', *Ecological Economics* **15** (2), 101–03.

Common, Mick S. (1995b), *Sustainability and Policy: Limits to Economics*, Cambridge: Cambridge University Press.

Common, Mick S., R.K. Blamey and T.W. Norton (1993), 'Sustainability and Environmental Valuation', *Environmental Values*, **2** (4), 299–334.

Converse, A.O. (1996), 'On Complete Recycling', *Ecological Economics*, **19** (3), 193–94.

Costanza, Robert (1989), 'What is Ecological Economics?', *Ecological Economics*, **1** (1), 1–7.

Costanza, Robert (1994), 'Three General Policies to Achieve Sustainability', in A. Jansson, M. Hammer, C. Folke and R. Costanza (eds), *Investing in Natural Capital: The Ecological Economics Approach to Sustainability*, Washington DC: Island Press, pp. 392–407.

Costanza, Robert, Ralph d'Arge, Rudolf de Groot, Stephen Farber, Monica Grasso, Bruce Hannon, Karin Limburg, Shahid Naeem, Robert V. O'Neill, José Paruelo, Robert G. Raskin, Paul Suttan and Marjan van den Belt (1997), 'The Value of the World's Ecostystem Services and Natural Capital', *Ecological Economics*, **25** (1), 3–15.

Crafts, Nicholas (2002), 'UK Real National Income, 1950–1998: Some Grounds for Optimism', *National Institute Economic Review*, **181** (1), 87–95.

Cropper, Maureen and Charles Griffiths (1994), 'The Interaction of Population Growth and Environmental Quality', *American Economic Review Papers and Proceedings*, **84** (2), 250–4.

Cropper, Maureen L., William N. Evans, Stephen .J. Berardi, Maria M. Ducla-Soares and Paul R. Portney (1992), 'The Determinants of Pesticide Regulation: A Statistical Analysis of EPA Decision Making', *Journal of Political Economy,* **100** (1), 175-97.

Crowards, Tom M. (1998), 'Safe Minimum Standards: Costs and Opportunities', *Ecological Economics*, **25** (3), 303–14.

Cummings, R.G. and G.W. Harrison (1995), 'The Measurement and Decomposition of Nonuse Values: A Critical Review', *Environmental and Resource Economics*, **5** (3), 225–47.

d'Arge, Ralph C. (1994), 'Sustenance and Sustainability: How Can We Preserve and Consume Without Major Conflict?', in A. Jansson, M. Hammer, C. Folke and R. Costanza (eds), *Investing in Natural Capital: the Ecological Economics Approach to Sustainability*, Washington DC: Island Press, pp. 113–27.

Daily, Gretchen C., Anne H. Ehrlich and Paul R. Ehrlich (1994), 'Optimum Human Population Size', *Population and Environment*, **15** (6), 469–75.

Daily, Gretchen, Partha Dasgupta, Bert Bolin, Pierre Crosson, Jacques du Guerny, Paul Ehrlich, Carl Folke, Ann Mari Jansson, Bengt-Owe Jansson, Nils Kautsky, Ann Kinzig, Simon Levin, Karl-Göran Mäler, Per Pinstrup-Andersen, Domenico Siniscalco and Brian Walker (1998), 'Food Production, Population Growth, and the Environment', *Science*, **281**, 28 August, 1291–2.

Daly, Herman E. (1988), 'On Sustainable Development and National Accounts', in David Collard, David W. Pearce and David Ulph (eds), *Economics, Growth and Sustainable Environments*, New York: St. Martin's Press, pp. 41–55.

Daly, Herman E. (1991), 'Towards an Environmental Macroeconomics', *Land Economics*, **67** (2), 255–9.

Daly, Herman E. (1992a), *Steady-state Economics — Second edition with new essays*, London: Earthscan, first published in 1977.

Daly, Herman E. (1992b), 'Towards an Environmental Macroeconomics: Reply', *Land Economics*, **68** (2), 244–5.

Daly, Herman E. (1994), 'Operationalizing Sustainable Development by Investing in Natural Capital', in A. Jansson, M. Hammer, C. Folke and R. Costanza (eds), *Investing in Natural Capital: The Ecological Economics Approach to Sustainability*, Washington DC: Island Press, pp. 22–37.

Daly, Herman E. (1995a), 'On Wilfred Beckerman's Critique of Sustainable Development', *Environmental Values*, **4** (1), 49–55.

Daly, Herman E. (1995b), 'On Nicholas Georgescu-Roegen's Contributions to Economics: An Obituary Essay', *Ecological Economics*, **13** (3), 149–54.

Daly, Herman E. (1996), *Beyond Growth*, Boston, MA: Beacon Press.

Daly, Herman E. (2005), 'Economics in a full world', *Scientific American*, **293** (3), 100–107.

Daly, Herman E. and John B. Cobb (1989), *For the Common Good*, Boston: Beacon Press.

Daly, Herman E. and John B. Cobb (2007), 'ISEW. The "Debunking" Interpretation and the Person-in-Community Paradox: Comment on Rafael Ziegler', *Environmental Values*, **16** (3), 287–8.

Daly, Herman E. and Kenneth N. Townsend (1993), 'Introduction', in Herman E. Daly and Kenneth N. Townsend (eds), *Economics, Ecology, Ethics*, Cambridge, MA: MIT Press, pp. 1–10.

Daly, Herman E. and Robert Costanza (1992), 'Natural Capital and Sustainable Development', *Conservation Biology*, **6** (1), 37–46.

Daly, Herman E. and Robert Goodland (1994), 'An Ecological-Economic Assessment of Deregulation of International Commerce Under GATT', *Ecological Economics*, **9** (1), 73–92.

Daly, Herman E., Brian Czech, David L. Trauger, William E. Rees, Mansi Grover, Tracy Dobson and Stephen C. Trombulak (2007), 'Are we consuming too much – for what?', *Conservation Biology*, **21** (5), 1359–62.

Dasgupta, Partha (1990), 'Well-Being and the Extent of its Realisation in Poor Countries', *Economic Journal*, **100** (400), 1–32.

Dasgupta, Partha (1994), 'Optimal versus Sustainable Development', in I. Serageldin and A. Steer (eds), *Valuing the Environment*, Proceedings of the First Annual International Conference on Environmentally Sustainable Development, Washington DC: World Bank, pp. 35–46.

Dasgupta, Partha (1997), *Environmental and Resource Economics in the World of the Poor*, Internet Edition, Washington DC: Resources for the Future. (http:\\www.rff.org).

Dasgupta, Partha (1998), 'Population, Consumption and Resources: Ethical Issues', *Ecological Economics*, **24** (2/3), 139–52.

Dasgupta, Partha (2001a), 'Valuing Objects and Evaluating Policies in Imperfect Economies', *Economic Journal*, **111** (471), C1–C29.

Dasgupta, Partha (2001b), *Human well-being and the natural environment*, Oxford: Oxford University Press.

Dasgupta, Partha (2007), 'Comments on the Stern Review's Economics of Climate Change', *National Institute Economic Review*, 199, 4–7.

Dasgupta, Partha (2008), 'Nature in Economics', *Environmental and Resource Economics*, **39** (1), 1–7.

Dasgupta, Partha (2009), 'The Welfare Economic Theory of Green National Accounts', *Environmental and Resource Economics*, **42** (1), 3–38.

Dasgupta, Partha and Geoffrey Heal (1974), 'The Optimal Depletion of Exhaustible Resources, *Review of Economic Studies* Symposium, 3–28.

Dasgupta, Partha and Geoffrey Heal (1979), *Economic Theory and Exhaustible Resources*, Cambridge: Cambridge University Press.

Dasgupta, Partha and Martin Weale (1992), 'On Measuring the Quality of Life', *World Development*, **20** (1), 119–31.

Dasgupta, Partha, Scott Barrett and Karl-Göran Mäler (1999), 'Intergenerational Equity, Social Discount Rates and Global Warming', in Paul R. Portney and John P. Weyant (eds), *Discounting and Intergenerational Equity*, Washington DC: Resources for the Future, pp. 51–77.

Dasgupta, Susmita, Kirk Hamilton, Kiran D. Pandey and David Wheeler (2006), 'Environment During Growth: Accounting for Governance and Vulnerability', *World Development*, **34** (9), 1597–1611.

Dasgupta, Swapan and Tapan Mitra (1983), 'Intergenerational Equity and Efficient Allocation of Exhaustible Resources', *International Economic Review*, **24** (1), 133–53.

Davis, Graham A. and David J. Moore (2000), 'Valuing Mineral Stocks and Depletion in Green National Income Accounts', *Environment and Development Economics*, **5** (1–2), 109–27.

De Bruyn, S.M. and J.B. Opschoor (1997), 'Developments in the Throughput-Income Relationship: Theoretical and Empirical Observations', *Ecological Economics*, **20** (3), 255–68.

De Bruyn, S.M., J.C.J.M. Van den Bergh and J.B. Opschoor (1998), 'Economic Growth and Emissions: Reconsidering the Empirical Basis of Environmental Kuznets Curves', *Ecological Economics*, **25** (2), 161–75.

Deadman, D. and R. Kerry Turner (1988), 'Resource Conservation, Sustainability and Technical Change', in R. Kerry Turner (ed.), *Sustainable Enironmental Management Principles and Practice*, London: Belhaven, pp. 67–101.

Dean, Judith M., Mary E. Lovely and Hua Wang (2009), 'Are Foreign Investors Attracted to Weak Environmental Regulations? Evaluating the Evidence form China', *Journal of Development Economics*, **90** (1), 1–13.

Deshmukh, Sudhakar D. and Stanley R. Pliska (1985), 'A Martingale Characterization of the Price of a Non-renewable Resource with Decisions Involving Uncertainty', *Journal of Economic Theory*, **35** (2), 322–42.

Devarajan, Shantayanan and Robert J. Weiner (1995), 'Natural Resource Depletion and National Income Accounting: Is GNP in Kuwait and Norway Really so High?', Working Paper No. 95-13, School of Business and Public Management, George Washington University, Washington DC.

Diamond, P.A. and J. Hausman (1994), 'Contingent Valuation: Is Some Number Better than No Number?', *Journal of Economic Perspectives*, **8** (4), 45–64.

Diefenbacher, Hans (1994), 'The Index of Sustainable Economic Welfare: A Case Study of the Federal Republic of Germany', in Clifford W. Cobb and John B. Cobb (eds), *The Green National Product: A Proposed Index of Sustainable Economic Welfare*, Lanham: University Press of America, pp. 215–45.

Dietz, Simon and Nicholas Stern (2008), 'Why Economic Analysis Supports Strong Action on Climate Change: A Response to the Stern Review's Critics', *Review of Environmental Economics and Policy*, **2** (1), 94–113.

Dietz, Simon, Chris Hope and Nicola Patmore (2007), 'Some Economics of "Dangerous" Climate Change: Reflections on the Stern Review', *Global Environmental Change*, **17** (3–4), 311–25.

Dincer, Ibrahim (2002), 'The Role of Exergy in Energy Policy Making', *Energy Policy,* **30** (2), 137–49.

Dixit, Avinash, Peter Hammond and Michael Hoel (1980), 'On Hartwick's Rule for Regular Maximin Paths of Capital Accumulation and Resource Depletion', *Review of Economic Studies*, **47** (3), 551–6.

Dobbs, Ian M. (1991), 'A Bayesian Approach to Decision-making under Ambiguity', *Economica*, **58** (232), 417–40.

Drèze, Jean and Amartya K. Sen (1989), *Hunger and Public Action*, Oxford: Clarendon Press.

Drèze, Jean, Amartya K. Sen and Athar Hussain (eds) (1995), *The Political Economy of Hunger*, Oxford: Clarendon Press.

Dyson, Tim (1994), 'Population Growth and Food Production: Recent Global and Regional Trends', *Population and Development Review*, **20** (2), 397–411.

Dyson, Tim (1996), *Population and Food — Global Trends and Future Prospects*, London: Routledge.

Dyson, Tim (2001), World food trends: a neo-Malthusian prospect?, *Proceedings of the American philosophical society*, **145** (4). 438–455

Easterlin, Richard A. (2003), 'Explaining happiness', Proceeding of the National Academy of Sciences, **100** (19), 11176–83.

Ehrenfeld, David (1986), 'Why Put a Value on Biodiversity?', in Edward O. Wilson (ed.), *Biodiversity*, Washington DC: National Academy Press, pp. 212–16.

Ehrlich, Paul R. (1989), 'The Limits to Substitution: Meta-resource Depletion and a New Economic–Ecological Paradigm', *Ecological Economics*, **1** (1), 9–16.

Ehrlich, Paul R. and Anne H. Ehrlich (1992), 'The Value of Biodiversity', *Ambio*, **21** (3), 219–26.

Eisner, Robert (1988), 'Extended Accounts for National Income and Product', *Journal of Economic Literature*, **26** (4), 1611–84.

Eisner, Robert (1990), *The Total Incomes System of Accounts*, Chicago: Chicago University Press.

Eisner, Robert (1994), 'The Index of Sustainable Economic Welfare: Comment', in Clifford W. Cobb and John B. Cobb (eds), *The Green National Product: A Proposed Index of Sustainable Economic Welfare*, Lanham: University Press of America, pp. 97–110.

Ekins, Paul (1994), 'The Environmental Sustainability of Economic Processes: A Framework for Analysis', in J.C.J.M. van den Bergh and Jan van der Straaten (eds), *Toward Sustainable Development: Concepts, Methods, and Policy*, Washington DC: Island Press, pp. 25–55.

Ekins, Paul (1995), 'Rethinking the Costs Related to Global Warming: A Survey of the Issues', *Environmental and Resource Economics*, **6** (3), 231–77.

Ekins, Paul (1996), 'The Secondary Benefits of CO_2 Abatement: How much Emission Reduction Do They Justify?', *Ecological Economics*, **16** (1), 13–24.

Ekins, Paul (1997), 'The Kuznets Curve for the Environment and Economic Growth: Examining the Evidence', *Environment and Planning A*, **29** (5), 805–30.

Ekins, Paul (2003), 'Identifying Critical Natural Capital: Conclusions about Critical Natural Capital', *Ecological Economics*, **44** (2–3), 277–92.

Ekins, Paul and Michael Jacobs (1995), 'Environmental Sustainability and the Growth of GDP: Conditions for Compatibility', in V. Bhaskar and Andrew Glyn (eds), *The North, the South and the Environment*, London: Earthscan, pp. 9–46.

Ekins, Paul and Sandrine Simon (1999), 'The Sustainability Gap: A Practical Indicator of Sustainability in the Framework of the National Accounts', *International Journal of Sustainable Development*, **2** (1), 32–58.

Ekins, Paul and Sandrine Simon (2001), 'Estimating Sustainability Gaps: Methods and Preliminary Applications for the UK and the Netherlands', *Ecological Economics*, **37** (1), 5–22.

Ekins, Paul, Carl Folke and Rudolf De Groot (2003), 'Identifying Critical Natural Capital', Editorial Introduction to Special Issue, *Ecological Economics*, **44** (2–3), 159–63.

El Serafy, Salah (1981), 'Absorptive Capacity, the Demand for Revenue, and the Supply of Petroleum', *Journal of Energy and Development*, **7** (1), 73–88.

El Serafy, Salah (1989), 'The Proper Calculation of Income from Depletable Natural Resources', in Yusuf J. Ahmad, Salah El Serafy and Ernst Lutz (eds), *Environmental Accounting for Sustainable Development: A UNDP–World Bank Symposium*, Washington DC: World Bank, pp. 10–18.

El Serafy, Salah (1991), 'The Environment as Capital', in Robert Costanza (ed.), *Ecological Economics: The Science and Management of Sustainability*, New York: Columbia University Press, pp. 168–75.

El Serafy, Salah (1993), 'Depletable Resources: Fixed Capital or Inventories?', in Alfred Franz and Carsten Stahmer (eds), *Approaches to Environmental Accounting: Proceedings of the IARIW Conference on Environmental Accounting 1991*, Heidelberg: Springer, pp. 245–58.

El Serafy, Salah (1997), 'Green Accounting and Economic Policy', *Ecological Economics*, **21** (3), 217–29.

El Serafy, Salah (2001), 'Steering by the Right Compass: the Quest for a Better Assessment of the National Product', in Ekko C. van Ierland, Jan van der Straaten and Herman R.J. Vollebergh (eds), *Economic Growth and Valuation of the Environment: A Debate*, Cheltenham, UK and Northampton, MA: Edward Elgar, pp. 189–210.

Eurostat (2002), *Material Use in the European Union 1980-2000: Indicators and Analysis*, Brussels: Statistical Office of the European Commission.

Faber, Malte, Reiner Manstetten and John Proops (1992), 'Humankind and the Environment: An Anatomy of Surprise and Ignorance', *Environmental Values*, **1** (3), 217–41.

Factor 10 Club (1997), *Statement to Government and Business Leaders*, Wuppertal: Wuppertal Institute for Climate, Environment and Energy.

Fankhauser, Samuel (1994), 'The Economic Costs of Global Warming Damage: A Survey', *Global Environmental Change*, **4** (4), 301–9.

Fankhauser, Samuel (1995), *Valuing Climate Change: The Economics of the Greenhouse*, London: Earthscan.

Fankhauser, Samuel and Richard S.J. Tol (1996), 'Climate Change Costs — Recent Advancements in the Economic Assessment', *Energy Policy*, **24** (7), 665–73.

Farrow, Scott (1985), 'Testing the Efficiency of Extraction from a Stock Resource', *Journal of Political Economy*, **93** (3), 452–87.

Farrow, Scott (1995), 'Extinction and Market Forces: Two Case Studies', *Ecological Economics*, **13** (2), 115–23.

Farzin, Y. Hossein (1995), 'Technological Change and the Dynamics of Resource Scarcity Measures', *Journal of Environmental Economics and Management*, **29** (1), 105–20.

Farzin, Y. Hossein and Craig A. Bond (2006), 'Democracy and Environmental Quality', *Journal of Development Economics*, **81** (1), 213–35.

Faucheux, Sylvie and Géraldine Froger (1995), 'Decision-making under Environmental Uncertainty', *Ecological Economics*, **15** (1), 29–42.

Faucheux, Sylvie and Martin O'Connor (eds) (1998), *Valuation for Sustainable Development – Methods and Policy Indicators*, Cheltenham, UK and Northampton, MA: Edward Elgar.

Faucheux, Sylvie, Eliot Muir and Martin O'Connor (1997), 'Neoclassical Natural Capital Theory and "Weak" Indicators for Sustainability', *Land Economics*, **73** (4), 528–52.

Faucheux, Sylvie, Martin O'Connor and Sybille van den Hove (1998), 'Towards a Sustainable National Income?', in Sylvie Faucheux and Martin O'Connor (eds), *Valuation for Sustainable Development – Methods and Policy Indicators*, Cheltenham, UK and Northampton, MA: Edward Elgar, pp. 261–79.

Ferguson, Andrew (1999), 'The Logical Foundations of Ecological Footprints', *Environment, Development and Sustainability*, **1**, 149–56.

Ferguson, Andrew (2002), 'The Assumptions Underlying Eco-Footprinting', *Population and Environment*, **23** (3), 303–13.

Ferguson, Dieneke, Christian Haas, Peter Reynard and Simon Zadek (1996), 'Dangerous Curves: Does the Environment Improve with Economic

Growth?', Report by the New Economics Foundation for WWF International, World Wide Fund for Nature, Gland.

Ferrari, Sylvie, Stephane Genoud and Jean-Baptiste Lesourd (2001), 'Thermodynamics and Economics: Towards Exergy-based Indicators of Sustainable Development', *Schweizerische Zeitschrift für Volkswirtschaft und Statistik*, **137** (3), 319–36.

Fiala, Nathan (2008), 'Measuring Sustainability: Why the Ecological Footprint is Bad Economics and Bad Environmental Science', *Ecological Economics*, **67** (4), 519–25.

Field, Barry and Charles Grebenstein (1980), 'Capital–Energy Substitution in US Manufacturing', *Review of Economics and Statistics*, **62** (2), 207–12.

Filion, Fern L., James P. Foley and Andre J. Jacquemot (1994), 'The Economics of Global Ecotourism', in Mohan Munasinghe and Jeffrey McNeely (eds), *Protected Area Economics and Policy: Linking Conservation and Sustainable Development*, Washington DC: World Bank, pp. 235–52.

Fischer-Kowalski (1998), 'Society's Metabolism – The Intellectual History of Materials Flow Analysis, Part I, 1860-1970', *Journal of Industrial Ecology*, **2** (1), 61-78.

Fischer-Kowalski and Walter Hüttler (1998), 'Society's Metabolism – The Intellectual History of Materials Flow Analysis, Part II, 1970-1998', *Journal of Industrial Ecology*, **2** (4), 107-36.

Fisher, Anthony C. (1979), 'Measures of Natural Resource Scarcity', in V. Kerry Smith (ed.), *Scarcity and Growth Reconsidered*, Baltimore: Johns Hopkins University Press, pp. 249–75.

Fisher, Irving (1906), *Nature of Capital and Income*. New York: A.M. Kelly.

Flores, Nicholas E. and Richard T. Carson (1997), 'The Relationship between the Income Elasticities of Demand and Willingness to Pay', *Journal of Environmental Economics and Management*, **33** (3), 287–95.

Foster, Vivien and Susana Mourato (2000), 'Valuing the Multiple Imapcts of Pesticide Use in the UK: A Contingent Ranking Approach', *Journal of Agricultural Economics*, **51** (1), 1–21.

Fredriksson, Per G., Eric Neumayer, Richard Damania and Scott Gates (2005), 'Environmentalism, Democracy, and Pollution Control', *Journal of Environmental Economics and Management*, **49** (2), 343–65.

Freeman, Myrick A. (1993), *The Measurement of Environmental and Resource Values*, Washington DC: Resources for the Future.

Galeotti, Marzio, Matteo Manera and Alessandro Lanza (2009), 'On the Robustness of Robustness Checks of the Environmental Kuznets Curve Hypothesis', *Environmental and Resource Economics*, **42** (4), 551–74.

Gardiner, Stephen M. (2004), 'Ethics and Global Climate Change', *Ethics*, **114** (3), 555–600.

Gawel, Erik (1998), 'Das Elend der Stoffstromökonomie – Eine Kritik', *Konjunkturpolitik* **44** (2), 173–206.

Gawel, Erik (2000), 'Probleme einer Stoffstromökonomik', *Konjunkturpolitik*, **46** (1–2), 164–89.

Georgescu-Roegen, Nicholas (1971), *The Entropy Law and the Economic Process*, Cambridge, MA: Harvard University Press.

Georgescu-Roegen, Nicholas (1975), 'Energy and Economic Myths', *Southern Economic Journal*, **41** (3), 347–81.

Georgescu-Roegen, Nicholas (1986), 'The Entropy Law and the Economic Process in Retrospect', *Eastern Economic Journal*, **12** (1), 3–25.

Georgiou, Stavros, Dale Whittington, David W. Pearce and Dominic Moran (1997), *Economic Values and the Environment in the Developing World*, Cheltenham, UK and Northampton, MA: Edward Elgar.

Gerlagh, Reyer and B.C.C. van der Zwaan (2002), 'Long-Term Substitutability between Environmental and Man-Made Goods', *Journal of Environmental Economics and Management*, **44** (2), 329–45.

Gerlagh, Reyer, Rob Dellink, Marjan Hofkes and Harmen Verbruggen (2001), 'An Applied General Equilibrium Model to Calculate a Sustainable National Income for the Netherlands', Report W-01/16, Free University, Institute for Environmental Studies, Amsterdam.

Gerlagh, Reyer, Rob Dellink, Marjan Hofkes and Harmen Verbruggen (2002), 'A Measure of Sustainable National Income for the Netherlands', *Ecological Economics*, **41** (1), 157–74.

Gillies, Donald (1993), *Philosophy of Science in the Twentieth Century: An Introduction*, Oxford: Blackwell.

Goeller, H.E. and A. Zucker (1984), 'Infinite Resources: The Ultimate Strategy', *Science*, **223** (4635), 456–62.

Goodland, Robert (1995), 'The Concept of Environmental Sustainability', *Annual Review of Ecological Systems*, **26** (1), 1–24.

Goodland, Robert and Herman E. Daly (1992), 'Ten Reasons Why Northern Income Growth Is Not the Solution to Southern Poverty', in Robert Goodland, Herman E. Daly and Salah El Serafy (ed.), *Population, Technology, and Lifestyle*, Washington DC: Island Press, pp. 128–45.

Gordon, Robert B., Tjalling C. Koopmans, William D. Nordhaus and Brian J. Skinner (1987), *Toward a New Iron Age? — Quantitative Modeling of Resource Exhaustion*, Cambridge, MA: Harvard University Press.

Goulder, Lawrence H. (1994), 'Environmental Taxation and the 'Double-dividend': A Reader's Guide', Working Paper No. 74, Center for Economic Studies, University of Munich, Munich, also printed in *International Tax and Public Finance*, **2** (2), 1995, 157–83.

Graham-Tomasi, Theodore, C. Ford Runge and William F. Hyde (1986), 'Foresight and Expectations in Models of Natural Resource Markets', *Land Economics*, **62** (3), 234–49.

Grazi, Fabio, Jeroen C.J.M. van den Bergh and Piet Rietveld (2007), 'Spatial Welfare Economics versus Ecological Footprint: Modeling Agglomeration, Externalities, and Trade', *Environmental and Resource Economics*, **38** (1), 135–53.

Greer, Mark R. (1995), 'Aggressive Greenhouse Gas Policies: How They Could Spur Economic Growth', *Journal of Economic Issues*, **29** (4), 1045–62.

Gren, I.M., C. Folke, R.K. Turner and I. Bateman (1994), 'Primary and Secondary Values of Wetland Ecosystems', *Environmental and Resource Economics*, **4** (1), 55–74.

Griffin, James M. (1981), 'The Energy–Capital Complementarity Controversy: a Progress Report on Reconciliation Attempts', in Ernst R. Berndt and Barry C. Field (eds), *Modeling and Measuring Natural Resource Substitution*, Cambridge, MA: MIT Press, pp. 70–80.

Griffin, James M. and Paul R. Gregory (1976), 'An Intercountry Translog Model of Energy Substitution Responses', *American Economic Review*, **66** (5), 845–57.

Gross, L.S. and E.C.H. Veendorp (1990), 'Growth with Exhaustible Resources and a Materials-Balance Production Function', *Natural Resource Modeling*, **4** (1), 77–94.

Grossman, Gene M. (1995), 'Pollution and Growth: What Do We Know?', in I. Goldin and L. Winters (eds), *The Economics of Sustainable Development*, Cambridge: Cambridge University Press, pp. 19–46.

Grossman, Gene M. and Alan B. Krueger (1993), 'Environmental Impacts of a North American Free Trade Agreement', in P. Garber (ed.), *The US–Mexico Free Trade Agreement*, Cambridge (Mass.): MIT Press.

Grossman, Gene M. and Alan B. Krueger (1995), 'Economic Growth and the Environment', *Quarterly Journal of Economics*, **110** (2), 353–77.

Grossman, Gene M. and Alan B. Krueger (1996), 'The inverted-U: what does it mean?', *Environment and Development Economics*, **1** (1), 119–122.

Grubb, Michael (1997), 'Technologies, Energy Systems and the Timing of CO2 Emissions Abatement', *Energy Policy*, **25** (2), 159–72.

Guenno, G. and S. Tiezzi (1998), 'An Index of Sustainable Economic Welfare for Italy', Working Paper 5/98, Fonazione Eni Enrico Mattei, Milano.

Guha, Ramachandra (1989), 'Radical American Environmentalism and Wilderness Preservation: A Third World Critique', *Environmental Ethics*, **11** (1), 71–83.

Gutes, Maite Cabeza (1996), 'The Concept of Weak Sustainability', *Ecological Economics*, **17** (2), 147–56.

Hall, Darwin C. and Jane V. Hall (1984), 'Concepts and Measures of Natural Resource Scarcity with a Summary of Recent Trends', *Journal of Environmental Economics and Management*, **11** (4), 363–79.

Halvorsen, Robert and Tim R. Smith (1991), 'A Test of the Theory of Exhaustible Resources', *Quarterly Journal of Economics*, **106** (1), 123–40.

Hamilton, Clive (1999), 'The Genuine Progress Indicator: Methodological Advances and Results from Australia', *Ecological Economics*, **30** (1), 13–28.

Hamilton, Clive and Richard Denniss (2000), 'Tracking Well-being in Australia – The Genuine Progress Indicator 2000', Discussion Paper Number 35. The Australia Institute, Canberra.

Hamilton, Kirk (1994), 'Green Adjustments to GDP', *Resources Policy*, **20** (3), 155–68.

Hamilton, Kirk (1995), 'Sustainable Development and Green National Accounts', Ph.D. thesis, London: University College London.

Hamilton, Kirk (1996), 'Pollution and Pollution Abatement in the National Accounts', *Review of Income and Wealth*, **42** (1), 13–33.

Hamilton, Kirk (1997), 'Forest Resources and National Income', World Bank, Environment Department, Working Paper, Washington DC: World Bank.

Hamilton, Kirk (2000), 'Genuine Saving as a Sustainability Indicator', Environment Department Paper No. 77, Washington DC: World Bank.

Hamilton, Kirk (2002), 'Sustaining Economic Welfare – Estimating Changes in Per Capita Wealth', Policy Research Working Paper 2498, Washington DC: World Bank.

Hamilton, Kirk and Giles Atkinson (1996), 'Air Pollution and Green Accounts', *Energy Policy*, **24** (7), 675–84.

Hamilton, Kirk and Giles Atkinston (2006), *Wealth, Welfare and Sustainability*. Cheltenham, UK and Northampton, MA: Edward Elgar.

Hamilton, Kirk and Giovanni Ruta (2009), 'Wealth Accounting, Exhaustible Resources and Social Welfare', *Environmental and Resource Economics*, **42** (1), 53–64.

Hamilton, Kirk and Michael Clemens (1999), 'Genuine Savings Rates in Developing Countries', *World Bank Economic Review*, **13** (2), 75–98.

Hamilton, Kirk, Giles Atkinson and David W. Pearce (1997), 'Genuine saving as an Indicator of Sustainability', Working Paper, World Bank and Centre for Social and Economic Research on the Global Environment, Washington DC, Norwich and London.

Hammond, P.J. (1988), 'Consequentialist Demographic Norms and Parenting Rights', *Social Choice and Welfare*, **5**, 127–45.

Hanemann, W. Michael (1991), 'Willingness to Pay and Willingness to Accept: How Much Can They Differ?', *American Economic Review*, **81** (3), 635–47.

Hanemann, W. Michael (1994), 'Valuing the Environment Through Contingent Valuation', *Journal of Economic Perspectives*, **8** (4), 19–43.

Hanley, Nick and Clive L. Spash (1993), *Cost–benefit Analysis and the Environment*, Cheltenham, UK and Northampton, MA: Edward Elgar.

Hanley, Nick and Jennifer Milne (1996), 'Ethical Beliefs and Behaviour in Contingent Valuation Surveys', *Journal of Environmental Planning and Management*, **39** (2), 255–72.

Hanley, Nick, Clive Spash and Lorna Walker (1995), 'Problems in Valuing the Benefits of Biodiversity Protection', *Environmental and Resource Economics*, **5** (3), 249–72.

Harbaugh, W., A. Levinson and D. Wilson (2002), 'Reexamining the Empirical Evidence for an Environmental Kuznets Curve', *Review of Economics and Statistics*, **84** (3), 541–51.

Hardin, Garrett (1968), 'The Tragedy of the Commons', *Science*, **162** (3859), 1243–8.

Harris, Michael (2007), 'On Income, Sustainability and the "Microfoundations" of the Genuine Progress Indicator', *International Journal of Environment, Workplace and Employment*, **3** (2), 119–31.

Harrison, G.W. (1992), 'Valuing Public Goods with the Contingent Valuation Method: A Critique of Kahneman and Knetsch', *Journal of Environmental Economics and Management*, **23** (3), 248–57.

Hartwick, John M. (1977), 'Intergenerational Equity and the Investing of Rents from Exhaustible Resources', *American Economic Review*, **67** (5), 972–4.

Hartwick, John M. (1978a), 'Substitution Among Exhaustible Resources and Intergenerational Equity', *Review of Economic Studies*, **45** (2), 347–54.

Hartwick, John M. (1978b), 'Investing Returns from Depleting Renewable Resource Stocks and Intergenerational Equity', *Economics Letters*, **1** (1), 85–8.

Hartwick, John M. (1990), 'Natural Resources, National Accounting and Economic Depreciation, *Journal of Public Economics*, **43** (3), 291–304.

Hartwick, John M. (1992), 'Deforestation and National Accounting', *Environmental and Resource Economics*, **2** (5), 513–21.

Hartwick, John M. (1993), 'Notes on Economic Depreciation of Natural Resource Stocks and National Accounting', in Alfred Franz and Carsten Stahmer (eds), *Approaches to Environmental Accounting: Proceedings of the IARIW Conference on Environmental Accounting 1991*, Heidelberg: Springer, pp. 167–98.

Hartwick, John M. (1995), 'Constant Consumption Paths in Open Economies with Exhaustible Resources', *Review of International Economics*, **3** (3), 275–83.

Hartwick, John M. and Anja Hageman (1993), 'Economic Depreciation of Mineral Stocks and the Contribution of El Serafy', in Ernst Lutz (ed.), *Toward Improved Accounting for the Environment*, Washington DC: World Bank, pp. 211–35.

Hartwick, John M. and Nancy D. Olewiler (1986), *The Economics of Natural Resource Use*, New York: Harper & Row.

Hausman, Daniel M. (1992), *The Inexact and Separate Science of Economics*, Cambridge: Cambridge University Press.

Hausman, J. (ed.) (1993), *Contingent Valuation: A Critical Assessment*, Amsterdam: Elsevier.

Heal, Geoffrey (2009), 'Climate Economics: A Meta-Review and Some Suggestions for Future Research', *Review of Environmental Economics and Policy*, **3** (1), 4–21.

Hecht, Joy (2001), *Environmental Accounting: What's it All About?*, Gland: International Union for the Conservation of Nature.

Heinen, J.T. (1994), 'Emerging, Diverging and Converging Paradigms on Sustainable Development', *International Journal of Sustainable Development and World Ecology*, **1** (1), 22–33.

Helm, Dieter (2008), 'Climate-change Policy: Why has so Little been Achieved?', *Oxford Review of Economic Policy*, **24** (2), 211–38.

Herendeen, Robert A. (1999), 'EMERGY, Value, Ecology and Economics', in Jeroen C.J.M. van den Bergh (ed.), *Handbook of Environmental and Resource Economics*, Cheltenham, UK and Northampton, MA: Edward Elgar, pp. 954–64.

Heyes, Anthony G. and Catherine Liston-Heyes (1995), 'Sustainable Resource Use: The Search for Meaning', *Energy Policy*, **23** (1), 1–3.

Hicks, John Richard (1939), 'The Foundations of Welfare Economics', *Economic Journal*, **49** (196), 696–712.

Hicks, John Richard (1946), *Value and Capital*, Oxford: Oxford University Press.

Hille, John (1997), *The Concept of Environmental Space*, Expert Corner no. 1997/2, Copenhagen: European Environment Agency.

Hinrichs, Doug (1997), '2500 Economists Agree on Risks to Global Climate Change', *Ecological Economics Bulletin*, **2** (2), 16–18.

Hinterberger, Friedrich and Fred Luks (1998), 'Dematerialization, Employment and Competitiveness in a Globalized Economy', Plenary Session Paper, Fifth Biennial Conference of the International Society for Ecological Economics, 15–19 November 1998, Santiago de Chile.

Hinterberger, Friedrich and Gerhard Wegner (1996), 'Limited Knowledge and the Precautionary Principle: On the Feasibility of Environmental Policies', Working Paper, Wuppertal Institute for Climate, Environment and Energy, Wuppertal.

Hinterberger, Friedrich and Maria Welfens (1996), 'Warum inputorientierte Umweltpolitik?', in Jörg Köhn and Maria Welfens (eds), *Neue Ansätze in der Umweltökonomie*, Marburg: Metropolis-Verlag, pp. 21–43.

Hinterberger, Friedrich, Fred Luks and Friedrich Schmidt-Bleek (1997), 'Material Flows vs. "Natural Capital" – What Makes an Economy Sustainable?', *Ecological Economics*, **23** (1), 1–15.

Hinterberger, Friedrich, Fred Luks and Marcus Stewen (1999), 'Wie ökonomisch ist die Stoffstromökonomik? Eine Gegenkritik', *Konjunkturpolitik*, **45** (4), 358–75.

Hoevenagel, Ruud (1996), 'The Validity of the Contingent Valuation Method: Perfect and Regular Embedding', *Environmental and Resource Economics*, **7** (1), 57–78.

Hofkes, Marjan, Reyer Gerlagh, Wietze Lise and Harmen Verbruggen (2002), 'Sustainable National Income: A Trend Analysis for the Netherlands for 1990–1995', Report R-02/02, Free University, Institute for Environmental Studies, Amsterdam.

Hohl, Andreas and Clement A. Tisdell (1993), 'How Useful are Environmental Safety Standards in Economics? — The Example of Safe Minimum Standards for Protection of Species', *Biodiversity and Conservation*, **2** (2), 168–81.

Hohmeyer, Olav (1992), *Adäquate Berücksichtigung der Erschöpfbarkeit nicht erneuerbarer Ressourcen, Fraunhofer-Institut für Systemtechnik und Innovationsforschung*, Bericht im Rahmen des Forschungsvorhabens 'Externe Kosten der Energie' der PROGNOS AG Basel, Karlsruhe: Fraunhofer-Institut.

Holling, C.S. (1995), 'Biodiversity in the Functioning of Ecosystems: an Ecological Synthesis', in Charles Perrings (ed.), *Biodiversity Loss: Economic and Ecological Issues*, Cambridge: Cambridge University Press, pp. 44–83.

Holtz-Eakin, Douglas and Thomas M. Selden (1995), 'Stoking the Fires? CO_2 Emissions and Economic Growth', *Journal of Public Economics*, **57** (1), 85–101.

Hotelling, Harold (1931), 'The Economics of Exhaustible Resources', *Journal of Political Economy*, **39** (2), 137–75.

Howarth, Richard B. (1991), 'Energy Use in US Manufacturing: The Impacts of the Energy Shocks on Sectoral Output, Industry Structure, and Energy Intensity', *Journal of Energy Development*, **14** (2), 175–91.

Howarth, Richard B. (1996), 'Climate Change and Overlapping Generations', *Contemporary Economic Policy*, **14** (4), 100–11.

Howarth, Richard B. (1997), 'Energy Efficiency and Economic Growth', *Contemporary Economic Policy*, **15** (4), 1–9.

Howarth, Richard B. and Richard B. Norgaard (1993), 'Intergenerational Transfers and the Social Discount Rate', *Environmental and Resource Economics*, **3** (4), 337–58.

Hudson, Edward and Dale Jorgenson (1974), 'US Energy Policy and Economic Growth', *Bell Journal of Economics*, **5** (2), 461–514.

Huesemann, M.H. (2003), 'The Limits of Technological Solutions to Sustainable Development', *Clean Technolgy and Environmental Policy*, **5** (1), 21-34.

Hueting, Roefie (1980), *New Scarcity and Economic Growth: More Welfare Through Less Production?*, Amsterdam, New York, Oxford: New Holland Publishing.

Hueting, Roefie (1991), 'Correcting National Income for Environmental Losses: A Practical Solution for a Theoretical Dilemma', in Robert Costanza (ed.), *Ecological Economics: The Science and Management of Sustainability*, New York: Columbia University Press, pp. 194–213.

Hueting, Roefie and Bart de Boer (2001), 'Environmental Valuation and Sustainable National Income According to Hueting', in Ekko C. van Ierland, Jan van der Straaten and Herman R.J. Vollebergh (eds), *Economic Growth and Valuation of the Environment: A Debate*, Cheltenham, UK and Northampton, MA: Edward Elgar, pp. 17–77.

Hueting, Roefie and Lucas Reijnders (1998), 'Sustainability is an Objective Concept', *Ecological Economics*, **27** (2), 139–47.

Hueting, Roefie and Peter Bosch (1990), 'On the Correction of National Income for Environmental Losses', *Statistical Journal of the United Nations ECE*, **7** (2), 75–83.

Hung, N.M. (1993), 'Natural Resources, National Accounting, and Economic Depreciation: Stock Effects', *Journal of Public Economics*, **51** (3), 379–89.

IEA (1997), *Indicators of Energy Use and Efficiency – Understanding the Link between Energy and Human Activity*, Paris: International Energy Agency.

Imhoff, Marc L., Lahouari Bounoua, Taylor Ricketss, Colby Loucks, Robert Harriss and William T. Lawrence (2004), 'Global Patterns in Human Consumption of Net Primary Production', *Nature*, **429** (24 June), 870–3.

IMV (2002), *Assessing the Ecological Footprint*, Copenhagen: Danish Environmental Institute.

Ingham, Alan and Alistair Ulph (1991), 'Market-based Instruments for Reducing CO_2 Emissions', *Energy Policy*, **19** (2), 138–48.

Ingham, Alan, James Maw and Alistair Ulph (1991), 'Empirical Measures of Carbon Taxes', *Oxford Review of Economic Policy*, **7** (2), 99–122.

IPCC (1996), *Climate Change 1995 — Economic and Social Dimensions of Climate Change — Contribution of Working Group III to the Second Assessment Report of the Intergovernmental Panel on Climate Change*, Cambridge: Cambridge University Press.

IPCC (2007a), *Climate Change 2007: The Physical Science Basis*, New York: Cambridge University Press.

IPCC (2007b), *Climate Change 2007: Impacts, Adaptation, and Vulnerability*, New York: Cambridge University Press.

IPCC (2007c), *Climate Change 2007: Mitigation of Climate Change*, New York: Cambridge University Press.

Jackson, Tim (1995), 'Price Elasticity and Market Structure — Overcoming Obstacles to Final Demand Energy Efficiency', in Terry Barker, Paul Ekins and Nick Johnstone (eds), *Global Warming and Energy Elasticities*, London: Routledge, pp. 254–66.

Jackson, Tim and Nick Marks (1994), *Measuring Sustainable Economic Welfare — A Pilot Index: 1950–1990*, Stockholm: Stockholm Environmental Institute.

Jackson, Tim and S. Stymne (1996), *Sustainable Economic Welfare in Sweden: A Pilot Index 1950–1992*, Stockholm: Stockholm Environment Institute.

Jackson, Tim, F. Laing, A. MacGillivray, N. Marks, J. Ralls and S. Stymne (1997), *An Index of Sustainable Economic Welfare for the UK 1950–1996*, Guildford: University of Surrey, Centre for Environmental Strategy.

Jacobs, Michael (1991), *The Green Economy — Environment, Sustainable Development and the Politics of the Future*, London: Pluto Press.

Jacobs, Michael (1995), 'Sustainable Development, Capital Substitution and Economic Humility: A Response to Beckerman', *Environmental Values*, **4** (1), 57–68.

Jacobs, Michael (1997a), 'Sustainability and Markets: On the Neoclassical Model of Environmental Economics', *New Political Economy*, **2** (3), 365–85.

Jacobs, Michael (1997b), 'Environmental Valuation, Deliberative Democracy and Public Decision-Making Institutions', in J. Foster (ed.), *Valuing Nature: Economics, Ethics and the Environment*, London: Routledge, pp. 232–46.

Jänicke, Martin, Harald Mönch and Manfred Binder (1992), *Umweltentlastung durch industriellen Strukturwandel? — Eine explorative Studie über 32 Industrieländer (1970 bis 1990)*, Berlin: Sigma.

Jevons, William Stanley (1865), *The Coal Question: An Inquiry Concerning the Prospects of the Nation and the Probable Exhaustion of Our Coal Mines*, London: Macmillan.

Jochem, Eberhard and Edelgard Gruber (1990), 'Obstacles to Rational Electricity Use and Measures to Alleviate Them', *Energy Policy*, **18** (4), 340–50.

Johnson, Manuel H., Frederick W. Bell and James T. Bennett (1980), 'Natural Resource Scarcity: Empirical Evidence and Public Policy', *Journal of Environmental Economics and Management*, **7** (3), 256–71.

Kahneman, Daniel and Jack Knetsch (1992), 'Valuing Public Goods: the Purchase of Moral Satisfaction', *Journal of Environmental Economics and Management*, **22** (1), 57–70.

Kaldor, Nicholas (1939), 'Welfare Propositions of Economics and Interpersonal Comparisons of Utility', *Economic Journal*, **49** (195), 549–52.

Kammen, Daniel M. (2006), 'The Rise of Renewable Energy', *Scientific American*, **295** (3), 84–93.

Kanbur, Ravi (1992), 'Heterogeneity, Distribution, and Cooperation in Common Property Resource Management', Working Paper No. 844, Washington DC: World Bank.

Kant, Immanuel (1785) [1968], *Grundlegung zur Metaphysik der Sitten*, Werke Band XI, Frankfurt: Suhrkamp.

Kaufmann, Robert K. (1992), 'A Biophysical Analysis of the Energy/Real GDP Ratio: Implications for Substitution and Technical Change', *Ecological Economics*, **6** (1), 35–56.

Kelsey, David and John Quiggin (1992), 'Theories of Choice under Ignorance and Uncertainty', *Journal of Economic Surveys* **6** (2), 133–53.

Khalil, E.L. (1994), 'Recycling of Matter. Further Comments', *Ecological Economics*, **9** (3), 193–94.

Khatib, Hisham (1995), 'Energy Intensity: A New Look', *Energy Policy*, **23** (8), 727–9.

Khazzoom, J. Daniel (1987), 'Energy Saving Resulting from the Adoptions of More Efficient Appliances', *The Energy Journal*, **10** (1), 85–89.

Klepper, Gernot and Frank Stähler (1998), 'Sustainability in Closed and Open Economies', *Review of International Economics*, **6** (3), 488–506.

Knetsch, Jack L. (1990), 'Environmental Policy Implications of Disparities between Willingness to Pay and Compensation Demanded Measures of Values', *Journal of Environmental Economics and Management*, **18** (3), 227–37.

Knetsch, Jack L. (2007), 'Biased Valuations, Damage Assessments, and Policy Choices: The Choice of Measure Matters', *Ecological Economics*, **63** (4), 684–9.

Knight, F. (1921), *Risk, Uncertainty and Profit*, Boston: Houghton Mifflin.

Kolar, Jan and Martin O'Connor (2000), 'Natural Resources and Environmental Accounting in the Czech Republic – An Overview of Methodology and Results', Paper Prepared for the EVE "Green Accounting" Workshop, 6–7 March 2000, Milan.

Kopp, Raymond J. and Paul R. Portney (1999), 'Mock Referenda for Intergenerational Decisionmaking', in Paul R. Portney and John P. Weyant (eds), *Discounting and Intergenerational Equity*, Washington DC: Resources for the Future, pp. 87–98.

Kot, Hagai (2008), A Genuine Progress Indicator for Israel – A Pilot Index: 1979-2004. MSc dissertation. London: London School of Economics and Political Science.

Kriström, Bengt and Pere Pere Riera (1996), 'Is the Income Elasticity of Environmental Improvements Less Than One?', *Environmental and Resource Economics*, **7** (1), 45–55.

Krutilla, John V. (1967), 'Conservation Reconsidered', *American Economic Review*, **57** (1), 777–86.

Krutilla, John V. and Anthony C. Fisher (1975), *The Economics of Natural Environments*, Washington DC: Resources for the Future.

Kuhn, Thomas S. (1962) [1996], *The Structure of Scientific Revolutions*, Third Edition 1996, Chicago: University of Chicago Press.

Kummel, R. (1994), 'Energy, Entropy–Economy, Ecology', *Ecological Economics*, **9** (3), 194–5.

Kunte, Arundhati, Kirk Hamilton, John Dixon and Michael Clemens (1998), *Estimating National Wealth — Methodology and Results*, Washington DC: World Bank.

Kuznets, S. (1955), 'Economic Growth and Income Inequality', *American Economic Review*, **45** (1), 1–28.

Lackner, Klaus S. and Jeffrey D. Sachs (2005), 'A Robust Strategy for Sustainable Energy', *Brookings Papers on Economic Activity*, **2**, 215-284.

Lawn, Philip A. (2003), 'A theoretical foundation to support the Index of Sustainable Economic Welfare (ISEW), Genuine Progress Indicator (GPI), and other related indexes', *Ecological Economics*, **44** (1), 105–18.

Lawn, Philip A. (2005), 'An Assessment of the Valuation Methods Used to Calculate the Index of Sustainable Economic Welfare (ISEW), Genuine Progress Indicator (GPI), and Sustainable Net Benefit Index (SNBI)', *Environment, Development and Sustainability*, **7** (2), 185-208.

Lawn, Philip A. (2008), The End of Economic Growth? A Contracting Threshold Hypothesis. Paper presented at the 10th Biennial International Society for Ecological Economics Conference, 7–11 August, Nairobi.

Lawn, Philip A. and R.D. Sanders (1999), 'Has Australia surpassed its optimal macroeconomic scale? Finding out with the aid of "benefit" and "cost" accounts and a sustainable net benefit index', *Ecological Economics*, **28** (2), 213–29.

Lecomber, R. (1975), *Economic Growth Versus the Environment*, London: Macmillan.

Leggett, Jeremy (ed.) (1990), *Global Warming: The Greenpeace Report*, Oxford: Oxford University Press.

Leipert, Christian (1989a), *Die heimlichen Kosten des Fortschritts — Wie Umweltzerstörung das Wirtschaftswachstum fördert*, Frankfurt am Main: Fischer.

Leipert, Christian (1989b), 'National Income and Economic Growth: The Conceptual Side of Defensive Expenditures', *Journal of Economic Issues*, **23** (3), 843–56.

Lenssen, Nicholas and Christopher Flavin (1996), 'Sustainable Energy for Tomorrow's World — The Case for an Optimistic View of the Future', *Energy Policy*, **24** (9), 769–81.

Levinson, Arik and M. Scott Taylor (2008), 'Unmasking the Pollution Haven Effect', *International Economic Review*, **49** (1), 223–54.

Li, Quan and Rafael Reuveny (2006), 'Democracy and Environmental Degradation', *International Studies Quarterly*, **50** (4), 935–56.

Lind, Robert C. (1995), 'Intergenerational Equity, Discounting, and the Role of Cost–Benefit Analysis in Evaluating Global Climate Policy', *Energy Policy*, **23** (4/5), 379–89.

Lipsey, Richard G. and Kelvin J. Lancaster (1956), 'The General Theory of Second-best', *Review of Economic Studies*, **63** (1), 11–32.

Lipton, Michael (1989), *New Seeds and Poor People*, London: Unwin Hyman.

List, J.A. and C.A. Gallet (1999), 'The Environmental Kuznets Curve: Does one Size Fit All?', *Ecological Economics*, **31** (3), 409–24.

Livernois, John (2008), 'On the Empirical Significance of the Hotelling Rule', *Review of Environmental Economics and Policy*, **3** (1), 22–41.

Löfgren, Karl-Gustaf (1992), 'Comment on C.R. Hulten, "Accounting for the Wealth of Nations: The Net versus Gross Output Controversy and its Ramifications"', *Scandinavian Journal of Economics*, **94** (0), S25–S28.

Loomes, Graham and Robert Sugden (1982), 'Regret Theory: An Alternative Theory of Rational Choice under Uncertainty', *Economic Journal*, **92** (368), 805–24.

Lopez, Ramon (1992), 'The Environment as a Factor of Production: The Economic Growth and Trade Policy Linkages', in Patrick Low (ed.), 'International Trade and the Environment, Discussion Paper No. 159, Washington DC: World Bank.

Low, Patrick (ed.) (1992), 'International Trade and the Environment', Discussion Paper No. 159, Washington DC: World Bank.

Lutz, Ernst (1992), 'Agricultural Trade Liberalization, Price Changes, and Environmental Effects', *Environmental and Resource Economics*, **2** (1), 79–89.

Lutz, Ernst (1993), 'Epilogue', in Ernst Lutz (ed.), *Toward Improved Accounting for the Environment — an UNSTAT–World Bank Symposium*, Washington DC: World Bank, pp. 315–18.

Machina, Mark J. (1987), 'Choice under Uncertainty: Problems Solved and Unsolved', *Journal of Economic Perspectives*, **1** (1), 121–54.

Machina, Mark J. (1989), 'Dynamic Consistency and Non-Expected Utility Models of Choice Under Uncertainty', *Journal of Economic Literature*, **27** (4), 1622–68.

Mackellar, F. Landis and Daniel R. Vining, Jr. (1989), 'Measuring Natural Resource Scarcity', *Social Indicators Research*, **21** (5), 517–30.

Magnus, J.A. (1979), 'Substitution between Energy and Non-energy Inputs in the Netherlands 1950–1976', *International Economic Review*, **2** (2), 465–84.

Mäler, Karl-Göran (1991), 'National Accounts and Environmental Resources', *Environmental and Resource Economics*, **1** (1), 1–15.

Malthus, Thomas Robert (1798), *An Essay on the Principle of Population*, London: J. Johnson.

Manne, A.S. and R.G. Richels (1995), 'The Greenhouse Debate: Economic Efficiency, Burden Sharing and Hedging Strategies', *Energy Journal*, **16** (4), 1–37.

Mansson, B.A. (1994), 'Recycling of Matter. A Response', *Ecological Economics*, **9** (3), 191–2.

Markandya, Anil and Charles Perrings (1991), 'Resource Accounting for Sustainable Development: A Review of Basic Concepts, Recent Debate and Future Needs', Discussion Paper DP 91-06, London Environmental Economics Centre, London.

Markandya, Anil and David W. Pearce (1988), 'Environmental Considerations and the Choice of the Discount Rate in Developing Countries', Environment Department Working Paper No. 3, Washington DC: World Bank.

Markandya, Anil and David W. Pearce (1991), 'Development, the Environment, and the Social Rate of Discount', *World Bank Research Observer*, **6** (2), 137–52.

Markandya, Anil and Suzette Pedroso-Galinato (2007), 'How Substitutable is Natural Capital?', *Environmental and Resource Economics*, **37** (1), 297–312.

Martinez-Alier, Joan (1995), 'The Environment as a Luxury Good or "Too Poor to be Green"?', *Ecological Economics*, **13** (1), 1–10.

Martinez-Alier, Joan (2002), *The Environmentalism of the Poor: a Study of Ecological Conflicts and Valuation*, Cheltenham, UK and Northampton, MA: Edward Elgar.

Martinot, Eric (2006), 'Renewable Energy Gains Momentum', *Environment*, **48** (6), 27–43.

Matthews et al. (2000), *The Weight of Nations – Material Outflows from Industrial Economies*, Washington DC: World Resources Institute.

Max-Neef, Manfred (1995), 'Economic Growth and Quality of Life: A Threshold Hypothesis', *Ecological Economics*, **15** (2), 115–18.

Mayo, Ed, Alex MacGillivray and Duncan McLaren (1997), *More Isn't Always Better – A Special Briefing on Growth and Quality of Life in the UK*, London: New Economics Foundation.

McCormick, John (1989), *The Global Environmental Movement*, London: Belhaven.

Meadows, Dennis, Donella Meadows, Erich Zahn and Peter Milling (1972), *The Limits to Growth*, New York: Universe Books.

Meadows, Donella, Denis Meadows and Jorgen Randers (1992), *Beyond the Limits: Global Collapse or a Sustainable Future*, London: Earthscan.

Meadows, Donella, Denis Meadows and Jorgen Randers (2004), *Limits to Growth: the 30-Year Update*, White River Junction: Chelsea Green Publishing Company.

Mendelsohn, Robert O., (2006), 'A Critique of the Stern Report', *Regulation* (Winter 2006-2007), 42–46.

Mikesell, Raymond F. (1994), 'Sustainable Development and Mineral Resources', *Resources Policy*, **20** (2), 83–6.

Mikesell, Raymond F. (1995), 'The Limits to Growth — A Reappraisal', *Resources Policy*, **21** (2), 127–31.

Mill, John Stuart (1862), *Principles of Political Economy*, Fifth edition, London: Parker, Son, and Bourn.

Miller, Merton H. and Charles W. Upton (1985), 'A Test of the Hotelling Valuation Principle', *Journal of Political Economy*, **93** (1), 1–25.

Mishan, Ezra J. (1974), 'Growth and Antigrowth: What Are the Issues?', in A. Weintraub, E. Schwartz and J. Richard Aronson (eds), *The Economic Growth Controversy*, London: Macmillan, pp. 3–38.

Mishan, Ezra J. (1994), 'Is A Welfare Index Possible?', in Clifford W. Cobb and John B. Cobb (eds), *The Green National Product: A Proposed Index of Sustainable Economic Welfare*, Lanham: University Press of America, pp. 169–92.

Mitchell, R.C. and R.T. Carson (1989), *Using Surveys to Value Public Goods*, Washington DC: Resources for the Future.

Moazzami, B. and F.J. Anderson (1994), 'Modelling Natural Resource Scarcity Using the "Error-Correction" Approach', *Canadian Journal of Economics*, **27** (4), 801–12.

Moffatt, I. and M.C. Wilson (1994), 'An Index of Sustainable Economic Welfare for Scotland, 1980-1991', *International Journal of Sustainable Development and World Ecology*, **1** (4), 264–91.

Moomaw, W.R. and G.C. Unruh (1997), 'Are Environmental Kuznets Curves Misleading Us? The Case of CO_2 Emissions', *Environment and Development Economics*, **2** (4), 451–63.

Moran, Daniel D., Mathis Wackernagel, Justian A. Kitzes, Steven H. Goldfinger and Aurélien Boutaud (2008), 'Measuring Sustainable Development – Nation by Nation', *Ecological Economics*, **64** (3), 470–4.

Myers, Norman (1993), 'Biodiversity and the Precautionary Principle', *Ambio*, **23** (1), 74–9.

Neumayer, Eric (1999a), *Weak versus Strong Sustainability: Exploring the Limits of Two Opposing Paradigms*, First Edition, Cheltenham, UK and Northampton, MA: Edward Elgar.

Neumayer, Eric (1999b), 'Global Warming: Discounting is not the Issue, but Substitutability is', *Energy Policy*, **27** (1), 33–43.

Neumayer, Eric (1999c), 'The ISEW: Not an Index of Sustainable Economic Welfare', *Social Indicators Research*, **48** (1), 77–101.

Neumayer, Eric (2000a), 'In Defence of Historical Accountability for Greenhouse Gas Emissions', *Ecological Economics*, **33** (2), 185–92.

Neumayer, Eric (2000b), 'On the Methodology of ISEW, GPI and Related Measures: Some Constructive Comments and Some Doubt on the Threshold Hypothesis', *Ecological Economics*, **34** (3), 347–61.

Neumayer, Eric (2000c), 'Resource Accounting in Measures of Unsustainability: Challenging World Bank's Conclusions', *Environmental and Resource Economics*, **15** (3), 257–78.

Neumayer, Eric (2000d), 'Scarce or Abundant? The Economics of Natural Resource Availability', *Journal of Economic Surveys*, **14** (3), 307–35.

Neumayer, Eric (2000e), 'The Human Development Index and Sustainability: A Constructive Proposal', *Ecological Economics*, **39** (1), 101–14.

Neumayer, Eric (2001a), *Greening Trade and Investment – Environmental Protection without Protectionism*, London: Earthscan.

Neumayer, Eric (2001b), 'Pollution havens: an analysis of policy options for dealing with an elusive phenomenon', *Journal of Environment & Development*, **10** (2), 147–77.

Neumayer, Eric (2002a), 'Do Democracies Exhibit Stronger International Environmental Commitment?', *Journal of Peace Research*, **39** (2), 139–64.

Neumayer, Eric (2002b), 'Does trade openness promote multilateral environmental cooperation?', *World Economy*, **25** (6), 815–32.

Neumayer, Eric (2003a), 'Are Left-Wing Party Strength and Corporatism Good for the Environment? A Panel Analysis of 21 OECD Countries, 1980-1998', *Ecological Economics*, **45** (2), 203–20.

Neumayer, Eric (2003b), 'Beyond income: Convergence in living standards, big time', *Structural Change and Economic Dynamics*, **14** (3), 275–96.

Neumayer, Eric (2003c), *Weak versus Strong Sustainability: Exploring the Limits of Two Opposing Paradigms*, Second Edition, Cheltenham, UK and Northampton, MA: Edward Elgar.

Neumayer, Eric (2004a), 'Sustainability Indicators', in Henk Folmer and Tom Tietenberg (eds), *International Yearbook of Environmental and Resource Economics 2004/05*, Cheltenham, UK and Northampton, MA: Edward Elgar.

Neumayer, Eric (2004b), 'Does the "resource curse" hold for growth in genuine income as well?', *World Development*, **32** (10), 1627–40.

Neumayer, Eric (2007), 'A Missed Opportunity: The Stern Review On Climate Change Fails to Tackle the Issue of Non-Substitutable Loss of Natural Capital', *Global Environmental Change*, **17** (3–4), 297–301.

Neumayer, Eric, Scott Gates and Nils Petter Gleditsch (2002), 'Environmental Commitment, Democracy and Conflict'. Background Paper for World Development Report 2003, Washington DC: World Bank.

Ng, Yew-Kwang (1983), *Welfare Economics*, London: Macmillan.

Nordhaus, William (2007), 'A Review of the Stern Review on the Economics of Climate Change', *Journal of Economic Literature*, **45** (3), 686-702.

Nordhaus, William D. (1973), 'World Dynamics: Measurement without Data', *Economic Journal*, **83** (332), 1156–83.

Nordhaus, William D. (1991a), 'To Slow or not to Slow: The Economics of the Greenhouse Effect', *Economic Journal*, **101** (407), 920–37.

Nordhaus, William D. (1991b), 'Economic Approaches to Greenhouse Warming', in Rüdiger Dornbusch and James M. Poterba (eds), *Global Warming: Economic Policy Responses*, Cambridge, MA: MIT Press, pp. 33–66.

Nordhaus, William D. (1992), 'Lethal Model 2: The Limits to Growth Revisited', *Brookings Papers on Economic Activity*, **0** (2), 1–59.

Nordhaus, William D. (1994), *Managing the Global Commons: The Economics of Climate Change*, Cambridge, MA: MIT Press.

Nordhaus, William D. (1999), 'Discounting and Public Policies that Affect the Distant Future', in Paul R. Portney and John P. Weyant (eds), *Discounting and Intergenerational Equity*, Washington DC: Resources for the Future, pp. 145–162.

Nordhaus, William D. (2008), *A Question of Balance – Weighting the Options on Global Warming Policies*. New Haven: Yale University Press.

Nordhaus, William D. and David Popp (1997), 'What is the Value of Scientific Knowledge? An Application to Global Warming Using the PRICE Model', *Energy Journal*, **18** (1), 1–45.

Nordhaus, William D. and Edward C. Kokkelenberg (eds.) (2000), *Nature's Numbers – Expanding the National Economic Accounts to Include the Environment*, Washington DC: National Academy Press.

Nordhaus, William D. and James Tobin (1972), 'Is Growth Obsolete?', in National Bureau of Economic Research, *Economic Growth*, Research General Series No. 96F, New York: Columbia University Press.

Nordhaus, William D. and Joseph Boyer (*2000), Warming the World – Economic Models of Global Warming*, Cambridge, MA: MIT Press.

Norgaard, Richard B. (1986), 'Thermodynamic and Economic Concepts as Related to Resource-Use Policies: Synthesis', *Land Economics*, **62** (3), 325–7.

Norgaard, Richard B. (1990), 'Economic Indicators of Resource Scarcity: A Critical Essay', *Journal of Environmental Economics and Management*, **19** (1), 19–25.

Norgaard, Richard B. (1991), 'Economic Indicators of Resource Scarcity: A More Critical Reply', *Journal of Environmental Economics and Management*, **21** (2), 195–9.

Norgaard, Richard B. (1994), *Development Betrayed: The End of Progress and a Coevolutionary Revisioning of the Future*, London and New York: Routledge.

Norton, Bryan G. (1986), 'Commodity, Amenity, and Morality — The Limits of Quantification in Valuing Biodiversity', in Edward O. Wilson (ed.), *Biodiversity*, Washington DC: National Academy Press, pp. 200–205.

Norton, Bryan G. (1995), 'Evaluating Ecosystem States: Two competing Paradigms', *Ecological Economics*, **14** (2), 113–27.

O'Connor, John (1994), 'Toward Environmentally Sustainable Development: Measuring Progress', in Thaddeus C. Trzyna (ed.), *A Sustainable World: Defining and Measuring Sustainable Development*, London: Earthscan, pp. 87–114.

O'Connor, Martin and Grant Ryan (1999), 'Macroeconomic Cost-Effectiveness and the Use of Multi-Sectoral Dynamic Modelling as an Environmental Valuation Tool', *International Journal of Sustainable Development*, **2** (1), 127–63.

O'Connor, Martin, Anton Steurer and Marialuisa Tamborra (2001), 'Greening National Accounts', Environmental Valuation in Europe Policy Research Brief Number 9, Cambridge: Cambridge Research for the Environment.

O'Hara, Sabine (1996), 'Discursive Ethics in Ecosystem Valuation and Policy', *Ecological Economics*, **16** (2), 95–107.

O'Riordan, Timothy and Andrew Jordan (1995), 'The Precautionary Principle in Contemporary Environmental Politics', *Environmental Values*, **4** (3), 191–212.

Odum, H.T. (1996), *Environmental Accounting: EMERGY and Environmental Decisionmaking*, New York: Wiley.

OECD (2007), *Measuring Material Flows and Resource Productivity. The OECD Guide*. Paris: Organisation for Economic Co-operation and Development.

OECD (2008a), *Measuring Material Flows and Resource Productivity. Synthesis Report*. Paris: Organisation for Economic Co-operation and Development.

OECD (2008b), *Measuring Material Flows and Resource Productivity. Inventory of Country Activities*. Paris: Organisation for Economic Co-operation and Development.

Olson, Mancur (1993), 'Dictatorship, Democracy, and Development', *American Political Science Review*, **87** (3), 567–76.

Opschoor, Hans (1991), 'GNP and Sustainable Income Measures: Some Problems and a Way Out', in Onno Kuik and Harmen Verbruggen (eds), *In Search of Indicators of Sustainable Development*, Dordrecht: Kluwer, pp. 39–44.

Opschoor, Hans and Lucas Reijnders (1991), 'Towards Sustainable Development Indicators', in Onno Kuik and Harmen Verbruggen (eds), *In Search of Indicators of Sustainable Development*, Dordrecht: Kluwer, pp. 7–27.

Özatalay, Savas, Stephen Grubaugh and Thomas Veach Long II (1979), 'Energy Substitution and National Energy Policy', *American Economic Review*, **69** (2), 369–71.

Page, Edward A. (2006), Climate Change, Justice and Future Generations. Cheltenham, UK and Northampton, MA: Edward Elgar.

Page, Talbot (1983), 'Intergenerational Justice as Opportunity', in Douglas MacLean and Peter Brown (eds), *Energy and the Future*, New Jersey: Rowman & Littlefield, pp. 38–57.

Page, Talbot and Douglas MacLean (1983), 'Risk Conservatism and the Circumstances of Utility Theory', *American Journal of Agricultural Economics*, **65** (5), 1021–26.

Palmer, Karen L. and David R. Simpson (1993), 'Environmental Policy as Industrial Policy', *Resources*, **112**, 17–21.

Panayotou, Theodore (1993), 'Empirical Tests and Policy Analysis of Environmental Degradation at Different Stages of Economic Development',

World Employment Programme Research Working Paper, International Labour Office, Geneva.

Panayotou, Theodore (1994), 'Conservation of Biodiversity and Economic Development: The Concept of Transferable Development Rights', *Environmental and Resource Economics*, **9** (1), 91–110.

Panayotou, Theodore (1997), 'Reducing Biodiversity Expenditure Needs: Reforming Perverse Incentives', in OECD, *Investing in Biological Diversity — The Cairns Conference*, Paris: OECD, pp. 217–33.

Parfit, Derek (1983), 'Energy Policy and the Further Future: The Identity Problem', in Douglas MacLean and Peter Brown (eds), *Energy and the Future*, New Jersey: Rowman & Littlefield, pp. 166–79.

Patterson, Murray G. (1996), 'What is Energy Efficiency?', *Energy Policy*, **24** (5), 377–90.

Pearce, David W. (1991), 'The Role of Carbon Taxes in Adjusting to Global Warming', *Economic Journal*, **101** (407), 938–48.

Pearce, David W. (1993a), *Economic Values and the Natural World*, London: Earthscan.

Pearce, David W. (1993b), 'Sustainable Development and Developing Country Economics', in R. Kerry Turner (ed.), *Sustainable Environmental Economics and Management: Principles and Practice*, London: Pinter, Belhaven, pp. 70–105.

Pearce, David W. (1994), 'The Precautionary Principle and Economic Analysis', in Timothy O'Riordan and James Cameron (eds), *Interpreting the Precautionary Principle*, London: Earthscan, pp. 132–51.

Pearce, David W. (1995), *Blueprint 4: Capturing Global Environmental Value*, London: Earthscan.

Pearce, David W. (1997), 'Substitution and Sustainability: Some Reflections on Georgescu-Roegen', *Ecological Economics*, **22** (3), 295–97.

Pearce, David W. (1998), 'Economic Valuation and Ecological Economics', in David Pearce (ed.), *Economics and Environment: Essays on Ecological Economics and Sustainable Development*, Cheltenham, UK and Northampton, MA: Edward Elgar, pp. 40–54.

Pearce, David W. and David Ulph (1998), 'A Social Discount Rate for the United Kingdom', in David PeaRce (ed.), *Economics and Environment: Essays on Ecological Economics and Sustainable Development*, Cheltenham, UK and Northampton, MA: Edward Elgar, pp. 268–85.

Pearce, David W. and Giles Atkinson (1993), 'Capital Theory and the Measurement of Sustainable Development: An Indicator of "Weak" Sustainability', *Ecological Economics*, **8** (2), 103–8.

Pearce, David W. and R. Kerry Turner (1990), *Economics of Natural Resources and the Environment*, New York: Harvester Wheatsheaf.

Pearce, David W., Anil Markandya and Edward Barbier (1989), *Blueprint for a Green Economy*, London: Earthscan.

Pearce, David W., Edward B. Barbier and Anil Markandya (1990), *Sustainable Development: Economics and Environment in the Third World*, Cheltenham, UK and Northampton, MA: Edward Elgar.

Pearce, David W., Kirk Hamilton and Giles Atkinson (1996), 'Measuring Sustainable Development: Progress on Indicators', *Environment and Development Economics*, **1** (1), 85–101.

Pearson, Mark (1995), 'The Political Economy of Implementing Environmental Taxes', *International Tax and Public Finance*, **2** (2), 357–73.

Perman, Roger, Yue Ma and James McGilvray (1996), *Natural Resource and Environmental Economics*, Harlow: Addison Wesley Longman.

Perrings, Charles (1989), 'Environmental Bonds and Environmental Research in Innovative Activities', *Ecological Economics*, **1** (1), 95–110.

Perrings, Charles (1994), 'Biotic Diversity, Sustainable Development, and Natural Capital', in A. Jansson, M. Hammer, C. Folke and R. Costanza (eds), *Investing in Natural Capital: The Ecological Economics Approach to Sustainability*, Washington DC: Island Press, pp. 92–112.

Perrings, Charles and David W. Pearce (1994), 'Threshold Effects and Incentives for the Conservation of Biodiversity', *Environmental and Resource Economics*, **4** (1), 13–28.

Perrings, Charles and Hans Opschoor (1994), 'The Loss of Biological Diversity: Some Policy Implications', *Environmental and Resource Economics*, **4** (1), 1–11.

Perrings, Charles, Carl Folke and Karl-Göran Mäler (1992), 'The Ecology and Economics of Biodiversity Loss: The Research Agenda', *Ambio*, **21** (3), 201–11.

Pezzey, John (1992a), 'Sustainability: An Interdisciplinary Guide', *Environmental Values*, **1** (4), 321–62.

Pezzey, John (1992b), 'Sustainable Development Concepts: An Economic Analysis', World Bank Environment Paper No. 2, Washington DC: World Bank.

Pezzey, John (1995), 'Sustainable Development, Intergenerational Equity and Environmental Policy', Department of Economics Discussion Paper No. 95-01, London: University College London.

Pezzey, John and Cees Withagen (1998), 'The Rise, Fall and Sustainability of Capital-Resource Economies', *Scandinavian Journal of Economics*, **100** (2), 513–27.

Pezzey, John C.V. (2002), 'One-sided Unsustainability Tests and NNP Measurement with Multiple Consumption Goods', Working Paper, Australian National University, Canberra.

Pezzey, John C.V. (2002b), 'The Economics of Sustainability: A Review of Journal Articles', Discussion Paper 02-03, Washington DC: Resources for the Future.

Pezzey, John C.V. and Michael A. Toman (2002a), 'Progress and Problems in the Economics of Sustainability', in Tom Tietenberg and Henk Folmer (eds.), *International Yearbook of Environmental and Resource Economics 2002/2003*, Cheltenham, UK and Northampton, MA: Edward Elgar, pp. 165–232.

Philibert, Cédric (1999), 'The Economics of Climate Change and the Theory of Discounting', *Energy Policy* **27** (15), 913–27.

Pigou, A.C. (1932), *The Economics of Welfare*, London: Macmillan.

Pindyck, Robert S. (1978), 'The Optimal Exploration and Production of Non-renewable Resources', *Journal of Political Economy*, **86** (5), 841–61.

Pindyck, Robert S. (1979), 'Interfuel Substitution and the Industrial Demand for Energy: An International Comparison', *Review of Economics and Statistics*, **61** (2), 169–79.

Plümper, Thomas and Eric Neumayer (2009), 'Famine Mortality and Rational Political Inactivity', *World Development*, **37** (1), 50–61.

Portney, Paul R. and John P. Weyant (eds) (1999), *Discounting and Intergenerational Equity*, Washington DC: Resources for the Future.

Poterba, James M. (1991), 'Tax Policy to Combat Global Warming: On Designing a Carbon Tax', in Rüdiger Dornbusch and James M. Poterba (eds), *Global Warming: Economic Policy Responses*, Cambridge, MA: MIT Press, pp. 33–98.

Prell, Mark A. (1996), 'Backstop Technology and Growth: Doomsday or Steady State?', *Journal of Environmental Economics and Management*, **30** (2), 254–64.

Preston, Samuel H. (1996), 'The Effect of Population Growth on Environmental Quality', *Population Research and Policy Review*, **15** (2), 95–108.

Price, Colin (1995), 'Emissions, Concentrations and Disappearing CO_2', *Resource and Energy Economics*, **17** (1), 87–97.

Proops, John L.R., Giles Atkinson, Burkhard Frhr. v. Schlotheim and Sandrine Simon (1999), 'International Trade and the Sustainability Footprint: a Practical Criterion for its Assessment', *Ecological Economics*, **29** (1), 75–97.

Prywes, Menahem (1986), 'A Nested CES Approach to Capital-Energy Substitution', *Energy Economics*, **8** (1), 22–8.

Pulselli, Federic Maria, Francesca Ciampalini, Enzo Tiezzi and Carlo Zappia, (2006), 'The Index of Sustainable Economic Welfare (ISEW) for a Local Authority: A Case Study in Italy', *Ecological Economics* **60** (1), 271–81.

Putnam, Robert D. (1993), *Making Democracy Work — Civic Traditions in Modern Italy*, Princeton: Princeton University Press.

Quiggin, John (2008), 'Stern and his Critics on Discounting: an Editorial Essay', *Climatic Change*, **89** (3–4), 195–205.

Rabl, Ari (1996), 'Discounting of Long-term Costs: What would Future Generations Prefer us to Do?', *Ecological Economics*, **17** (3), 137–45.

Ramsamy, M. Sen (1994), 'Sustainable Tourism', in Wolfgang Lutz (ed.), *Population, Development, Environment*, New York: Springer, pp. 175–90.

Ramsey, F.P. (1928), 'A Mathematical Theory of Saving', *Economic Journal*, **38** (152), 543–59.

Randall, Alan (1991), 'The Value of Biodiversity', *Ambio*, **20** (2), 64–8.

Ravaioli, Carla (1995), *Economists and the Environment: What the Top Economists Say about the Environment*, London: Zed Books.

Rawls, John (1972), *A Theory of Justice*, Oxford: Oxford University Press.

Ray, George F. (1983), 'Industrial Materials: Past, Present and Future', in S.F. Frowen (ed.), *Controlling Industrial Economies*, London: Macmillan, pp. 61–82.

Ray, George F. (1984), 'Mineral Reserves: Projected Lifetimes and Security of Supply', *Resources Policy*, **10** (2), 75–80.

Ready, Richard C. and Richard C. Bishop (1991), 'Endangered Species and the Safe Minimum Standard', *American Journal of Agricultural Economics*, **73** (2), 309–12.

Redclift, Michael (1994), 'Reflections on the "Sustainable Development" Debate', *International Journal of Sustainable Development and World Ecology*, **1** (1), 3–21.

Redefining Progress (1999), *The 1998 U.S. Genuine Progress Indicator: Methodology Handbook*, San Francisco.

Redefining Progress (2001), *The 2000 Genuine Progress Indicator*, San Francisco.

Redefining Progress (2006), *The Genuine Progress Indicator 2006*, Oakland.

Rees, William and Mathis Wackernagel (1996), 'Urban Ecological Footprints: Why Cities Cannot be Sustainable – And Why They are a Key to Sustainability', *Environmental Impact Assessment Review*, **16**, 223–48.

Rees, William E. and Mathis Wackernagel (1994), 'Ecological Footprints and Appropriated Carrying Capacity: Measuring the Natural Capital Requirements of the Human Ecology', in A. Jansson, M. Hammer, C. Folke and R. Costanza (eds), *Investing in Natural Capital*, Washington DC: Island Press, pp. 362–90.

Reich, Utz-Peter (1994), 'Der falsche Glanz am Ökosozialprodukt', *Zeitschrift für Umweltpolitik und Umweltrecht*, **17** (1), 25–41.

Repetto, Robert and Wilfrido Cruz (1991), *Accounts Overdue: Natural Resource Depreciation in Costa Rica*, Washington DC: World Resources Institute.

Repetto, Robert, Dale Rothman, Paul Faeth and Duncan Austin (1997), 'Has Environmental Protection Really Reduced Productivity Growth?', *Challenge*, **40** (1), 46–57.

Repetto, Robert, W. Magrath, M. Wells, C. Beer and F. Rossini (1989), *Wasting Assets: Natural Resources in the National Income Accounts*, Washington DC: World Resources Institute.

Ricardo, David (1817), *Principles of Political Economy and Taxation*, London: John Murray.

Richter, Wolfgang (1994), *Monetäre Makroindikatoren für eine nachhaltige Umweltnutzung: eine Diskussion theoretischer und praktischer Aspekte des Ökosozialproduktkonzeptes*, Marburg: Metropolis.

Riddel, Mary (2003), 'Candidate Eco-labelling and Senate Campaign Contributions', *Journal of Environmental Economics and Management*, **45** (2), 177–94.

Robinson, Warren C. (1998), 'Global Population Trends — The Prospects for Stabilization', *Resources*, **131**, 6–9.

Rosenberg, D., P. Oegema, and M. Bovy (1995), *ISEW for the Netherlands: Preliminary Results and Some Proposals for Further Research*, Amsterdam: IMSA.

Royal Society (1992), *Risk: Analysis, Perception, Management*, London: The Royal Society.

Rueschemeyer, Dietrich, Evelyne Huber Stephens and John D. Stephens (1991), *Capitalist Development and Democracy*, Cambridge: Cambridge University Press.

Ruttan, Vernon W. (1991), 'Constraints on Sustainable Growth in Agricultural Production: Into the 21st Century', *Canadian Journal of Agricultural Economics*, **39** (4), 567–80.

Sachs, Jeffrey D. and Andrew M. Warner (2001), 'The Curse of Natural Resources', *European Economic Review*, **45** (4–6), 827–38.

Sammarco, Giuseppe (1996), 'Environmental Accounting: Problems and Proposals', in Ignazio Musu and Domenico Siniscalco (eds), *National Accounts and the Environment*, Dordrecht: Kluwer, pp. 33–47.

Santopietro, George D. (1998), 'Alternative Methods for Estimating Resource Rent and Depletion Cost: the Case of Argentina's YPF', *Resources Policy*, **24** (1), 39–48.

Sauré, Philip (2008), Overreporting Oil Reserves. Working Paper. Zurich: Swiss National Bank.

Schelling, Thomas C. (1991), 'Economic Responses to Global Warming: Prospects for Cooperative Approaches', in Rüdiger Dornbusch and James M. Poterba (eds), *Global Warming: Economic Policy Responses*, Cambridge (Mass.): MIT Press, pp. 197–221.

Schelling, Thomas C. (1995), 'Intergenerational Discounting', *Energy Policy*, **23** (4/5), 395–401.

Schmidt-Bleek, Friedrich (1993a), 'MIPS — A Universal Ecological Measure?', *Fresenius Environmental Bulletin* **2**, 306–11.

Schmidt-Bleek, Friedrich (1993b), 'MIPS Re-Visited', *Fresenius Environmental Bulletin*, **2**, 407–12.

Scott, Anthony and Peter Pearse (1992), 'Natural Resources in a High-tech Economy — Scarcity Versus Resourcefulness', *Resources Policy*, **18** (3), 154–66.

Scruggs, Lyle A. (1998) 'Political and Economic Inequality and the Environment', *Ecological Economics*, **26** (3), 259–75.

Sefton, J.A. and M.R. Weale (1996), 'The Net National Product and Exhaustible Resources: The Effects of Foreign Trade', *Journal of Public Economics*, **61** (1), 21–47.

Selden, Thomas M. and Daqing Song (1994), 'Environmental Quality and Development: Is There a Kuznets Curve for Air Pollution Emissions?', *Journal of Environmental Economics and Management*, **27** (2), 147–62.

Selden, Thomas M., Anne S. Forrest and James E. Lockhart (1999), 'Analyzing the Reductions in US Air Pollution Emissions: 1970 to 1990', *Land Economics*, **75** (1), 1–21.

Sen, Amartya K. (1967): 'Isolation, Assurance and the Social Rate of Discount', *Quarterly Journal of Economics*, **81** (322), 112–24.

Sen, Amartya K. (1982), 'The Choice of Discount Rates for Social Benefit-Cost Analysis', in R.C. Lind (ed.), *Discounting for Time and Risk in Energy Policy*, Washington DC: Resources for the Future, pp. 325–52.

Sen, Amartya K. (1987), *On Ethics and Economics*, Oxford: Blackwell.

Serageldin, Ismail (1996), *Sustainability and the Wealth of Nations: First Steps in An Ongoing Journey*, Washington DC: World Bank.

Serôa da Motta, Ronaldo and Carlos Young (1995), 'Measuring Sustainable Income from Mineral Extraction in Brazil', *Resources Policy*, **21** (2), 113–25.

Serôa da Motta, Ronaldo and Ferraz do Amaral, Claudio A. (2000), 'Estimating Timber Depreciation in the Brazilian Amazon', *Environment and Development Economics*, **5** (1–2), 129–42.

Serôa da Motta, Ronaldo and Peter H. May (1996), 'Measuring Sustainable Income: The Case of Mineral and Forest Depletion in Brazil', in Peter H. May and Ronaldo Serôa da Motta (eds), *Pricing the Planet — Economic Analysis for Sustainable Development*, New York: Columbia University Press, pp. 197–208.

Shafik, Nemat (1994), 'Economic Development and Environmental Quality: An Econometric Analysis', *Oxford Economic Papers*, **46** (5), 757–73.

Shafik, Nemat and Sushenjit Bandyopadhyay (1992), 'Economic Growth and Environmental Quality — Time-series and Cross-country Evidence', Working Paper No. 904, Washington DC: World Bank.

Shavell, Steven (1993), 'Contingent Valuation of the Nonuse Value of Natural Resources: Implications for Public Policy and the Liability System', in Jerry A. Hausman (ed.), *Contingent Valuation: A Critical Assessment*, Amsterdam: Elsevier, pp. 371–88.

Shogren, Jason F., Joseph A. Herriges and Ramu Govindasamy (1993), 'Limits to Environmental Bonds', *Ecological Economics*, **8** (2), 109–33.

Simon, H.A. (1982), *Models of Bounded Rationality*, 2 vols, Cambridge, MA: MIT Press.

Simon, Julian L. (1990), *Population Matters: People, Resources, Environment, and Immigration*, New Brunswick: Transactions Press.

Simon, Julian L. (1996), *The Ultimate Resource*, Second Edition, Princeton: Princeton University Press.

Slade, Margaret E. (1982), 'Trends in Natural-resource Commodity Prices: An Analysis of the Time Domain', *Journal of Environmental Economics and Management*, **9** (2), 122–37.

Slade, Margaret E. (1987), 'Natural Resources, Population Growth, and Economic Well-being', in D. Gale Johnson and Ronald D. Lee (eds), *Population Growth and Economic Development: Issues and Evidence*, Wisconsin: University of Wisconsin Press, pp. 331–69.

Slade, Margaret E. (1988), 'Grade Selection Under Uncertainty: Least Cost Last and Other Anomalies', *Journal of Environmental Economics and Management*, **15** (2), 189–205.

Slade, Margaret E. (1992), 'Do Markets Underprice Natural-resource Commodities?', Working Paper No. 962, Washington DC: World Bank.

Smil, Vaclav (1994), 'How Many People Can the Earth Feed?', *Population and Development Review*, **20** (2), 255–92.

Smil, Vaclav (2000), *Feeding the world: a challenge for the twenty-first century*, Cambridge, MA: MIT Press.

Smil, Vaclav (2003), *Energy at the Crossroads. Global Perspectives and Unvertainties*. Boston, MA: MIT Press.

Smil, Vaclav (2006), 'Peak Oil: A Catastrophist Cult and Complex Realities', *World Watch* January/February, 22-24.

Smith, V. Kerry and Carol Mansfied (1998), 'Buying Time: Real and Hypothetical Offers', *Journal of Environmental Economics and Management*, **36** (3), 209–24.

Smith, V. Kerry and John V. Krutilla (1979), 'Endangered Species, Irreversibilities, and Uncertainty: A Comment', *American Journal of Agricultural Economics*, **58** (2), 371–5.

Smulders, Sjak (1995), 'Environmental Policy and Sustainable Economic Growth', *De Economist*, **143** (2), 163–95.

Söllner, Fritz (1997), 'A Reexamination of the Role of Thermodynamics for Environmental Economics', *Ecological Economics*, **22** (3), 175–201.

Solow, John L. (1987), 'The Capital–Energy Complementarity Debate Revisited', *American Economic Review*, **77** (4), 605–14.

Solow, Robert M. (1974a), 'Intergenerational Equity and Exhaustible Resources', *Review of Economic Studies*, Symposium, 29–46.

Solow, Robert M. (1974b), 'Is the End of the World at Hand?', in A. Weintraub, E. Schwartz and J. Richard Aronson (eds), *The Economic Growth Controversy*, London: Macmillan, pp. 39–61.

Solow, Robert M. (1974c), 'The Economics of Resources or the Resources of Economics', *American Economic Review*, **64** (2), 1–14.

Solow, Robert M. (1986), 'On the Intergenerational Allocation of Natural Resources', *Scandinavian Journal of Economics*, **88** (1), 141–9.

Solow, Robert M. (1993a), 'An Almost Practical Step Toward Sustainability', *Resources Policy*, **19** (3), 162–72.

Solow, Robert M. (1993b), 'Sustainability: An Economist's Perspective', in R. Dorfman and N. Dorfman (eds), *Selected Readings in Environmental Economics*, New York: Norton, pp. 179–87.

Solow, Robert M. (1997), 'Georgescu-Roegen versus Solow/Stiglitz', *Ecological Economics*, **22** (3), 267–8.

Spangenberg, Joachim., Friedrich Hinterberger, Stephan Moll and Helmut Schütz (1999), 'Material Flow Analysis, TMR and the MIPS Concept: A Contribution to the Development of Indicators for Measuring Changes in Consumption and Production Patterns', *International Journal of Sustainable Development*, **2** (1), 491–505.

Spash, Clive L. (1993), 'Economics, Ethics, and Long-term Environmental Damages', *Environmental Ethics*, **10** (1), 117–32.

Spash, Clive L. (1994), 'Double CO_2 and Beyond: Benefits, Costs and Compensation', *Ecological Economics*, **10** (1), 27–36.

Spash, Clive L. (2000), 'Ecosystems, Contingent Valuation and Ethics: The Case of Wetland Recreation', *Ecological Economics*, **34** (2), 195–215.

Spash, Clive L. (2002), *Greenhouse Economics – Value and Ethics*, London and New York: Routledge.

Spash, Clive L. (2008), 'Contingent Valuation Design and Data Treatment: if You can't Shoot the Messenger, Change the Message', *Environment and Planning C*, **26** (1), 34-53.

Spash, Clive L. and Nick Hanley (1995), 'Preferences, Information and Biodiersity Preservation', *Ecological Economics*, **12** (3), 191–208.

Stahmer, Carsten (1995), 'Utz-Peter Reichs Kritik am Ökosozialprodukt: Eine Erwiderung', *Zeitschrift für Umweltpolitik und Umweltrecht*, **18** (1), 101–10.

Stern, David I. and Michael S. Common (2001), 'Is there an Environmental Kuznets Curve for Sulfur?', *Journal of Environmental Economics and Management*, **41** (2), 162–78.

Stern, David I.(2004), 'The Rise and Fall of the Environmental Kuznets Curve', *World Development*, **32** (8), 1419–39.

Stern, David I., Michael S. Common and Edward B. Barbier (1996), 'Economic Growth and Environmental Degradation: The Environmental Kuznets Curve and Sustainable Development', *World Development*, **24** (7), 1151–60.

Stern, Nicholas (2007), *The Economics of Climate Change – The Stern Review*, Cambridge: Cambridge University Press.

Stern, Nicholas (2008), 'The Economics of Climate Change', *American Economic Review: Papers & Proceedings*, **98** (2), 1–37.

Sterner, Thomas and U. Martin Persson (2008), 'An Even Sterner Review: Introducing Relative Prices into the Discounting Debate', *Review of Environmental Economics and Policy*, **2** (1), 61–76.

Steurer, A., G. Gie, C. Leipert, C. Pasurka and D. Schäfer (1998), 'Environmental Protection Expenditure and its Representation in National Accounts', in K. Uno and P. Bartelmus (eds), *Environmental Accounting in Theory and Practice*, Dordrecht: Kluwer, pp. 309–19.

Stevens, Thomas H., Jaime Echeverria, Ronald J. Glass, Tim Hager and Thomas A. More (1991), 'Measuring the Existence Value of Wildlife: What Do CVM Estimates Really Show?', *Land Economics*, **67** (4), 390–400.

Stiglitz, Joseph (1974), 'Growth with Exhaustible Natural Resources: Efficient and Optimal Growth Paths', *Review of Economic Studies*, Symposium, 123–37.

Stockhammer, Engelbert, Harald Hochreiter, Bernhard Obermayr and Klaus Steiner (1997), 'The Index of Sustainable Economic Welfare (ISEW) as an Alternative to GDP in Measuring Economic Welfare. The Results of the Austrian (Revised) ISEW Calculation 1955–1992', *Ecological Economics*, **21** (1), 19–34.

Swanson, Timothy M. (1994), 'The Economics of Extinction Revisited and Revised: A Generalised Framework for the Analysis of the Problems of Endangered Species and Biodiversity Loss', *Oxford Economic Papers*, **46** (5), 800–821.

Swanson, Timothy M. (1996), 'The Reliance of Northern Economies on Southern Biodiversity: Biodiversity as Information', *Ecological Economics*, **17** (1), 1–8.

Swanson, Timothy M. (1997), *Global Action for Biodiversity*, London: Earthscan.

Swierzbinski, Joseph and Robert Mendelsohn (1989), 'Information and Exhaustible Resources: A Bayesian Analysis', *Journal of Environmental Economics and Management*, **16** (3), 193–208.

Tahvonen, Olli and Jari Kuuluvainen (1993), 'Economic Growth, Pollution, and Renewable Resources', *Journal of Environmental Economics and Management*, **24** (2), 101–18.

Thage, Bent (1989), 'The National Accounts and the Environment', in Yusuf J. Ahmad, Salah El Serafy and Ernst Lutz (eds), *Environmental Accounting for Sustainable Development: A UNDP–World Bank Symposium*, Washington DC: World Bank, pp. 314–36.

Tilton, John E. (1977), *The Future of Nonfuel Minerals*, Washington DC: The Brookings Institution.

Tilton, John E. (1996), 'Exhaustible Resources and Sustainable Development', *Resources Policy*, **22** (1/2), 91–7.

Tol, Richard S.J. (1994), 'Communication — The Damage Costs of Climate Change: A Note on Tangibles and Intangibles, Applied to DICE', *Energy Policy*, **22** (5), 436–8.

Tol, Richard S.J. (2005), 'On dual-rate discounting', *Economic Modelling*, **21** (1), 95–8.

Tol, Richard S.J. and Gary W. Yohe (2006), 'A Review of the Stern Review', *World Economics*, **7** (4), 233–50.

Toman, Michael A. (1985), 'Optimal Control with an Unbounded Horizon', *Journal of Economic Dynamics and Control*, **9** (3), 291–316.

Toman, Michael A., John Pezzey and Jeffrey Krautkraemer (1995), 'Neoclassical Economic Growth Theory and "Sustainability"', in Daniel W. Bromley (ed.), *Handbook of Environmental Economics*, Cambridge: Cambridge University Press, pp. 139–65.

Torras, Mariano and James K. Boyce (1998), 'Income, Inequality, and Pollution: A Reassessment of the Environmental Kuznets Curve', *Ecological Economics*, **25** (2), 147–60.

Torsello, Loredana and Allessandro Vercelli (1998), 'Environmental Bonds: A Critical Assessment', in Graciela Chichilnisky, Geoffrey Heal and Alessandro Vercelli (eds), *Sustainability: Dynamics and Uncertainty*, Dordrecht: Kluwer, pp. 243–55.

Trainer, F.E. (1995), 'Can Renewable Energy Sources Sustain Affluent Society?', *Energy Policy*, **23** (12), 1009–26.

Turner, R. Kerry (1995), 'Sustainable Development and Climate Change', Working Paper PA 95-01, Centre for Social and Economic Research on the Global Environment, Norwich and London.

Turner, R. Kerry and David W. Pearce (1992), 'Sustainable Development: Ethics and Economics', Working Paper PA 92-09, Centre for Social and Economic Research on the Global Environment, Norwich and London.

Turnovsky, Michelle, Michael Folie and Alistair Ulph (1982), 'Factor Substitutability in Australian Manufacturing with Emphasis on Energy Inputs', *Economic Record*, **58** (160), 61–72.

UNCED (1992), *Agenda 21*, New York: United Nations.

United Nations (1993), *Integrated Environmental and Economic Accounting — Interim Version. Studies in Methods, Handbook of National Accounting*, Series F, No. 61, New York: United Nations.

United Nations (1997), *World Population Prospects*, New York: United Nations Department for Economic and Social Information and Policy Analysis, Population Division.

Unruh, G.C. and Moomaw, W.R. (1998), 'An Alternative Analysis of Apparent EKC-type Transitions', *Ecological Economics*, **25** (2), 221–29.

Uri, N.D. and R. Boyd (1995), 'Scarcity and Growth Revisited', *Environment and Planning A*, **27** (11), 1815–32.

US Bureau of Mines (various years), *Mineral Commodity Summaries*, Washington DC: US Department of the Interior.

US Congress (1978), *Endangered Species Act Amendments of 1978*, Report No. 95-1625 on the Endangerd Species Act of 1973 (Public Law 93-205) as amended by the 95th Congres, Washington DC: US Congress.

US President's Materials Policy Commission (1952a), *Resources for Freedom – Volume I: Foundations for Growth and Security*, Washington, DC: United States Government Printing Office.

US President's Materials Policy Commission (1952b), *Resources for Freedom – Volume IV: The Promise of Technology*, Washington, DC: United States Government Printing Office.

Usher, Dan (1994), 'Income and the Hamiltonian', *Review of Income and Wealth*, **40** (2), 123–41.

Vadnjal, Dan and Martin O'Connor (1994), 'What is the Value of Rangitoto Island?', *Environmental Values*, **3** (4), 369–80.

Van den Bergh, Jeroen C.J.M. and Harmen Verbruggen (1999), 'Spatial Sustainability, Trade and Indicators: an Evaluation of the "Ecological Footprint"', *Ecological Economics*, **29** (1), 61–72.

van der Voet, Ester, Lauran van Oers and Igor Nikolic (2003), Dematerialisation: not just a matter of weight. CML Report 160. Centre of Environmental Science (CML), Section Substances & Products, Leiden University.

van der Voet, Ester, Lauran van Oers and Igor Nikolic (2005), 'Dematerialisation: not just a matter of weight', *Journal of Industrial Ecology*, **8** (4), 121–37.

Van Tongeren, Jan, Stefan Schweinfest, Ernst Lutz, Maria Gomez Luna and Guillen Martin (1993), 'Integrated Economic and Environmental Accounting: A Case Study for Mexico', in E. Lutz (ed.), *Toward Improved Accounting for the Environment — An UNSTAT–World Bank symposium*, Washington DC: World Bank, pp. 85–107.

Varian, Hal R. (1992), *Microeconomic Analysis*, New York: Norton.

Vatn, A. and D.W. Bromley (1994), 'Choices without Prices without Apologies', *Journal of Environmental Economics and Management*, **26** (2), 129–48.

Veisten, Knut, Ståle Navrud and Johnny S.Y. Valen (2006), 'Lexicographic Preferences in Biodiversity Valuation: Tests of Inconsistencies and Willingness to Pay', *Journal of Environmental Planning and Management*, **49** (2), 167–80.

Vercelli, Alessandro (1998), 'Sustainable Development and the Freedom of Future Generations', in Graciela Chichilnisky, Geoffrey Heal and Alessandro Vercelli (eds), *Sustainability: Dynamics and Uncertainty*, Dordrecht: Kluwer, pp. 171–87.

Victor, Peter A. (1991), 'Indicators of Sustainable Development: Some Lessons from Capital Theory', *Ecological Economics*, **4** (3), 191–213.

Victor, Peter A., J.E. Hanna and A. Kubursi (1995), 'How Strong is Weak Sustainability', *Economie Appliquée*, **48** (2), 75–94.

Vincent, Jeffrey R. (1997), 'Resource Depletion and Economic Sustainability in Malaysia', *Environment and Development Economics*, **2** (1), 19–37.

Vincent, Jeffrey R., Theodore Panayotou and John M. Hartwick (1997), 'Resource Depletion and Sustainability in Small Open Economies', *Journal of Environmental Economics and Management*, **33** (3), 274–86.

Vitousek, Peter M., Paul R. Ehrlich, Anne H. Ehrlich and Pamela A. Mason (1986), 'Human Appropriation of the Products of Photosynthesis', *BioScience*, **36** (6), 368–73.

Wackernagel, Mathis and J. David Yount (2000), 'Footprints for Sustainability: The Next Steps', *Environment, Development and Sustainability*, **2**, 21–42.

Wackernagel, Mathis and Judith Silverstein (2000), 'Big Things First: Focusing on the Scale Imperative with the Ecological Footprint', *Ecological Economics*, **32** (3), 391–4.

Wackernagel, Mathis and William E. Rees (1997), 'Perceptual and Structural Barriers to Investing in Natural Capital: Economics from an Ecological Footprint Perspective', *Ecological Economics*, **20** (1), 3–24.

Wackernagel, Mathis, Larry Onisto, Patricia Bello, Alejandro Callejas Linares, Ina Susana López Falfán, Jesus Méndez García, Ana Isabel Suárez Guerrero, Ma. Guadalupe Suárez Guerrero (1999), 'National Natural Capital Accounting with the Ecological Footprint Analysis', *Ecological Economics*, **29** (3), 375–90.

Wackernagel, Mathis, Niels B. Schulz, Diana Deumling, Alejandro Callejas Linares, Martin Jenkins, Valerie Kapos, Chad Monfreda, Jonathan Loh, Norman Myers, Richard Norgaard and Jørgen Randers (2002), 'Tracking the ecological overshoot of the human economy', *Proceedings of the National Academy of Sciences*, **99** (14), 9266–71.

Waggoner, Paul E. (1994), *How Much Land Can Ten Billion People Spare for Nature?*, Task Force Report No. 121, Ames: Council for Agricultural Science and Technology.

Wagner, Martin (2008), 'The Carbon Kuznets Curve: A Cloudy Picture Emitted by Bad Econometrics?', *Resource and Energy Economics*, **30** (3), 388–408.

Watkins, G.C. (2006), 'Oil Scarcity: What have the Past Three Decades Revealed?', *Energy Policy*, **34** (5), 508–14.

Weber, Max (1922), *Gesammelte Aufsätze zur Wissenschaftslehre*, edited by Marianne Weber, Tübingen: J.C.B. Mohr.

Weikard, Hans-Peter, and Xuegin Zhu (2005), 'Discounting and environmental quality: When should dual rates be used?', *Economic Modelling*, **22** (5), 868–78.

Weisbrod, Burton A. (1964), 'Collective Consumption Services of Individual Consumption Goods', *Quarterly Journal of Economics*, **77** (3), 71–7.

Weitzman, Martin L. (1997), 'Sustainability and Technical Progress', *Scandinavian Journal of Economics*, **99** (1), 1–13.

Weitzman, Martin L. (1998), 'Why the Far-Distant Future Should be Discounted at Its Lowest Possible Rate', *Journal of Environmental Economics and Management*, **36** (1), 201–8.

Weitzman, Martin L. (2009a), 'On Modeling and Interpreting the Economics of Catastrophic Climate Change', *Review of Economics and Statistics*, **91** (1), 1–19.

Weitzman, Martin L. (2009b), Reactions to the Nordhaus Critique, Working Paper. Harvard University: Department of Economics.

Weitzman, Martin L. and Karl-Gustaf Löfgren (1997), 'On the Welfare Significance of Green Accounting as Taught by Parable', *Journal of Environmental Economics and Management*, **32** (2), 139–53.

Weizsäcker, Ernst von, Amory B. Lovins and L. Hunter Lovins (1997), *Factor Four: Doubling Wealth – Halving Resource Use*, The New Report to the Club of Rome. London: Earthscan.

Wheeler, D. and P. Martin (1992), 'Prices, Policies and the International Diffusion of Clean Technology: The Case of Wood Pulp Production', in Patrick Low (ed.), *International Trade and the Environment*, Discussion Paper No. 159, Washington DC: World Bank, pp. 197–224.

Willey, David and Andrew Ferguson (1999): *Carrying Capacity Ethics*, London: Optimum Population Trust.

Willis, Ken and Guy Garrod (1995), 'Transferability of Benefit Estimates', in Ken Willis and J. Corkindale (eds), *Environmental Valuation — New Perspectives*, Oxon: CAB International, pp. 191–212.

Wilson, E.O. (1988), *Biodiversity*, Washington DC: National Academy Press.

Withagen, Cees (1996), 'Sustainability and Investment Rules', *Economics Letters*, **53** (1), 1–6.

World Bank (1992), *World Development Report 1992 — Development and the Environment*, New York: Oxford University Press.

World Bank (1997), *Expanding the Measure of Wealth: Indicators of Environmentally Sustainable Development*. Washington DC: World Bank.

World Bank (2002), *Adjusted Net Savings Data*. Washington DC: World Bank.

World Bank (2003), *Wealth Estimates*. Washington DC: World Bank.

World Bank (2006), *Where is the Wealth of Nations? Measuring Capital for the 21st Century*. Washington DC: World Bank.

World Bank (2009a), *Adjusted Net Savings Data*. Washington DC: World Bank

World Bank (2009b), *World Development Indicators Online*. Washington DC: World Bank

World Commission on Environment and Development (1987), *Our Common Future*, Oxford: Oxford University Press.

WRI (various years), *World Resources* — a joint publication from the World Resources Institute, United Nations' Environment Programme, Washington DC: United Nations' Development Programme and World Bank.

WWF (2008), *Living Planet Report 2008*. Gland: World Wide Fund for Nature.

Yang, Zili (2003), 'Dual-rate Discounting in Dynamic Economic-Environmental Modelling', *Economic Modelling*, **20** (5), 941–57.

Zeckhauser, Richard J. and W. Kip Viscusi (1995), 'Risk Within Reason', in Julian L. Simon (ed.), *The State of Humanity*, Cambridge, MA: Blackwell, pp. 628–36.

Ziegler, Rafael (2007), 'Political Perception and Ensemble of Macro Objectives and Measures: The Paradox of the Index of Sustainable Economic Welfare', *Environmental Values* **16** (1), 43–60.

Zolotas, Xenophon (1981), *Economic Growth and Declining Social Welfare*, New York: New York University Press.

Index